THE

CELEBRITY

LISTS BOOK

Also available:
The Lists Book

THE CELEBRITY LISTS BOOK

MITCHELL SYMONS

To my three favourite celebrities:
Penny, Jack and Charlie

First published in in 1998 by Chameleon Books,
an imprint of André Deutsch Ltd, 76 Dean Street, London WC1V 5HA
(www.vci.co.uk)

André Deutsch is a VCI plc company

Book design by Suzanne Perkins/Grafica

A catalogue record for this title is available from the British Library

ISBN 0 233 99413 0

Printed in Great Britain by WBC, Bridgend

TABLE OF CONTENTS

ACKNOWLEDGEMENTS

First and foremost, I would like to thank Louise Dixon and Anna Kiernan at André Deutsch for doing and being everything an author could wish for.

Other people whose kind help I would like to gratefully acknowledge include: Gilly Adams, Russell Ash, Jeremy Beadle, Marcus Berkmann, Penny Chorlton, Anne Kay, Richard Littlejohn, Tricia Martin, Simon Rose, Andy Simpson, Nigel Stoneman, Alan Symons, Jenny Symons, Louise Symons, David Thomas and Rob Woolley.

Finally, I would like to acknowledge the huge debt I owe to David Wallechinsky, a man I've never even met. If it hadn't been for the seminal list books compiled by him and his family, this book – and all other lists books – would never have seen the light of day.

Chapter 1

Family Affair

28 CELEBRITIES BORN OUT OF WEDLOCK

1. Demi Moore
2. Macaulay Culkin
3. Ella Fitzgerald
4. Oprah Winfrey
5. Ryan Giggs
6. Naomi Campbell
7. Coco Chanel
8. Jane Lapotaire
9. Dame Catherine Cookson
10. Sir Cyril Smith
11. Ruud Gullit
12. Samantha Janus
13. Fidel Castro
14. Franco Zeffirelli
15. Mr Motivator (Derrick Evans)
16. The Duchess of Windsor
17. Tony O'Reilly
18. Elsa Lanchester
19. Ray Brooks
20. Manuel Noriega
21. Marilyn Monroe
22. Eric Clapton
23. Pat Barker
24. Bruce Oldfield
25. James Baldwin
26. Billie Holiday
27. Mike Tyson
28. Saddam Hussein (not much of a celebrity, I know, but there's no bigger bastard)

2 CELEBRITIES WHO HAVE A SON NAMED SATCHEL

1. Woody Allen
2. Spike Lee

8 CELEBRITIES WHO ARE THE FATHERS OF 1-8 CHILDREN

1. Tom Conti (has one child)

2. Paddy Ashdown (two)

3. Paul Daniels (three)

4. Donald Sutherland (four)

5. Mike Reid (five)

6. Sting (six)

7. Joss Ackland (seven)

8. Joe Johnson (eight)

8 CELEBRITIES WHO ARE MOTHERS OF 1-8 CHILDREN

1. Lulu (has one child)

2. Wendy Craig (two)

3. Cilla Black (three)

4. Judy Finnegan (four)

5. June Brown (five)

6. Loretta Lynn (six)

7. Elizabeth Longford (seven)

8. Soraya Khashoggi (eight)

2 CELEBRITIES WHOSE FATHERS WERE GREEK RESTAURATEURS

1. George Michael

2. Yusuf Islam (Cat Stevens)

10 CELEBRITIES BORN ON CHRISTMAS EVE

1. Lord Colin Cowdrey
2. Sir Ivan Lawrence
3. Dr John Marek MP
4. Christopher Neame
5. Carol Vorderman
6. Matthew Arnold
7. Ava Gardner
8. Lemmy
9. Jill Bennett
10. Howard Hughes

14 CELEBRITIES BORN ON NEW YEAR'S EVE

1. Michale Bonallack (1934)
2. Steve Bruce (1960)
3. Tony Dorigo (1965)
4. Alex Ferguson (1941)
5. Sir Anthony Hopkins (1937)
6. Ben Kingsley (1943)
7. Trevor Phillips (1953)
8. Alex Salmond (1954)
9. Donna Summer (1948)
10. Jean Pierre Rives (1952)
11. Andy Summers (1943)
12. Sarah Miles (1943)
13. Simon Wiesenthal (1908)
14. Joey McIntyre (1972)

2 CELEBRITIES WHO BECAME MOTHERS AGAIN AFTER BECOMING GRANDMOTHERS

1. Priscilla Presley

2. Claudia Cardinale

10 CELEBRITIES WITH 1-10 SIBLINGS

1. The Queen (has one sibling – i.e. Princess Margaret)

2. Tony Adams (two)

3. Kate Winslet (three)

4. Michael Johnson (four)

5. Madonna (five)

6. Sir Jimmy Savile (six)

7. Barry McGuigan (seven)

8. Brenda Blethyn (eight)

9. Lewis Carroll (nine)

10. David Emanuel (ten)

17 CELEBRITIES AND THEIR ANCESTORS

1. Issy Van Renderwick: William of Orange
2. Sir John Gielgud: Ellen Terry
3. Glenn Ford: President Martin Van Buren
4. Prince Philip: Queen Victoria
5. Matthew Fleming: Ian Fleming
6. Helena Bonham Carter: Herbert Asquith
7. Judy Garland: President General Ulysses S. Grant
8. Dame Barbara Cartland: Robert the Bruce
9. Joyce Grenfell: Nancy Astor
10. David 'Kid' Jensen: Robert Louis Stevenson
11. Queen Sofia of Spain: Queen Victoria
12. William Holden: President Warren G. Harding
13. General Colin Powell: King Edward I
14. Errol Flynn: Fletcher Christian
15. Basil Rathbone: King Henry IV
16. Joanna Trollope: Anthony Trollope
17. Daniel Farson: Bram Stoker

81 CELEBRITIES WHO ADOPTED CHILDREN

1. Diane Keaton
2. Lyndall Hobbs
3. Honor Blackman
4. John Ridgway
5. Ilie Nastase
6. Michael Nicholson
7. Eamonn Andrews
8. Ronald Reagan
9. Lionel Richie
10. Colin Welland
11. Marlon Brando
12. Bob Monkhouse
13. David Bellamy
14. Sir David Steel
15. Michelle Pfeiffer
16. Burt Reynolds and Loni Anderson
17. Linda Ronstadt
18. Sheena Easton
19. Steven Spielberg and Kate Capshaw
20. Liz Tilberis
21. Burt Bacharach and Carole Bayer Sager
22. Jill Ireland and Charles Bronson
23. Michael Landon
24. Ted Danson
25. Patricia Kluge
26. Sylvia Syms
27. Graham Chapman
28. Pearl Bailey
29. Graham Gouldman
30. Joan Lestor
31. Magic Johnson
32. Prue Leith
33. Dora Bryan
34. Muhammad Ali
35. Connie Francis
36. David Niven
37. Roy Rogers
38. Pat Booth
39. Sir Nicholas Scott
40. Jane Russell
41. Burl Ives
42. Una Stubbs
43. Henry Fonda
44. Rosie O'Donnell
45. Isabella Rossellini
46. Robin Givens
47. Don Ameche
48. Ella Fitzgerald
49. Woody Allen
50. Kate Jackson
51. Baroness Emma Nicholson
52. Kevin Lloyd
53. Barbara Stanwyck
54. Aileen Getty
55. Lord Hanson
56. Ian Wright
57. John Denver
58. Doris Stokes
59. Julius Caesar
60. Joan Crawford
61. Floyd Patterson
62. George Burns
63. Patti LaBelle
64. Walt Disney
65. James Cagney
66. Louis Gossett Jr.
67. Valerie Harper
68. Bob Hope
69. Jerry Lewis
70. Paul Newman and Joanne Woodward
71. Bette Davis
72. Gloria Swanson
73. Sammy Davis Jr.
74. Phil and Ronnie Spector
75. Bernard Matthews
76. Jill Summers
77. George Orwell
78. Paul Verhoeven
79. Josephine Baker
80. Imelda Marcos
81. Harpo Marx

124 PAIRS OF CELEBRITIES WHO SHARE THE SAME DATE OF BIRTH

1. Joan Baez and Susannah York (9.1.41)

2. Freddie Starr and Scott Walker (9.1.41)

3. Anthony Andrews and Brendan Foster (12.1.48)

4. David Bellamy and John Boorman (18.1.33)

5. Robert Palmer and Dennis Taylor (19.1.49)

6. Alan Alda and Bill Jordan (28.1.36)

7. Tony Blackburn and Katharine Ross (29.1.43)

8. Vanessa Redgrave and Boris Spassky (30.1.37)

9. Patrick Macnee and Denis Norden (6.2.22)

10. Sandy Lyle and Cyrille Regis (9.2.58)

11. Alan Bates and Barry Humphries (17.2.34)

12. Yoko Ono and Bobby Robson (18.2.33)

13. Paul Rendall and John Travolta (18.2.54)

14. Roberto Baggio and Colin Jackson (18.2.67)

15. Prince Andrew and Leslie Ash (19.2.60)

16. Sheila Hancock and Princess Michael of Kent (22.2.33)

17. Mike D'Abo and Roger Daltrey (1.3.44)

18. Dame Naomi James and J.P.R. Williams (2.3.49)

19. Patsy Kensit and Lorna Vincent (4.3.68)

20. Michael Grade and Lynn Redgrave (8.3.43)

21. Virginia Bottomley and James Taylor (12.3.48)

22. Michael Caine and Quincy Jones (14.3.33)

23. William Shatner and Leslie Thomas (22.3.31)

24. John Major and Eric Idle (29.3.43)

25. Marlon Brando and Doris Day (3.4.24)

26. Francis Coppola and Sir David Frost (7.4.39)

27. Julian Lloyd Webber and Anthea Redfern (14.4.51)

28. Clare Francis and Henry Kelly (17.4.46)

29. Louise Jameson and Luther Vandross (20.4.51)

30. Alan Bond and Glen Campbell (22.4.38)

31. Bruno Brookes and Paula Yates (24.4.60)

32. Sir David Attenborough and Don Rickles (8.5.26)

33. Albert Finney and Glenda Jackson (9.5.36)

34. Maureen Lipman and Donovan (10.5.46)

35. Ian Dury and Susan Hampshire (11.5.42)

36. Alan Ball and Nicky Henson (12.5.45)

37. Bob Carolgees and Steve Winwood (12.5.48)

38. Peter Gabriel and Stevie Wonder (13.5.50)

39. Olga Korbut and Debra Winger (16.5.55)

40. Liz McColgan and Adrian Moorhouse (24.5.64)

41. Helena Bonham Carter and Zola Budd (26.5.66)

42. Duncan Goodhew and Siouxsie Sioux (27.5.57)

43. Faith Brown and Gladys Knight (28.5.44)

44. Jonathan Pryce and Ronnie Wood (1.6.47)

45. Gemma Craven and Tom Robinson (1.6.50)

46. Stacy Keach and Charlie Watts (2.6.41)

47. Bruce Dern and Bill Treacher (4.6.36)

48. Mike Gatting and Javed Miandad (6.6.57)

49. Gene Wilder and Jackie Stewart (11.6.39)

50. Paul Boateng MP and Mike Yarwood (14.6.41)

51. Paula Abdul and Rory Underwood (19.6.63)

52. Sir Malcolm Rifkind and Lord Maurice Saatchi (21.6.46)

53. Meryl Streep and Lindsay Wagner (22.6.49)

54. Alan Coren and Tommy Cannon (27.6.38)

55. Shirley Ann Field and Eric Richard (27.6.40)

56. Majid Khan and Helen Shapiro (28.9.46)

57. Vince Clarke and Suzanne Dando (3.7.61)

58. Michael Howard and Bill Oddie (7.7.41)

59. Tony Jacklin and Glenys Kinnock (7.7.44)

60. John Motson and Virginia Wade (10.7.45)

61. Sir Alastair Burnet and Kathy Staff (12.7.28)

62. Stanley Kubrick and Danny La Rue (26.7.28)

63. Sir Clive Sinclair and Roy Walker (30.7.40)

64. Kate Bush and Daley Thompson (30.7.58)

65. Geraldine Chaplin and Jonathan Dimbleby (31.7.44)

66. Robert Culp and Ted Hughes (16.8.30)

67. Belinda Carlisle and Kirk Stevens (17.8.58)

68. Neil Diamond and Ray Stevens (24.1.40)

69. Dame Janet Baker and Barry Norman (21.8.33)

70. Elvis Costello and Jim Wallace MP (25.8.54)

71. Lenny Henry and Michael Jackson (29.8.58)

72. Pauline Collins and Raquel Welch (3.9.40)

73. Carol Barnes and Jacqueline Bisset (13.9.44)

74. Paul Allott and Ray Wilkins (14.9.56)

75. Tommy Lee Jones and Oliver Stone (15.9.46)

76. Charles Haughey and B.B. King (16.9.25)

77. Julio Iglesias and Ian Ogilvy (23.9.43)

78. Michele Dotrice and Meatloaf (27.9.47)

79. Sir Terence Conran and Basil D'Oliviera (4.10.31)

80. Chris Lowe and Tony Meo (4.10.59)

81. Charles Dance and Chris Tarrant (10.10.46)

82. Luciano Pavarotti and Joan Rivers (12.10.35)

83. Sir Cliff Richard and Christopher Timothy (14.10.40)

84. Gary Kemp and Graeme Sharp (16.10.60)

85. Geofffrey Boycott and Manfred Mann (21.10.40)

86. Mark Fisher and Denny Laine (29.10.44)

87. Juliet Mills and Bruce Welch (2.11.41)

88. Mark Hateley and Dee Hepburn (7.11.61)

89. Andy Kershaw and Tony Slattery (9.11.59)

90. Mark Chamberlain and Meg Ryan (19.11.61)

91. Jamie Lee Curtis and Tim Robinson (21.11.58)

92. Ian Botham and Jamie, the Marquis of Blandford (24.11.55)

93. Jacques Chirac and Diane Ladd (29.11.32)

94. Andy Gray and Billy Idol (30.11.55)

95. Robert Lindsay and Ted Nugent (13.12.49)

96. Jane Birkin and Peter Lorimer (14.12.48)

97. Benny Andersson (of ABBA) and Christopher Ellison (16.12.46)

98. Uri Geller and Lesley Judd (20.12.46)

99. Robin Campbell (of UB40) and Annie Lennox (25.12.54)

100. Harvey Smith and Jon Voight (29.12.38)

101. Victoria Principal and Stephen Stills (3.1.45)

102. Windsor Davies and Ben Gazzara (28.8.30)

103. George Foreman and Linda Lovelace (10.1.49)

104. Paul Newman and David Jenkins (former Bishop of Durham) (26.1.25)

105. Fred Trueman and Rip Torn (6.2.31)

106. Stockard Channing and Peter Tork (13.2.44)

107. Aimi Macdonald and Graeme Pollock (27.2.44)

108. Mikhail Gorbachev and Tom Wolfe (2.3.31)

109. Carl Perkins and Jack Smethurst (9.4.32)

110. Adrian Henri and Omar Sharif (10.4.32)

111. Bobby Hatfield (of The Righteous Brothers) and Gloria Hunniford (10.4.40)

112. Al Green and Christopher Strauli (13.4.46)

113. Joe Cocker and Keith Fletcher (20.5.44)

114. Clive Allen and Nick Heyward (20.5.61)

115. George Best and Howard Kendall (22.5.46)

116. Mark Goodier and Dee C. Lee (6.6.61)

117. Patricia Brake and Eddie Large (25.6.42)

118. Karen Black and Genevieve Bujold (1.7.42)

119. Henri Leconte and Jan Molby (4.7.63)

120. Mark Cox and Robbie Robertson (5.7.43)

121. Pauline Quirk and Imre Varadi (8.7.59)

122. Ben De Haan and Jim Kerr (9.7.59)

123. Harrison Ford and Roger McGuinn (of The Byrds) (13.7.42)

124. Blake Edwards and Jason Robards (26.7.22)

5 CELEBRITIES WHO PUT THEIR BABIES UP FOR ADOPTION

1. Clare Short

2. Roseanne

3. Pauline Collins

4. Joni Mitchell

5. Marilyn Monroe

2 CELEBRITIES WHO HAVE A DAUGHTER NAMED ALLEGRA

1. Vanessa Feltz

2. Tony Curtis

2 CELEBRITIES WHO BABYSAT FOR THE CHILDREN OF OTHER CELEBRITIES

1. Little Eva: Carole King

2. Lindsay Wagner: Glen Campbell

6 CELEBRITIES WHO WERE TEENAGE RUNAWAYS

1. Courtney Love

2. Oprah Winfrey

3. Bob Dylan

4. Daniel Day-Lewis

5. Billy Connolly

6. Errol Flynn

2 CELEBRITIES WHO WERE SEVENTH SONS OF SEVENTH SONS

1. Glen Campbell
2. Perry Como

2 CELEBRITIES WHOSE FATHERS WERE BOOKMAKERS

1. Peter O'Toole
2. Perry Como

2 CELEBRITIES WHO HAVE GRANDFATHERS WHO WON NOBEL PRIZES IN THE YEAR 1954

1. Olivia Newton-John (Max Born, won for Physics)
2. Mariel Hemingway (Ernest Hemingway, won for Literature)

3 CELEBRITIES WHO HAD MOTHERS WHO, AS FAR AS THE REST OF THE WORLD WERE CONCERNED, WERE THEIR 'SISTERS'

1. Eric Clapton
2. Jack Nicholson
3. Dame Catherine Cookson

80 CELEBRITES WHO ARE ONLY CHILDREN

1. Dale Winton
2. Teri Hatcher
3. Alan Bleasdale
4. David Essex
5. Barbara Windsor
6. Sir Elton John
7. Mick Hucknall
8. Bob Hoskins
9. Ulrika Jonsson
10. Uri Geller
11. Cherie Lunghi
12. Paul Nicholas
13. Melvyn Bragg
14. David Gower
15. Penelope Keith
16. Robert De Niro
17. Robin Cook
18. Terry Venables
19. Clive James
20. Lester Piggott
21. Harold Pinter
22. Sir Peter Hall
23. Miriam Margolyes
24. Tony Blair
25. Nanette Newman
26. Michael Heseltine
27. Dame P.D. James
28. Vanessa-Mae Nicholson
29. Sian Phillips
30. Jean-Paul Gaultier
31. Dame Ruth Rendell
32. Jimmy Young
33. Jacques Chirac
34. Frederick Forsyth
35. Julia McKenzie
36. Sir Edward Heath
37. Anton Mosimann
38. Penny Vincenzi
39. Nick Faldo
40. Barbara Taylor Bradford

41. John Redwood

42. Betty Boothroyd

43. Chris Tarrant

44. Paul Merton

45. Dr David Starkey

46. John Mortimer

47. Michael Parkinson

48 Paula Yates

49. Virginia McKenna

50. John Savident

51. John Stapleton

52. Jack Shepherd

53. Ken Hom

54. Gillian Lynne

55. David Copperfield

56. John Nettles

57. Ruby Wax

58. Aled Jones

59. Tammy Wynette

60. Mike McShane

61. Gayle Hunnicutt

62. Screaming Lord Sutch

63. Martina Hingis

64. Sam Mendes

65. Harry Enfield

66. Lord Roy Jenkins

67. Dame Iris Murdoch

68. Susan Hill

69. Michael Bond

70. Gemma Craven

71. Burt Bacharach

72. Sir Anthony Hopkins

73. Sir Peter Ustinov

74. Sam Torrance

75. Julie Burchill

76. Anita Brookner

77. Scott Walker

78. Simon Callow

79. Annette Crosbie

80. Noel Edmonds

11 CELEBRITIES WHO WERE FOSTER CHILDREN

1. John Fashanu
2. Vidal Sassoon
3. Leslie Thomas
4. George Cole
5. Kathy Burke
6. Bruce Oldfield
7. Gary Glitter
8. Jane Lapotaire
9. Kriss Akabusi
10. Eartha Kitt
11. Neil Morrissey

79 CELEBRITIES AND WHAT THEIR FATHERS DID FOR A LIVING

1. David Bailey (Tailor)
2. Peter Bowles (Chauffeur)
3. Francesca Annis (Banker)
4. Michael Parkinson (Miner)
5. John Cleese (Insurance salesman)
6. Vanessa Feltz (Knicker manufacturer)
7. Malcolm McDowell (Publican)
8. Anthony Andrews (BBC musical arranger)
9. Melvyn Bragg (Publican)
10. Dennis Waterman (Railwayman)
11. Freddie Starr (Carpenter)
12. Greta Scacchi (Artist)
13. Jeremy Irons (Accountant)
14. Mike Read (Publican)
15. Bryan Ferry (Mineworker)
16. Lord Andrew Lloyd Webber (Organist)
17. Julie Walters (Builder)
18. Robert Wyatt (Journalist)
19. Elizabeth Taylor (Art dealer)
20. Alexei Sayle (Railwayman)
21. Bill Wyman (Bricklayer)
22. Edwina Currie (Tailor)
23. George Harrison (Bus driver)
24. Len Deighton (Chauffeur)
25. Koo Stark (Film producer)
26. Jean Shrimpton (Builder)
27. Stewart Copeland (CJA agent)

28. Nancy Reagan (Car salesman)

29. George Cole (Butcher)

30. Lesley-Anne Down (Caretaker)

31. Neil Young (Journalist)

32. Bob Geldof (Commercial traveller)

33. Bruce Oldfield (Boxer)

34. Bruce Forsyth (Garage owner)

35. Sir Jimmy Savile (Bookmaker's clerk)

36. Morrissey (Hospital porter)

37. Steve Wright (Tailor)

38. Anne Diamond (Scientist)

39. Jerry Hall (Lorry driver)

40. Rupert Everett (Army major)

41. Mark Knopfler (Architect)

42. Gloria Hunniford (Newspaper advertising manager)

43. Paul Daniels (Cinema projectionist)

44. Simon Le Bon (Foreign Office civil servant)

45. Boy George (Builder)

46. Robert Wagner (Metal manufacturer)

47. Sir Peter Hall (Stationmaster)

48. Harvey Goldsmith (Tailor)

49. Dudley Moore (Railway electrician)

50. David Emanuel (Steelworker)

51. Cheryl Tiegs (Undertaker)

52. Rik Mayall (Teacher)

53. Will Smith (Refrigeration engineer)

54. Frank Johnson (Pastry cook and confectioner)

55. Keith Chegwin (Timber firm rep)

56. Joe Strummer (Diplomat)

57. Sean Connery (Lorry driver)

58. Elaine Paige (Estate agent)

59. Sir David Puttnam (Photographer)

60. Mick Jagger (P.E. teacher)

61. Frederick Forsyth (Furrier)

62. Robert Redford (Milkman)

63. Ed Asner (Scrap iron dealer)

64. John Stapleton (Co-op manager)

65. Jimmy Young (Baker)

66. Barbara Windsor (Bus driver)

67. Jack Lemmon (Flour mixer)

68. Suggs (Photographer)

69. Glenda Jackson (Bricklayer)

70. Jon Bon Jovi (Hairdresser)

71. Oliver Stone (Stockbroker)

72. Alan Bennett (Butcher)

73. Olivia Newton-John (Headmaster)

74. Peter Stringfellow (Steelworker)

75. Lynn Faulds-Wood (Accountant)

76. Zandra Rhodes (Lorry Driver)

77. Robert Carlyle (Painter and decorator)

78. Emma Bunton (Milkman)

79. Matthew Modine (Boss of a drive-in cinema)

15 CELEBRITIES WITH FAMOUS MOTHERS

1. Baroness Shirley Williams (Vera Brittain)
2. Liza Minnelli (Judy Garland)
3. Sophie Dahl (Tessa Dahl)
4. Caron Keating (Gloria Hunniford)
5. Joely Richardson (Vanessa Redgrave)
6. Rudi Davies (Beryl Bainbridge)
7. Emma Forbes (Nanette Newman)
8. Beatie Edlley (Sylvia Syms)
9. Mia Farrow (Maureen O'Sullivan)
10. Jennifer Ehle (Rosemary Harris)
11. Susannah Harker (Polly Adams)
12. Finty Williams (Dame Judi Dench)
13. Carrie Fisher (Debbie Reynolds)
14. Caspian Mills (Hayley Mills)
15. Melanie Griffith (Tippi Hedren)

4 CELEBRITIES WITH FAMOUS STEP-PARENTS

1. Sally Field – Jock Mahoney
2. David Cassidy – Shirley Field
3. Julian Lennon – Yoko Ono
4. Paloma Picasso – Jonas Salk

6 CELEBRITIES WITH CELEBRITY FATHERS-IN-LAW

1. Gregor Fisher: Peter Vaughan
2. Woody Allen: André Previn
3. Jonny Lee Miller: Jon Voight
4. Dean Martin: Carl Wilson
5. William Somerset Maugham: Dr Barnado
6. Artie Shaw: Jerome Kern

20 CELEBRITIES WITH FAMOUS FATHERS

1. Zoë Ball (Johnny Ball)
2. Lucy Davis (Jasper Carrott)
3. Helen Storey (David Storey)
4. Lucy Briers (Richard Briers)
5. Sophie Ward (Simon Ward)
6. Damon Hill (Graham Hill)
7. Abigail McKern (Leo McKern)
8. Jason Connery (Sean Connery)
9. Kiefer Sutherland (Donald Sutherland)
10. Julian Lennon (John Lennon)
11. Stella McCartney (Sir Paul McCartney)
12. Jacques Villeneuve (Gilles Villeneuve)
13. Kim Wilde (Marty Wilde)
14. Andrea Boardman (Stan Boardman)
15. Suzanne Charlton (Sir Bobby Charlton)
16. Emilio Estevez (Martin Sheen)
17. Kirsty MacColl (Ewan MacColl)
18. Julia Sawalha (Nadim Sawalha)
19. Linus Roache (William Roache)
20. Paula Yates (Hughie Green)

33 CELEBRITIES WITH DOCTOR FATHERS

1. Glenn Close
2. Roger Black
3. Pamela Stephenson
4. Katharine Hepburn
5. Mike Oldfield
6. Jacqueline Bisset
7. Brian de Palma
8. Tony Blackburn
9. Jane Seymour
10. Bill Pullman
11. Frances Edmonds
12. Baroness Tessa Jowell
13. Sister Wendy Beckett
14. Edvard Munch
15. William Roache
16. Sandra Bernhard
17. John Dunlop
18. Mary Killen
19. Willem Dafoe
20. Kate Bush
21. Adnan Khashoggi
22. W. H. Auden
23. Mike Leigh
24. Dame Judi Dench
25. Paul Bradley
26. Nigel Hawthorne
27. Sir Tom Stoppard
28. Humphrey Bogart
29. Stephen Hawking
30. Fred Zinnemann
31. Ben Kingsley
32. Hillary Clinton
33. Joan Rivers

6 CELEBRITIES WITH CELEBRITY AUNTS

1. Nigel Havers: Dame Elizabeth Butler-Sloss
2. Michael Korda: Merle Oberon
3. Jemma Redgrave: Vanessa Redgrave
4. Macaulay Culkin: Bonnie Bedelia
5. Alessandra Mussolini: Sophia Loren
6. Bridget Fonda: Jane Fonda

8 CELEBRITIES WITH CELEBRITY UNCLES

1. Alan Howard: Leslie Howard
2. Judge Jules (Radio 1 D J): Rick Stein
3. Michael Grade: Lord Lew Grade
4. Peter Francisco: Silvino Francisco
5. Christy O'Connor Jnr: Christy O'Connor Snr
6. Scott Quinnell: Barry John
7. David Graveney: Tom Graveney
8. Sir Bobby Charlton: Jackie Milburn

8 CELEBRITIES WHOSE FATHERS HAVE BEEN IN JAIL

1. Ronnie O'Sullivan
2. Keanu Reeves
3. Jools Holland
4. Heather Mills
5. Woody Harrelson
6. Steffi Graf
7. Tatum O'Neal
8. Benazir Bhutto

43 CELEBRITIES WITH AT LEAST ONE JEWISH PARENT

1. Alicia Silverstone
2. Joel Stransky
3. Gary Kasparov
4. Calvin Klein
5. Manfred Mann
6. Claire Bloom
7. Olivia Newton-John
8. Vidal Sassoon
9. Herb Alpert
10. Kevin Kline
11. Lauren Bacall
12. Dyan Cannon
13. Peter Green
14. Sidney Lumet
15. Peter Shaffer
16. Cyd Charisse
17. Milos Forman
18. Joan Collins
19. Johan Neeskens
20. Gloria Steinem
21. Arlo Guthrie
22. Debra Winger
23. Stanley Kubrick
24. Alan Arkin
25. Marcel Marceau
26. Michael Douglas
27. Arthur Penn
28. Walter Matthau
29. Nadine Gordimer
30. Carly Simon
31. Daniel Day-Lewis
32. Roman Polanski
33. Phil Spector
34. Mel Torme
35. Jody Scheckter
36. Larry King
37. Dame Muriel Spark
38. Paul Newman
39. Neil Sedaka
40. Norman Mailer
41. James Caan
42. Anouk Aimee
43. Billy Joel

9 CELEBRITIES WITH MORE FAMOUS YOUNGER BROTHERS

1. Jack Charlton (Sir Bobby)
2. Paul Ross (Jonathan)
3. Terry Major-Ball (John Major)
4. Sheila Mercier (Lord Brian Rix)
5. Sir Samuel Brittan (Sir Leon)
6. Jay Osmond (Donny)
7. Jermaine Jackson (Michael)
8. Justin Fashanu (John)
9. Manuel Ballesteros (Severiano)

35 CELEBRITIES WHO ARE PARENTS OF TWINS

1. Jeremy Paxman
2. Cheryl Baker
3. Dickie Davies
A. Robert De Niro
5. Earl Spencer
6. Ivan Lendl
7. Jane Seymour
8. Nigel Benn
9. Madeleine Albright
10. Nigel Spackman
11. Fern Britton
12. Mollie Sugden
13. James Galway
14. Michael Buerk
15. Gary Oldman
16. David Batty
17. Dean Gaffiney
18. Willie Thorne
19. Pelé
20. Pat Cash
21. Graham Gooch
22. Alan Bates
23. Corbin Bernsen
24. David Essex
25. David Coleman
26. Sir Louis Blom-Cooper
27. Roy Boulting (himself a twin)
28. Paul Broadhurst
29. Chris Cowdrey
30. Jonathan Meades
31. Charles Moore
32. Ronald Searle
33. Desmond Wilcox
34. Fred Winter
35. Lou Diamond Phillips

4 CELEBRITIES WHO ARE GRANDPARENTS OF TWINS

1. Alex Ferguson
2. Tammy Wynette
3. Tony Britton
4. Frances Shand-Kydd

12 CELEBRITIES WITH FAMOUS GODPARENTS

1. Winona Ryder (Timothy Leary)
2. Henry Brocklehurst (Camilla Parker Bowles)
3. Whitney Houston (Aretha Franklin)
4. Joel Cadbury (Douglas Bader)
5. Scott Quinnell (Mervyn Davies)
6. Daniel Massey (Noel Coward)
7. Bertrand Russell (John Stuart Mill)
8. Jennifer Aniston (Telly Savalas)
9. Peter Scott (J. M. Barrie)
10. Chris Cowdrey (Peter May)
11. Jonathan Aitken (Queen Juliana)
12. Mia Farrow (George Cukor)

9 CELEBRITIES WHOSE FATHERS WERE RABBIS

1. Harry Houdini
2. Erich Segal
3. Jackie Mason
4. Lord Victor Mishcon
5. Mickey Duff
6. Isaac Asimov
7. Josh Salzmann
8. Isaac Bashevis Singer
9. Chaim Bermant

13 CELEBRITIES WITH CLERGYMAN FATHERS

1. Gordon Brown
2. Otis Redding
3. John Motson
4. Virginia Wade
5. Jane Austen
6. Sir David Frost
7. Alice Cooper
8. John Hurt
9. Ike Turner
10. Lord David Steel
11. Denzel Washington
12. John Wells
13. Frances McDormand

13 CELEBRITIES WITH POLICEMEN FATHERS

1. Roger Moore
2. Selina Scott
3. Hywel Bennett
4. Kevin Lloyd
5. Gordon Sherry
6. David May
7. Julian Clary
8. Jacques Santer
9. Liz Robertson
10. Simon Gregson
11. Burt Reynolds
12. Terry Waite
13. Richard Littlejohn

Chapter 2

Education

19 CELEBRITIES WHO GOT FIRSTS AT UNIVERSITY

1. Imogen Stubbs (English, Cambridge)

2. Martin Bell (English, Cambridge)

3. David Baddiel (English, Cambridge)

4. Denzil Davies, MP (Law, Oxford)

5. Sir Roy Strong (History, Queen Mary College, London)

6. Arthur C. Clarke, (Joint honours Physics and Maths – in two years – King's College, London)

7. Lord Douglas Hurd (History, Cambridge)

8. Vanessa Feltz (English, Cambridge)

9. Keith Vaz, MP (Law, Cambridge)

10. Michael Portillo (History, Cambridge)

11. Lord Maurice Saatchi (Economics, London School of Economics, London)

12. Gordon Brown, MP (History, Edinburgh)

13. Peter Jay (PPE, Oxford)

14. Paul Condon (Law, Oxford)

15. Adair Turner (History and Economics, Cambridge)

16. David Elstein (History, Cambridge)

17. Lord Denis Healey (Greats, Oxford)

18. Chris Smith, MP (English, Cambridge)

19. Darius Guppy (History, Oxford)

10 CELEBRITIES WHO ATTENDED THE SORBONNE

1. Rose Tremain
2. Verity Lambert
3. Spencer Batiste
4. Michael Bogdanov
5. Dale Campbell-Savours
6. Lord Killanin
7. Prue Leith
8. Magnus Linklater
9. Sir Julian Critchley
10. Christian Lacroix

2 CELEBRITIES WHO ENDOWED UNIVERSITY PROFESSORSHIPS

1. Barbra Streisand (in 'Intimacy & Sexuality')
2. Cameron Mackintosh (in Musical Theatre)

37 CELEBRITIES WHO WERE IN THE CAMBRIDGE UNIVERSITY FOOTLIGHTS (*=President)

1. Emma Thompson
2. Peter Cook*
3. Sir David Frost
4. Clive Anderson*
5. Fred Emery
6. Stephen Fry
7. Richard Vranch
8. Steve Punt
9. Morwenna Banks
10. Tony Slattery*
11. Sandi Toksvig
12. Hugh Laurie*
13. Jimmy Mulville*
14. Rory McGrath
15. Griff Rhys Jones
16. Douglas Adams
17. Sarah Dunant
18. Rob Buckman
19. Clive James*
20. Eric Idle*
21. Julie Covington
22. Germaine Greer
23. Lord Killanin*
24. Graeme Garden*
25. Tim Brooke-Taylor*
26. John Cleese
27. Bill Oddie
28. Jonathan Lynn
29. Graham Chapman
30. Eleanor Bron
31. John Bird
32. Bamber Gascoigne
33. Michael Frayn
34. Jonathan Miller
35. Leslie Bricusse*
36. Frederic Raphael
37. David Baddiel

12 PAIRS OF CELEBRITIES WHO ATTENDED THE SAME UNIVERSITIES

1. Harry Enfield and Harriet Harman (York)

2. Mick Jagger & John F. Kennedy (London School of Economics)

3. Rowan Atkinson & Kate Adie (Newcastle)

4. Sian Lloyd & Glenys Kinnock (Cardiff)

5. Carol Thatcher & Jonathan Dimbleby (University College, London)

6. Paul Boateng MP & Sue Lawley (Bristol)

7. Andrew Logan & Tim Rodber (Oxford Brookes)

8. D. H. Lawrence & Brian Moore (Nottingham)

9. Julie Walters & Mick Hucknall (Manchester Metropolitan)

10. Simon Mayo & Timmy Mallett (Warwick)

11. Keith Chegwin & Bill Clinton (Oxford)

12. Andrew Neil & William Boyd (Glasgow)

3 CELEBRITIES WHO JOINED THE INSTITUTE OF ADVANCED MOTORISTS

1. Sir Jimmy Savile

2. Pam St Clement

3. Prince Michael of Kent

15 CELEBRITIES WHO WERE APPOINTED UNIVERSITY CHANCELLORS

1. Prince Philip: Edinburgh

2. Sarah, Duchess of York: Salford

3. Betty Boothroyd: Open

4. Lord Glenamara: Northumbria

5. Dame Margot Fonteyn: Durham

6. Baroness Helena Kennedy: Oxford Brookes

7. Prince Charles: Cardiff

8. Lord Roy Jenkins: Oxford

9. Sir David Puttnam: Sunderland

10. Lord MacLaurin: Hertfordshire

11. Baroness Margaret Thatcher: Buckingham

12. Lord Peter Palumbo: Portsmouth

13. Lord Brian Rix: East London

14. Lord Jack Ashley: Staffordshire

15. Lord Richard Attenborough: Sussex

54 CELEBRITIES WHO WERE AWARDED HONORARY UNIVERSITY DOCTORATES

1. Liam Neeson (Ulster)
2. Jack Higgins (Leeds Metropolitan)
3. Gary Player (St Andrews)
4. Michael Heseltine (Liverpool)
5. Virginia Wade (Sussex)
6. Richard Wilson (Glasgow)
7. Jack Rowell (Bath)
8. Denise Robertson (Sunderland)
9. John Cleese (St Andrews)
10. Tony Blair (Northumbria)
11. Sir Freddie Laker (City)
12. Mark Knopfler (Leeds)
13. Sir David Puttnam (Leicester)
14. Dame Cleo Laine (Open)
15. Joanna Lumley (Kent)
16. Sir Edward Heath (Oxford)
17. Johnny Ball (Sheffield Hallam)
18. Dame Kiri Te Kanawa (Durham)
19. Michael Holroyd (East Anglia)
20. Michael Foot (Nottingham)
21. Sir Peter Ustinov (Durham)
22. Dame Janet Baker (Bradford)
23. Sir Trevor Huddleston (Warwick)
24. Sue Lawley (Wolverhampton)
25. Pat Jennings (Ulster)
26. Richard Baker (Strathclyde)
27. Jack Charlton (Northumbria)
28. Neil Kinnock (Cardiff)
29. Sting (Northumbria)
30. Lord Denis Healey (Bradford)
31. John Tusa (London)
32. Sir Jimmy Savile (Leeds)
33. Sandy Gall (Aberdeen)
34. Nigel Mansell (Birmingham)
35. Lord Brian Rix (Dundee)
36. Sean Bean (Sheffield Hallam)
37. Betty Boothroyd (Cambridge)
38. Trevor McDonald (Plymouth)
39. Dame Iris Murdoch (Cambridge)
40. Sir John Gielgud (London)
41. Virginia Bottomley (Portsmouth)
42. Sir Roger Bannister (Sheffield)
43. Alex Ferguson (Robert Gordon University, Aberdeen)
44. John Mortimer (Nottingham)
45. Baroness Barbara Castle (Manchester)
46. Paul Scofield (Sussex)
47. Placido Domingo (Georgetown)
48. Sir David Attenborough (Bristol)
49. Nigel Kennedy (Bath)
50. Sir Ludovic Kennedy (Strathclyde)
51. Terry Waite (Durham)
52. Victoria Wood (Lancaster)
53. Margaret Drabble (East Anglia)
54. Sir John Harvey-Jones (Exeter)

101 PAIRS OF CELEBRITIES WHO ATTENDED THE SAME SCHOOL

1. Richard Branson and George Melly (Stowe)
2. Stephen Fry and Jonathan Agnew (Uppingham)
3. Lord Colin Cowdrey and Frederick Forsyth (Tonbridge)
4. Lord Brian Rix and A.J.P. Taylor (Bootham)
5. Andy Kershaw and John Stapleton (Hulme Grammar [Boys])
6. Bob Willis and Terry Jones (Royal Grammar [Guildford])
7. Rory Underwood and Craig Raine (Barnard Castle)
8. Peter Sissons and Steven Norris (Liverpool Institute High School For Boys)
9. Stewart Copeland and Gareth Edwards (Millfield)
10. Sir Malcolm Rifkind and Gavin Hastings (George Watson's)
11. Michael Atherton and John Crawley (Manchester Grammar)
12. Edward Fox and Mark Thatcher (Harrow)
13. Edwina Currie MP and Gillian Reynolds (Liverpool Institute HS For Girls)
14. Mollie Sugden and Lord Denis Healey (Drake and Tonsons' Kindergarten)
15. Richard Baker and Sir Samuel Brittan (Kilburn GS)
16. Mick Fleetwood and Jeremy Irons (Sherborne)
17. Birt and Laurie Taylor (St Mary's College, Liverpool)
18. Bruce Dickinson and Al Alvarez (Oundle)
19. David Hare and Christopher Hampton (Lancing)
20. Jonathan King and David Dimbleby (Charterhouse)
21. Sarah Brightman and Nigel Havers (Arts Educational, London)
22. Bob Monkhouse and Peter Lilley MP (Dulwich)
23. Imogen Stubbs and Shirley Conran (St Paul's [Girls])
24. Claire Rayner and Elizabeth Emanuel (City of London [Girls])
25. Sir Tim Rice and Tom Sharpe (Lancing)
26. Rob Andrew and Kevin Whately (Barnard Castle)
27. Chris Patten and Julian Clary (St Benedict's)
28. David Gilmour, & Sir Peter Hall (The Perse School, Cambridge)
29. Frances Ruffelle and Letitia Dean (Sylvia Young)
30. Ian Hislop and Terry-Thomas (Ardingly)
31. Harriet Harman, MP and Celia Brayfield (St Paul's [Girls])
32. Ken Russell and Jeffrey Bernard (Pangbourne)
33. Barry Norman and Geoffrey Palmer (Highgate)
34. Tony Newton, MP and Tom Robinson (Friends' School [Saffron Walden])
35. Beryl Reid and Judith Chalmers (Withington)
36. Nicky Campbell and Magnus Magnusson (Edinburgh Academy)
37. Paul Gascoigne and Steve Stone (Heathfield Senior School)
38. Chris Lowe & Jimmy Armfield (Arnold)
39. Gordon Kennedy and Gavin Hastings (George Watson's)
40. Jeremy Paxman and Denholm Elliott (Malvern [Boys])
41. Neil Diamond and Barbra Streisand (Erasmus Hall High, New York)
42. John Major, MP and Raymond Briggs (Rutlish School, Merton)
43. Roger Lloyd Pack and Gyles Brandreth (Bedales)
44. Rupert Everett and Piers Paul Read (Ampleforth)
45. Katherine Hamnett and Mary Archer (Cheltenham Ladies)
46. Stirling Moss and Alan Ayckbourn (Haileybury)
47. Chris De Burgh and Captain Mark Phillips (Marlborough)
48. Denis Norden and Mike Brearley (City of London [Boys])
49. Patricia Hodge and Barbara Mills (the DPP) (St Helen's)

50. Sir Arthur Conan Doyle and Charles Laughton (Stonyhurst)

51. Jeremy Clarkson and Graeme Garden (Repton)

52. Julian Glover and Simon Ward (Alleyn's)

53. Kenneth Clarke, MP and Leslie Crowther (Nottingham HS)

54. Penny Junor and The Princess Royal (Benenden)

55. Dame Judi Dench and Margaret Drabble (The Mount, York)

56. Mark Ramprakash and Angus Fraser (Gayton HS)

57. Debbie Greenwood and Bel Mooney (Aigburth Vale HS)

58. Chubby Checker and Eddie Fisher (South Philadelphia High)

59. Des Lynam and Paul Scofield (Varndean GS)

60. Sir Alastair Burnet and Martin Bell (The Leys)

61. John Cleese and Chris Serle (Clifton)

62. Ben Kingsley and Robert Powell (Manchester Grammar)

63. Lucinda Green and Emma Nicholson, MP (St Mary's [Wantage])

64. Michael Winner and Sir Ralph Halpern (St Christopher, Letchworth)

65. John Gummer and Dinsdale Landen (King's [Rochester])

66. Brough Scott and Ted Dexter (Radley)

67. Jools Holland and William G. Stewart (Shooters' Hill)

68. Robert Redford and Stacy Keach (Van Nuys High, California)

69. Kriss Akabusi and Lord Norman Tebbit (Edmonton Comprehensive/Grammar)

70. Michael Aspel and Geoffrey Robinson, MP (Emanuel)

71. Sir Ian McKellen and Nigel Short (Bolton Boys)

72. Jenny Agutter and Fiona Fullerton (Elmhurst)

73. John Motson and Gary Newbon (Culford)

74. Dame Maggie Smith and Miriam Margolyes (Oxford High)

75. Barry Cryer and Gerald Kaufman (Leeds Grammar)

76. Jane Seymour and Stephanie Lawrence (Arts Educational, Tring)

77. Kenneth Baker MP and John Simpson (St Paul's)

78. Les Dennis and Paul McCartney (Stockton Wood Primary)

79. Helena Bonham Carter and Fay Weldon (South Hampstead HS)

80. Peter Snow and Robin Oakley (Wellington College)

81. Michael Buerk and Johnnie Walker (Solihull)

82. Graham Greene and Michael Meacher MP (Berkhamsted)

83. Desmond Morris and Andrew Gardner (Dauntsey's)

84. Indira Gandhi and Dame Iris Murdoch (Badminton)

85. David Hockney and Adrian Moorhouse (Bradford GS)

86. Michael Fish and Michael Praed (Eastbourne)

87. Emma Thompson and Sue Carpenter (Camden School For Girls)

88. Sir David Attenborough and Mark Cox (Wyggeston GS)

89. Ann-Margret and Bruce Dern (New Trier High, Illinois)

90. Michael Palin and Sir Rex Harrison (Birkdale)

91. Lucy Irvine and Anne Nightingale (Lady Eleanor Holles)

92. Tony Blackburn and Duncan Goodhew (Millfield)

93. Anthony Andrews and Brent Sadler (Royal Masonic)

94. Lord David Owen and Richard Adams (Bradfield)

95. Gary Davies and Roland Joffe (Carmel College)

96. David Gower and Tristan Garel-Jones MP (King's [Canterbury])

97. Bamber Gascoigne and Patrick Macnee (Eton)

98. P.G. Wodehouse and Raymond Chandler (Dulwich)

99. Esther Rantzen and Eleanor Bron (North London Collegiate)

100. Alan Bennett and John Craven (Leeds Modern)

101. Harold Pinter and Michael Caine (Hackney Downs)

4 CELEBRITIES WITH HGV LICENCES

1. Rowan Atkinson
2. Tim Healy
3. Ken Tyrrell
4. Rick Astley

10 CELEBRITIES WHO LEFT SCHOOL AT 15

1. **George Carey, Archbishop of Canterbury**. Dr Carey left Bifrons Secondary Modern School having failed his Eleven Plus four years earlier. But you don't get to become an archbishop on the strength of a good report from the woodwork teacher so, eventually, he returned to full-time education and went on to gain a PhD at King's College, London.

2. **Paul Shane**. The roly-poly actor who found fame as Ted Bovis in *Hi-De-Hi!* left school at 15 to go down the pits as a miner.

3. **David Bailey**. The photographer who came to represent 'Swinging London' in the 1960s hated school so much that he left on the day of his 15th birthday.

4. **Debbie Moore**. The business woman left school at 15, without a single qualification. After working as a model, she started the Pineapple Dance Studios in 1979 and took it public in 1982. She was voted Business Woman of The Year in 1984 and wrote a bestselling autobiography in 1989 entitled *When A Woman Means Business*. Education? Who needs it!

5. **Jennifer D'Abo**. Like Debbie Moore, a former Businesswoman of The Year, Jennifer D'Abo turned round Ryman, the stationery company, before going on to head up the society florists, Moyses Stevens. And, no, she's <u>not</u> related to Mike (of Manfred Mann) or Maryam (of Bond Girl fame) but she is the mother of the successful restaurateur, Joel Cadbury.

6. **Sir Philip Harris**. Like so many entrepreneurs (e.g. Peter De Savary, Richard Branson, Alan Sugar and Sophie Mirman), the multi-millionaire businessman and carpet magnate is another graduate of the University of Life.

7. **Jeremy Beadle**. The TV presenter and prankster wasn't destined for a lengthy formal education but he's more than made up for it since. An auto-didact, he owns what is probably the most wide-ranging private reference library in the country and would have walked *Mastermind* if he had ever bothered to go in for it.

8. **Kevin Keegan**. The Newcastle United manager left school to become a professional footballer. His first club was Scunthorpe United but he became a star at Liverpool (where he first exhibited signs of a perm) and became captain of the England team. He went on to play for Hamburg and, after several years of bad hair days, became an extremely successful manager.

9. **Twiggy**. As Lesley Hornby, she left school as soon as possible to become a model and, very soon, the face of the 1960s.

10. **Shirley Bassey.** The girl from Tiger Bay, who could tell that you were a man of distinction the minute you walked in the joint, left school aged 15 and soon left home to work in a factory wrapping chamber pots.

10 CELEBRITIES WHO TRAINED AS COMMERCIAL ARTISTS

1. Lynsey De Paul
2. David Bowie
3. Bob Hoskins
4. Roy Hudd
5. Sir Dirk Bogarde
6. Gene Hackman
7. Ian Hunter
8. Len Deighton
9. Pete Townshend
10. Leo Sayer

6 CELEBRITIES WHO STUDIED AT RADA

1. Mike Leigh
2. Lynne Reid Banks
3. Jonathan Meades
4. Pete Murray
5. Valerie Singleton
6. Brian Matthew

11 CELEBRITIES WHO WERE RHODES SCHOLARS

1. Bill Clinton
2. Bryan Gould
3. Bill Bradley
4. Kris Kristofferson
5. Bob Hawke
6. Terrence Malick (Director of *Badlands* and *Days of Heaven*)
7. Eddie Eagan (1920s Olympic Heavyweight Boxing Champion)
8. Naomi Wolf
9. David Kirk (former captain of the All Blacks)
10. Dom Mintoff
11. Edward de Bono

7 AMERICAN CELEBRITIES AND HOW THEY WERE RATED BY THEIR CLASSMATES

1. Billy Crystal – voted Wittiest Student In His Class

2. Tom Cruise – voted Least Likely To Succeed

3. Caprice – voted Homecoming Queen

4. Sandra Bullock – voted Most Likely To Brighten Your Day

5. Robin Williams – voted Least Likely To Succeed

6. Meg Ryan – voted Cutest Girl In Class

7. Monica Lewinsky – voted "The Girl Most Likely To Get Her Name In Lights'

13 CELEBRITIES WHO WERE HEAD GIRLS AT SCHOOL

1. Sarah, Duchess of York (Hurst Lodge)

2. Norma Major (Peckham Comprehensive)

3. Baroness Margaret Thatcher (Kesteven And Grantham Girls' School)

4. Mo Mowlam MP (Coundon Court Comprehensive)

5. Dame Thora Hird (Morecambe Preparatory School)

6. Joan Bakewell (Stockport High School For Girls)

7. Gillian Shephard MP (North Walsham High School For Girls)

8. Kate Winslet (Redroofs)

9. Baroness Lynda Chalker (Roedean)

10. Emma Nicholson (St Mary's, Wantage)

11. Victoria Smurfit (Aravon)

12. Baroness Sarah Hogg (St Mary's Convent, Ascot)

13. Francine Stock (St Catherine's, Guildford)

21 CELEBRITIES WHO WERE HEAD BOYS AT SCHOOL

1. Ian Hislop (Ardingly)
2. Hugh Dennis (University College School)
3. Sir Peter Hall (The Perse School)
4. Brian Moore (Cranbrook)
5. Richard Hill (Bishop Wordsworth's School)
6. Jonah Lomu (Wesley College)
7. Jeremy Paxman (Malvern College)
8. Prince Edward (Gordonstoun)
9. Frank Bruno (Oak Hall)
10. Simon MacCorkindale (Haileybury)
11. Peter Jay (Winchester)
12. John Fowles (Bedford)
13. Lord William Rees-Mogg (Charterhouse)
14. Lord Douglas Hurd (Eton)
15. Lord David Owen (Mudd House Prep School)
16. Prince Philip (Gordonstoun)
17. Prince Charles (Gordonstoun)
18. Peter Phillips (Gordonstoun)
19. Boris Johnson (Eton)
20. Sir Robin Butler (Harrow)
21. Rory Knight Bruce (Stowe)

26 CELEBRITIES WHO WERE CONVENT SCHOOLGIRLS

1. Karren Brady
2. Helen Mirren
3. Joanna Lumley
4. Barbara Windsor
5. Donna D'Errico
6. Caroline Aherne
7. Zoë Ball
8. Sue Barker
9. Samantha Fox
10. Patsy Kensit
11. Genevieve Bujold
12. Janet Dibley
13. Marianne Faithfull
14. Carole Bouquet
15. Nicola Pagett
16. Cherie Booth Blair
17. Emma Nicholson
18. Kathy Burke
19. Ann Widdecombe
20. Sarah Kennedy
21. Tiggy Legge-Bourke
22. Mia Farrow
23. Jennifer Paterson
24. Dillie Keane
25. Stephanie Beacham
26. Kristin Scott Thomas

10 CELEBRITIES WHO TRAINED AS BALLET DANCERS

1. Victoria Principal
2. Leslie Caron
3. Sally Meen
4. Elizabeth Emanuel
5. Annabel Croft
6. O.J. Simpson
7. Holly Aird
8. Stephanie Lawrence
9. Ken Russell
10. Clare Francis

11 CELEBRITIES WHO TRAINED TO BE DOCTORS BUT DIDN'T QUALIFY

1. Neil Diamond
2. Giorgio Armani
3. Lew Ayres (who went on to play Dr Kildare)
4. Bob Dole
5. Sir Nicholas Fairbairn
6. Luca Cumani
7. Alessandra Mussolini
8. Wim Wenders
9. Christopher Isherwood
10. Michael Bywater
11. Roger Black

10 CELEBRITIES WHO STUDIED TO BE ARCHITECTS

1. Art Garfunkel
2. Rifat Ozbek
3. Janet Street-Porter
4. Queen Noor of Jordan
5. Justine Frischmann
6. Carla Bruni
7. Alan Plater
8. Lord Snowdon
9. Justin De Blank
10. Chris Lowe

Chapter 3

Distinguishing Features

13 CELEBRITY REDHEADS

1. The Duchess of York
2. Mick Hucknall
3. Neil Kinnock
4. Dennis Pennis
5. Geri Halliwell
6. Chloe Newsome
7. Chris Evans
8. Rula Lenska
9. Patsy Palmer
10. Alex Kingston
11. Barbara Knox
12. Nicholas Witchell
13. Jane Asher

9 CELEBRITIES WHO BOUGHT ROLLS-ROYCES

1. Gary Glitter
2. Zia Mahmood
3. Noel Gallagher
4. Shane Ritchie
5. Ruth Madoc
6. Sir Jimmy Savile
7. Michael Caine
8. Donovan
9. Cilla Black

2 CELEBRITIES WHO EACH HAVE EYES OF DIFFERENT COLOURS

1. Jane Seymour (one green and one brown)
2. David Bowie (one green and one blue)

9 CELEBRITIES WHO ARE COLOUR-BLIND

1. William Hague
2. Paul Newman
3. Rod Stewart
4. Jack Nicklaus
5. Nicky Piper
6. Peter Bowles
7. Peter Ebdon
8. Sir Donald Sinden
9. David Millns

64 CELEBRITIES WHO ARE LEFT-HANDED

1. Brian Lara
2. Rik Mayall
3. Goldie Hawn
4. Sir Bobby Charlton
5. Graham Thorpe
6. Shirley MacLaine
7. Henry Cooper
8. Phil Mickelson
9. John Barnes
10. Juliet Morris
11. Steve Ovett
12. Michael Crawford
13. Greg Rusedski
14. Diane Keaton
15. Robert De Niro
16. Carol Barnes
17. Emma Thompson
18. Nicholas Lyndhurst
19. Harvey Goldsmith
20. William Roache
21. Matthew Broderick
22. Paul Nicholas
23. Faith Brown
24. Cheryl Baker
25. Janet Street-Porter
26. Paul Shane
27. Ringo Starr
28. George Michael
29. Tom Cruise
30. Julia Sawalha
31. Syd Little
32. Su Pollard
33. Monica Seles
34. Loyd Grossman
35. Ian Rush
36. Richard Dreyfuss
37. Robert Redford
38. Sir Bob Geldof
39. Anthony Newley
40. Jean Boht
41. Mark Spitz
42. Jennifer Saunders
43. Jean Shrimpton
44. Tony Robinson
45. Bill Treacher
46. Ruud Gullitt
47. Jimmy Connors
48. Mary Hopkin
49. Martina Navratilova
50. Phil Collins
51. Jimmy Greaves
52. John McEnroe
53. Oprah Winfrey
54. Magnus Magnusson
55. Terry Venables
56. Julian Clary
57. Julia Roberts
58. Bjorn Borg
59. Jimmy White
60. Michael Parkinson
61. Terry Waite
62. Ross Kemp
63. Ryan O'Neal
64. Prince William

4 CELEBRITIES WHO HAVE LOST PART OF A FINGER

1. Dave Allen
2. Tony Bullimore
3. Auberon Waugh
4. Terry Nutkins

13 CELEBRITIES WITH GYPSY BLOOD

1. Pat Phoenix
2. Elvis Presley
3. Eric Clapton
4. Vita Sackville-West
5. Django Reinhardt
6. Eric Cantona
7. David Essex
8. Bob Hoskins
9. Charlie Chaplin
10. Ava Gardner
11. Pablo Picasso
12. Nadja Auermann
13. Miguel de Cervantes

14 CELEBRITIES WITH FLAT FEET

1. Stan Collymore
2. Linda Lusardi
3. Roger Black
4. Zoë Ball
5. Edwina Currie
6. Lord Colin Cowdrey
7. Dame Alicia Markova
8. Newt Gingrich
9. Lord Longford
10. Prince Charles
11. Cyndi Lauper
12. Stephen King
13. Lord Young of Graffham
14. Robin Smith

49 CELEBRITIES WITH TATTOOS

1. Roseanne (Pink rose on left foot; ex-husband's (Tom Arnold) name on shoulder and bottom now replaced with flowers and fairies)
2. Gerard Depardieu (Star on arm)
3. Patsy Kensit ("Liam" with shamrock on ankle)
4. Oliver Reed (Eagle on penis)
5. Ulrika Jonsson (Devil on bottom)
6. George Shultz (Tiger on bottom)
7. Mel C (Celtic band on arm)
8. Lord Patrick Lichfield (Seahorse on arm)
9. Princess Stephanie of Monaco (Dragon on hip)
10. Mick Hucknall (Federal symbol of Europe on arm)
11. Pamela Anderson (Tommy Lee's name on wedding finger)
12. Johnny Depp ('Winona Forever' on arm)
13. Cher (Flower on bottom)
14. Alexander McQueen (Japanese fish symbol on chest)
15. Rachel Williams (Arrow on bottom)
16. Vanilla Ice (Leaf on stomach)
17. Drew Barrymore (Butterfly and flower sprig on bottom)
18. Dean Holdsworth ('Let He Without Sin Cast The First Stone' on arm)
19. Ringo Starr (Half moon on arm)
20. Vinnie Jones ('Leeds Utd' on leg)
21. Paula Yates (Fish on arm)
22. Brian Harvey ('Eastside' on arm)
23. Joan Baez (Flower on back)
24. Sean Bean ('100% Blade' on arm)
25. Madonna ('MP' - standing for 'Madonna's Property' - and Marilyn Monroe's face on bottom)
26. Glen Campbell (Dagger on arm)
27. Sharron Davies (Elephant on bottom)
28. Tony Copsey ('Made In England' on bottom)
29. Julia Roberts (Red heart with a Chinese character meaning 'strength of heart' on shoulder)
30. Brian Conley ('No Entry' on bottom)
31. Kelly McGillis (Red rose on ankle)
32. John Kennedy Jnr. (Irish shamrock on shoulder)
33. Suzi Quattro (Star on wrist)
34. Sean Connery ('Scotland Forever' and 'Mum and Dad' on arms)
35. Brigitte Nielsen (Heart on bottom)
36. Tommy Lee (Wife's name on penis, Pamela Anderson)
37. Christy Turlington (Heart shape on ankle)
38. Shaznay Lewis (Year of the Rabbit above her right breast)
39. Liam Gallagher ('Patsy' on arm)
40. Björk (Icelandic rune on shoulder)
41. Melanie Blatt (Chinese-style dragon climbing up her ribcage and musical notes dancing across one shoulder)
42. Melanie Griffith (Pear on bottom)
43. Geri Halliwell (Sundial design on top of back and jaguar further down)
44. Marianne Faithfull (Bird on hand)
45. Chrissie Hynde (Dolphin on arm)
46. Helen Mirren (Pair of crosses on hand)
47. Nicole Appleton (Year of the Tiger on her torso)
48. Julian Dicks (Taz the Tasmanian devil on leg)
49. Whoopi Goldberg (Woodstock on breast)

10 CELEBRITIES IMMEDIATELY RECOGNISABLE BY THEIR GLASSES

1. Chris Evans
2. Dennis Taylor
3. Ian McCaskill
4. Andre Agassi
5. Lord Norman Tebbit
6. Ronnie Barker
7. Timmy Mallett
8. Sir Robin Day
9. Dame Edna Everage
10. Jim Bowen

10 CELEBRITIES IMMEDIATELY RECOGNISABLE BY THEIR TEETH

1. Esther Rantzen
2. Shane MacGowan
3. David Mellor
4. Robin Gibb
5. Janet Brown
6. Ken Dodd
7. Sally Thomsett
8. Mick Hucknall
9. Lance Percival
10. Janet Street-Porter

13 CELEBRITIES IMMEDIATELY RECOGNISABLE FROM THEIR EYEBROWS

1. Denis Healey
2. Madonna
3. Eric Cantona
4. Chris De Burgh
5. Norman Lamont
6. Patrick Moore
7. Sir Rhodes Boyson
8. Brooke Shields
9. Morrissey
10. Major Ronald Ferguson
11. Helena Bonham Carter
12. Liam Gallagher
13. Noel Gallagher

10 CELEBRITIES WHO HAD LIP IMPLANTS

1. Madonna
2. Lynne Perrie
3. Suzanne Mizzi
4. Cher
5. Loni Anderson
6. Pamela Anderson
7. Caprice
8. Melanie Griffith
9. Ivana Trump
10. Elizabeth Taylor

12 CELEBRITIES WHO HAD NOSE JOBS

1. Peter O'Toole
2. Cilla Black
3. Edwina Currie
4. Caroline Aherne
5. Bonnie Langford
6. Graeme Souness
7. Tom Jones
8. Cher
9. Belinda Lang
10. Dale Winton
11. Stefanie Powers
12. Cheryl Ladd

12 CELEBRITIES WHO DESCRIBE THEMSELVES AS "PERSONALITIES" (i.e. in their official biographies.)

1. Anthea Turner
2. Michael Barrymore
3. Noel Edmonds
4. Matthew Kelly
5. Timmy Mallett
6. Sir Jimmy Savile
7. Carol Vorderman
8. Christopher Biggins
9. Gloria Hunniford
10. David 'Kid' Jensen
11. Valerie Singleton
12. Richard Skinner

9 CELEBRITIES WHO HAVE HAD LIPOSUCTION

1. Michael Ball (from his stomach)
2. Demi Moore (from her thighs, bottom and stomach)
3. Joan Rivers (from her thighs)
4. Anna Nicole Smith (from her stomach)
5. Michael Caine (from his stomach)
6. Melanie Griffith (from her stomach and thighs)
7. Kenny Rogers (from his stomach)
8. Roseanne (from her stomach)
9. Don Johnson (from his chin and cheeks)

17 CELEBRITIES WHO HAVE HAD FACELIFTS

1. Loni Anderson
2. Cher
3. Jane Fonda
4. Dolly Parton
5. Joan Rivers
6. Ivana Trump
7. Mary Tyler Moore
8. Angela Lansbury
9. Fay Weldon
10. Roseanne
11. Lynne Perrie
12. Nicholas Parsons
13. Julie Christie
14. Bea Arthur
15. Roger Moore
16. Molly Parkin
17. Farrah Fawcett

10 CELEBRITIES AND THE ORGANISATIONS OF WHICH THEY'RE PATRONS

1. Anthea Turner (Born Free Foundation)
2. Stephen Fry (Norwich Play House)
3. Lord Richard Attenborough (Kingsley Hall Community Centre)
4. Brian Blessed (Dearne Community Miners' Welfare Scheme)
5. Jean Boht (British Homoeopathic Association)
6. Sue Cook (Parents At Work)
7. John Craven (Rainforest Action Fund)
8. Elizabeth Dawn (Manchester Taxi Drivers Association)
9. Chris Tarrant (Phoenix Centre For The Physically Handicapped)
10. Martyn Lewis (Youth For Britain)

4 CELEBRITIES WHO BOUGHT OTHER CELEBRITIES' HOUSES

1. Brian Jones bought A. A. Milne's house

2. Pete Townshend bought the Poet Laureate, Alfred Lord Tennyson's, house

3. Lord Jeffrey Archer bought Rupert Brooke's house

4. Nick Mason bought Camilla Parker Bowles's house

3 CELEBRITIES WHO BITE THEIR NAILS

1. Gordon Brown MP

2. Dustin Hoffman

3. Phil Collins

14 CELEBRITIES WHO WEAR WIGS OR HAIRPIECES

1. Ted Danson

2. Terry Wogan

3. Tommy Lee Jones

4. Burt Reynolds

5. Frank Sinatra

6. Tina Turner

7. Gary Glitter

8. Charlton Heston

9. Joan Collins

10. William Shatner

11. Debbie Harry

12. Jimmy Young

13. Bruce Forsyth

14. Ken Morley

5 CELEBRITIES WHO CAN USE THE ROMAN NUMERAL III AFTER THEIR NAMES

1. Loudon Wainwright

2. Ted Turner

3. Davis Love

4. Ted Danson

5. Alec Baldwin

5 CELEBRITIES WHO HAD THEIR NIPPLES PIERCED

1. Tim Roth
2. Tommy Lee
3. Howard Donald
4. Jaye Davidson
5. Billy Connolly

4 CELEBRITIES WHO HAD THEIR TONGUES PIERCED

1. Mel B
2. Keith Flint (of Prodigy)
3. Kathy Acker
4. Ross Hale (former British & Commonwealth Light-Welterwight champion)

9 CELEBRITIES WHO NEVER GIVE INTERVIEWS

1. Bjorn Borg
2. Peter Green
3. The Queen
4. Marlon Brando
5. Michael Jackson
6. Charlie Watts
7. Tom Bell
8. J.D. Salinger
9. Warren Beatty

30 CELEBRITIES WHO HAVE MADE THE TOP 10 IN RICHARD BLACKWELL'S ANNUAL 'WORST-DRESSED WOMEN' LISTS

1. The Duchess of York (1996 "The bare-toed terror of London town. She looks like an unemployed barmaid in search of a crown". Also made the list in 1988 when she was accused of looking "like a horse that came in last". Blackwell went on to say "she looks terrible, like she should be making beds on the second floor of a motel")

2. Geena Davis (1992 "Big Bird in heels")

3. Yoko Ono (1972 "Oh no Yoko")

4. Roseanne (1989 "Bowling alley reject")

5. David Bowie (1973 "A cross between Joan Crawford and Marlene Dietrich doing a glitter revival of New Faces")

6. Faye Dunaway (1991 "The Depressing Diva of Designer Dreck")

7. Bette Midler (1978 "She didn't go to a rummage sale, she wore it")

8. Barbra Streisand (1990 "What can I say? Yentl's gone mental". 1983 "A boy version of Medusa")

9. Jane Seymour (1991 "A paisley peepshow on parade")

10. Debbie Harry (1979 "Ten cents a dance with a nickel change")

11. Madonna (1992 "The Bare-bottomed Bore of Babylon". 1988 "Helpless, hopeless and horrendous")

12. Dennis Rodman (1996 "The 'Fashion Menace' may be the Bad Boy of basketball, but in fishnet and feathers he's a unisex wreck")

13. Glenn Close (1992 "Dracula's Daughter")

14. Helen Reddy (1974 "Isn't ready")

15. Tyne Daly (1991 "Tyne's a train wreck in Technicolor")

16. Camilla Parker Bowles (1995 "The Queen of Frump" and The biggest bomb to hit Britain since the Blitz". 1994 "Her fashion image is way off track: she looked in the mirror and watched it crack")

17. Kathy Bates (1991 "At play in the basement of K Mart")

18. The Queen (1990 "God save the mothballs, the Stonehenge of style strikes again")

19. Cher (1986 "Popular Mechanics Playmate of the Month. Someone must have thrown a monkey wrench into her fashion taste". 1984 "A plucked cockatoo setting femininity back 20 years")

20. Sir Elton John (1975 "Would be the campiest spectacle in the Rose Parade")

21. Demi Moore (1989 "A Spandexed nightmare on Willis Street")

22. Jodie Foster (1991 "Her fashions would look better on Hannibal Lecter")

23. Linda Ronstadt (1977 "Bought her entire wardrobe during a five-minute bus stop")

24. Julia Roberts (1992 "Hand out the hook for rag doll Roberts")

25. Tina Turner (1985 "Some women dress for men, some dress for women, some dress for laughs")

26. Sinead O'Connor (1992 "No tresses, no dresses. The high priestess of pretence downright depresses". 1990 "Nothing compares to the bald-headed banshee of MTV")

27. Boy George (1983 "Victor/Victoria in bad drag")

28. Olivia Newton-John (1983 "From toes to nose, a shredded tragedy")

29. Imelda Marcos (1988 "An over-the-hill actress auditioning for Evita")

30. Sheena Easton (1981 "A London road runner dressed for the fog")

Chapter 4

What's in a Name?

95 CELEBRITIES WHO CHANGED THEIR NAMES

1. Eric Clapton (Eric Clapp)
2. Tina Turner (Annie Mae Bullock)
3. Doris Day (Doris Kapelhoff)
4. Axl Rose (William Bailey)
5. Michael Barrymore (Michael Parker)
6. Whoopi Goldberg (Caryn Johnson)
7. Billy Idol (William Broad)
8. Cheryl Baker (Rita Crudgington)
9. Adam Faith (Terry Nelhams)
10. Meatloaf (Marvin Aday)
11. Michael Crawford (Michael Dumble-Smith)
12. Dave Allen (David Tynan-O'Mahoney)
13. Chevy Chase (Cornelius Chase)
14. Lulu (Marie Lawrie)
15. Elaine Paige (Elaine Bickerstaff)
16. Grandmaster Flash (Joseph Saddler)
17. Elle Macpherson (Eleanor Gow)
18. Tom Jones (Thomas Woodward)
19. Demi Moore (Demetria Guynes)
20. Georgie Fame (Clive Powell)
21. Siouxsie Sioux (Susan Ballion)
22. Russ Abbot (Russell Roberts)
23. Sir Cliff Richard (Harry Webb)
24. Winona Ryder (Winona Horowitz)
25. Jane Seymour (Joyce Frankenberg)
26. Christian Slater (Christian Hawkins)
27. Michael Caine (Maurice Micklewhite)
28. Manfred Mann (Michael Lubowitz)
29. Sigourney Weaver (Susan Weaver)
30. Elvis Costello (Declan McManus)
31. Julie Andrews (Julia Wells)
32. Anne Bancroft (Anna Italiano)
33. Bobby Davro (Robert Nankeville)
34. Mel Brooks (Melvin Kaminsky)
35. Charles Aznavour (Shahnour Aznourian)
36. Iggy Pop (James Osterberg)
37. Stevie Wonder (Steveland Judkins)
38. Jean-Claude Van Damme (Jean-Claude Van Varenberg)
39. Shakin' Stevens (Michael Barrett)
40. Diane Keaton (Diane Hall)
41. Gary Numan (Gary Webb)
42. Les Dennis (Leslie Heseltine)
43. Jennifer Jason Leigh (Jennifer Morrow)
44. Paul Jones (Paul Pond)

45. Dana (Rosemary Brown)

46. The Edge (David Evans)

47. Nicolas Cage (Nicholas Coppola)

48. Adam Ant (Stewart Goddard)

49. Tammy Wynette (Virginia Pugh)

50. Billy Ocean (Leslie Charles)

51. Mica Paris (Michelle Wallen)

52. Sting (Gordon Sumner)

53. Janis Ian (Janis Fink)

54. Chris de Burgh (Christopher Davidson)

55. Freddie Starr (Freddie Powell)

56. Captain Sensible (Ray Burns)

57. Lou Reed (Louis Firbank)

58. Tony Curtis (Bernard Schwartz)

59. Jack Palance (Walter Palanuik)

60. Charles Bronson (Charles Buchinski)

61. Donna Summer (Donna Gaines)

62. David Essex (David Cook)

63. Sir Elton John (Reginald Dwight)

64. Meg Ryan (Margaret Hyra)

65. Alice Cooper (Vincent Furnier)

66. P.J. Proby (James Smith)

67. Elkie Brooks (Elaine Bookbinder)

68. Victor Borge (Borge Rosenbaum)

69. Brigitte Bardot (Camille Javal)

70. Joan Rivers (Joan Molinsky)

71. Kiki Dee (Pauline Matthews)

72. Woody Allen (Allen Konigsberg)

73. Martin Sheen (Ramon Estevez)

74. John Cleese (John Cheese)

75. Calvin Klein (Richard Klein)

76. Engelbert Humperdinck (Gerry Dorsey)

77. Bono (Paul Hewson)

78. Bo Derek (Cathleen Collins)

79. Hammer (Stanley Burrell)

80. Don Johnson (Donald Wayne)

81. David Copperfield (David Kotkin)

82. Bill Wyman (William Perks)

83. Omar Sharif (Michael Shalhoub)

84. James Garner (James Baumgarner)

85. David Bowie (David Jones)

86. Vic Reeves (Jim Moir)

87. Cilla Black (Priscilla White)

88. Jodie Foster (Alicia Foster)

89. Snoop Doggy Dogg (Calvin Broadus)

90. Pat Benatar (Patricia Andrejewski)

91. Sid Owen (David Sutton)

92. Barry Manilow (Barry Pincus)

93. Michael Keaton (Michael Douglas)

94. Theresa Russell (Theresa Paup)

95. Christopher Walken (Ronald Walken)

44 CELEBRITIES WHO DIDN'T CHANGE THEIR NAMES

1. Art Garfunkel
2. Goldie Hawn
3. Marianne Faithfull
4. Rush Limbaugh
5. Rowan Atkinson
6. Macaulay Culkin
7. Gordon Honeycombe
8. Clint Eastwood
9. Errol Flynn
10. Aaron Spelling
11. Cloris Leachman
12. Woody Harrelson
13. Brooke Shields
14. Danny De Vito
15. Kirstie Alley
16. Liam Neeson
17. Quentin Tarantino
18. Kelsey Grammer
19. Marlon Brando
20. Glenn Close
21. Julian Clary
22. Wesley Snipes
23. Gene Hackman
24. Joan Armatrading
25. Arnold Schwarzenegger
26. Johnny Depp
27. Billy Crystal
28. Keanu Reeves
29. Noel Edmonds
30. Richard Gere
31. Lyle Lovett
32. Harrison Ford
33. Uma Thurman
34. Val Kilmer
35. Gareth Hale
36. Norman Pace
37. Robert De Niro
38. Oprah Winfrey
39. Dustin Hoffman
40. Al Pacino
41. Denzel Washington
42. Luther Vandross
43. Tom Petty
44. Sheryl Crow

10 PAIRS OF CELEBRITY SIBLINGS WITH DIFFERENT SURNAMES

1. Joan Fontaine and Olivia de Havilland
2. A.S. Byatt and Margaret Drabble
3. Emilio Estevez and Charlie Sheen
4. Warren Beatty and Shirley MacLaine
5. John Major and Terry Major-Ball
6. Keith Chegwin and Janice Long
7. Sheila Mercier and Lord Brian Rix
8. Lord Lew Grade and Lord Bernard Delfont
9. George Sanders and Tom Conway
10. Talia Shire and Francis Coppola

22 CELEBRITIES WITH EXTRAORDINARY MIDDLE NAMES

1. Mark FREUDER Knopfler
2. Ben CAINE Hollioake
3. Bob PRIMROSE Wilson
4. John MARWOOD Cleese
5. Paul EMERSON CARLYLE Ince
6. Robson GOLIGHTLY Green
7. Emile IVANHOE Heskey
8. Anthea MILLICENT Turner
9. Lawrence BRUNO NERO Dallaglio
10. Jeremy DICKSON Paxman
11. Uma KARUNA Thurman
12. Damon ERNEST DEVERAUX Hill
13. Hugh JOHN MUNGO Grant
14. Michael CIARAN Barrymore
15. Sir Terence ORBY Conran
16. Paul YAW Boateng
17. Joan HENRIETTA Collins
18. Rowan SEBASTIAN Atkinson
19. Mel COLUMCILLE Gibson
20. Gene ALDEN Hackman
21. Woody TRACY Harrelson
22. Rob HEPLER Lowe

15 CELEBRITIES WITH THE NAME 'JUNIOR' AS PART OF THEIR TITLE

1. Harry Connick
2. Louis Gossett
3. Sammy Davis
4. Martin Luther King
5. Bill Cotton
6. Cuba Gooding
7. Lon Chaney
8. Larry Mullen
9. Christy O'Connor
10. John Kennedy
11. Buster Mathis
12. Gordon Brand
13. Efrem Zimbalist
14. Ed Begley
15. Douglas Fairbanks

5 CELEBRITIES WHO WERE BORN WITH THE FIRST NAME MARY

1. Lauren Hutton
2. Dame Barbara Cartland
3. Dusty Springfield
4. Kathleen Turner
5. George Eliot

2 CELEBRITIES WHO MARRIED A WOMAN NAMED KELLY PRESTON (THOUGH NOT THE SAME WOMAN!)

1. Lou Diamond Phillips
2. John Travolta

30 CELEBRITIES WHOSE NAMES APPEAR IN THE DICTIONARY OF COCKNEY RHYMING SLANG

1. George Best: Guest
2. Jeremy Beadle: Needle
3. Tommy Steele: Eel
4. Melvyn Bragg: Shag
5. Richard Todd: Cod
6. Cilla Black: Back
7. Jimmy Young: Bung
8. David Bowie: Blowy (in the sense of windy)
9. Michael Caine: Pain
10. Barry McGuigan: Big 'un
11. Sir Edward Heath: Teeth
12. Oliver Reed: Weed (as in tobacco)
13. Frankie Vaughan: Prawn
14. Sebastian Coe: Toe
15. Glenn Hoddle: Doddle
16. Gregory Peck: Cheque
17. Ian Rush: Brush
18. Jane Russell: Mussel
19. Acker Bilk: Milk
20. Doris Day: Way
21. Ken Dodd: Wad
22. Screaming Lord Sutch: Clutch
23. Marty Wilde: Mild (as in ale)
24. Bernhard Langer: Banger
25. Dudley Moore: Sore
26. Mickey Rooney: Loony
27. Enoch Powell: Towel
28. Danny La Rue: Blue
29. Ronnie Biggs: Digs (as in lodgings)
30. Alan Minter: Splinter

14 CELEBRITIES WHOSE NAMES ARE USED IN NEW RHYMING SLANG

1. Giorgio Armani – Sarnie
2. Douglas Hurd – Third (as in University degree)
3. Niki Lauda – Powder
4. Christian Slater – Later
5. Darren Gough – Cough
6. Roberta Flack – Sack
7. Calvin Klein – Fine
8. Jim Bowen – Goin'
9. Geoff Hurst – First (as in University degree)
10. Thelonius Monk – Skunk
11. Claire Rayner – Trainer (e.g. Claire Rayners = Trainers)
12. Kate Moss – Toss
13. Pete Tong – Wrong
14. Terry Waite – Late

THE ANAGRAMS OF 150 CELEBRITIES

1. BLOB RECREATION: Robbie Coltrane

2. BAD IN HER: Dani Behr

3. ANGRY BOILS: Gaby Roslin

4. I AM CHEAP SELL: Michael Aspel

5. NO, I DECLINE: Celine Dion

6. ERROR ON BIDET: Robert De Niro

7. NO, SARDONIC ONE: Sinead O'Connor

8. IF HELL IS POP CHILD: Phillip Schofield

9. ORDER IN YAWN: Winona Ryder

10. CASUAL PIG - GONE: Paul Gascoigne

11. IS LASS INFLATED?: Lisa Stansfield

12. NO! DO CENSOR!: Des O'Connor

13. SO CHECK JAIL, MAN: Michael Jackson

14. SEND MY OLD MAN: Desmond Lynam

15. TINY TRASH CRIER: Terry Christian

16. SCREEN ANNOY: Sean Connery

17. BIG LEMONS: Mel Gibson

18. TALLY-HO! FLIRT AGAIN!: Gillian Taylforth

19. SCANS TOILET: Selina Scott

20. JOINS POSH? HERESY!: Sophie Rhys-Jones

21. BRAIN CREEPS ON: Pierce Brosnan

22. SOME TASK: Kate Moss

23. TIGHT SWERVE: Steve Wright

24. NARCOLEPTIC: Eric Clapton

25. RISK BIG NAME?: Kim Basinger

26. I MEAN PHALLIC!: Michael Palin

27. HMM! A SNOT POEM: Emma Thompson

28. SHUT BEAK: Kate Bush

29. I'M A LOVE-BITING TORY: Virginia Bottomley

30. GIRLIE LAW HELL: Geri Halliwell

31. I'M THAT CLEAN HERO: Michael Atherton

32. SEX ADVISED: David Essex

33. AH! NUTTER NEAR: Anthea Turner

34. LARGE FAT NOISE: Gloria Estefan

35. RAW BRAINS BROAD: Barbara Windsor

36. A GENEROUS MESS: Graeme Souness

37. LEMMINGS SERENADE: Melinda Messenger

38. ME THIN MAN: Tim Henman

39. I LIKE 'EM YOUNG: Kylie Minogue

40. DIET? TREMBLE!: Bette Midler

41. AND I AM SAVED: David Seaman

42. "CREEP," SHE'LL MOAN: Elle Macpherson

43. REAR LOBOTOMY KIT: Tim Brooke-Taylor

44. SHOOK BUM BONE: Bob Monkhouse

45. HIDDEN WAR CRY: Wendy Richard

46. ANIMAL WHISTLER: William Shatner

47. STRANGE CRAP MISER: Princess Margaret

48. BBC? NOW HURRY BOY!: Roy 'Chubby' Brown

49. CARNAL ROBES: Carol Barnes

50. HE'S THE GRIM DANDY: Teddy Sheringham

51. SARDONIC WHIRL: Richard Wilson

52. SOFA MEMBER: Emma Forbes

53. A RESTLESS BRAVE LOONIE: Severiano Ballesteros

54. REVIEW AGONY SURE: Sigourney Weaver

55. DREARY MILD ACHE: Richard Madeley

56. SOLD BRAIN ON: Linda Robson

57. I'M SO CUTER: Tom Cruise

58. INJURED FANS SNEER: Jennifer Saunders

59. OLD WEST ACTION: Clint Eastwood

60. PAST CREATURE: Stuart Pearce

61. CLINICAL MASK: Ian McCaskill

62. FINE TICKLE LADY: Felicity Kendal

63. BRAINY CLONE: Brian Conley

64. ONLY I CAN THRILL: Hillary Clinton

65. DEAR DEAR, RUDE PIG: Gerard Depardieu

66. BASH RED WALLY: Bradley Walsh

67. MY GOD, AN ORANGE!: Gayner Goodman

68. MERRY WARDROBE: Drew Barrymore

69. I'M A ROCKET PRO: Patrick Moore

70. BAD MORALS RUN RAW: Malandra Burrows

71. FOUL HARD IN GROIN: Gloria Hunniford

72. I'M THE LOCAL NOB: Michael Bolton

73. PLAY NOT, LORD: Dolly Parton

74. APRICOT VALUATION: Luciano Pavarotti

75. SLOVENLY STEEL STAR: Sylvester Stallone

76. I, THE LAZY BLOATER: Elizabeth Taylor

77. MANURE PLOT: Paul Merton

78. HE'S GROWN LARGE 'N' CRAZED: Arnold Schwarzenegger

79. GERMANY: Meg Ryan

80. AS A ROAD VICTIM: Victoria Adams (Posh Spice)

81. HORRID BUG DEVASTATION: Sir David Attenborough

82. ANORAK'S IN TOWN: Rowan Atkinson

83. I COLLAR SLIME: Carol Smillie

84. PEDESTRIAN: Andi Peters

85. I AM A NICE LECH: Michael Caine

86. CATCHES CIGAR: Greta Scacchi

87. TWO RED RATS: Rod Stewart

88. ME MOODIER: Demi Moore

89. HEROIC MALE EGG: George Michael

90. ASK TINY PEST: Patsy Kensit

91. COAL PAIN: Al Pacino

92. A PRETENDER: Peter Andre

93. I WARM BILLIONS: Robin Williams

94. CROWD FIND RACY: Cindy Crawford

95. GRR! TOY CHARM: Rory McGrath

96. CALL DIRE LESBIAN: Belinda Carlisle

97. LIBRARY WOMAN: Barry Manilow

98. I ROCK BONO: Robin Cook

99. TRY LARGE GIT: Gary Glitter

100. AVOID COW RIOT: Victoria Wood

101. DEAL VAIN GENITALS: Linda Evangelista

102. CLOSE EVIL SLOT: Elvis Costello

103. LOVELIEST IN ANGER: Valerie Singleton

104. WIN CALL GIRL: Will Carling

105. HALT! SEARCH MANIAC: Michaela Strachan

106. STORY BLUNDER: Burt Reynolds

107. HUGE MAIL WAIL: William Hague

108. AUTUMN HARM: Uma Thurman

109. AN APE LUSH: Paul Shane

110. HELD LONG END: Glenn Hoddle

111. NATIVE NODDY: Danny De Vito

112. INTERNAL SCUM: Martin Clunes

113. BUM NOT MEAN: Emma Bunton (Baby Spice)

114. DIVIDE BAD LAD: David Baddiel

115. FRY WHORE PAIN: Oprah Winfrey

116. DEFINED SNARL: Les Ferdinand

117. NUDE YELLS PAY: Lynsey De Paul

118. JET LONGER? OH NO!: Joe Longthorne

119. MATE IS LOONY: Alison Moyet

120. ROAM BEACH MERRILY: Michael Barrymore

121. GOT SO WEIRD: Tiger Woods

122. GROAN MADLY: Gary Oldman

123. CONSIDER NAVEL: Clive Anderson

124. AIRPLANE PONG: Angela Rippon

125. MASK ON MIRROR: Mark Morrison

126. SEE POSH JELLY: Lesley Joseph

127. CATCH DRY JOKE: Jack Docherty

128. HERE IS SHINY CD: Chrissie Hynde

129. NOW MAIN REBEL: Melanie Brown (Scary Spice)

130. NASTILY ON RED: Dennis Taylor

131. BORN INSANE? NO!: Anne Robinson

132. TART BLINKED: Britt Ekland

133. GAIN SAD ARSE: Andre Agassi

134. BRAWL OR GAY: Gary Barlow

135. BLOW FREE BIRO: Robbie Fowler

136. A WILD OLD MENACE: Andie MacDowell

137. EH BRICK ANUS?: Chris Eubank

138. BID A VILE DAY: David Bailey

139. OK SNOBBISH: Bob Hoskins

140. EVIL LASS IN EROTICA: Alicia Silverstone

141. TO PROJECT NHS: John Prescott

142. AGONIES RISE: Rosie Gaines

143. TART JEERS TO REPENT: Janet Street-Porter

144. GIRL SAW MALE TWIT: William G. Stewart

145. LIMP CYCLE BANK: Nicky Campbell

146. I WAR THING: Ian Wright

147. HANG THEN, BANKER: Kenneth Branagh

148. TA, VAIN RUMP!: Ivana Trump

149. SO GLORY DAMNS: Loyd Grossman

150. JUNK LIARS SOON: Ulrika Jonsson

12 CELEBRITIES AND WHO (OR WHAT) THEY WERE NAMED AFTER

1. Dale Winton (after the actor Dale Robertson)

2. Dustin Hoffman (after the cowboy star of the silent movies Dustin Farnum)

3. Mariel Hemingway (after a bay in Cuba)

4. Gloria Hunniford (after the actress Gloria Swanson)

5. Glenn Hoddle (after the bandleader Glenn Miller)

6. Sugar Ray Leonard (after the musician Ray Charles)

7. Whitney Houston (after the American TV soap star Whitney Blake)

8. Shirley MacLaine (after Shirley Temple)

9. Chelsea Clinton (after the song *Chelsea Morning*)

10. Dame Thora Hird (after the song *Thora, Speak To Me Thora*)

11. Martina Hingis (after the tennis star Martina Navratilova)

12. Dennis Bergkamp (after the footballer Denis Law)

15 CELEBRITIES AND THEIR CHILDHOOD NICKNAMES

1. Prince Andrew: The Sniggerer

2. Prince Edward: Jaws

3. Prince Philip: Flop

4. Prince William: Wombat

5. George Michael: Yog

6. Kate Moss: Mosschops

7. Cindy Crawford: Crawdaddy

8. Felicity Kendal: Fatty Foo

9. Beryl Bainbridge: Basher

10. Bob Geldof: Liver Lips

11. Kate Winslet: Blubber

12. Steven Spielberg: The Retard

13. Tony Robinson: Mighty Mouse

14. Michael Caine: The Professor

15. Steve Wright: Concorde

22 CELEBRITIES WHO HAD ROSES NAMED AFTER THEM

1. Anna Ford
2. Gary Player
3. Penelope Keith
4. Cardinal Hume
5. Sir Paul McCartney
6. Ingrid Bergman
7. Clive Lloyd
8. Mary Hayley Bell
9. Chevy Chase
10. Nigel Hawthorne
11. Geoffrey Boycott
12. Pam Ayres
13. Dame Vera Lynn
14. Judy Garland
15. Prince Philip
16. Tina Turner
17. Jane Asher
18. Harold Macmillan
19. Princess Michael of Kent
20. William Shakespeare
21. Dame Thora Hird
22. Princess Royal

11 CELEBRITIES WITH FOUR INITIALS

1. V.H.B.M. Bottomley (Virginia Bottomley: Conservative MP)
2. M.B.G.C. Williamson (Malcolm Williamson: Master of The Queen's Music)
3. S.W.R.D. Bandaranaike (Solomon Bandaranaike: Late Sri Lankan politician)
4. J.P.M.S. Clary (Julian Clary: Comedian)
5. D.G.C.P. Ogilvy (The Earl of Airlie)
6. N.K.A.S. Vaz (Keith Vaz: Labour Politician)
7. S.F.A.F. Bacchus (Faoud Bacchus: Former West Indian Test Cricketer)
8. W.A.T.T. Garel-Jones (Tristan Garel-Jones: Conservative Politician)
9. P.A.C.L. Oppenheim (Phillip Oppenheim: Conservative Politician)
10. K.P.T.F. Duffy (Keith Duffy: Member of Boyzone)
11. C.P.A.G. Windsor (Prince Charles)

44 CELEBRITIES WHO USED THEIR MIDDLE NAMES AS FIRST NAMES

1. Patrick Ryan O'Neal
2. Lee Alexander McQueen
3. Keith Rupert Murdoch
4. Robert Oliver Reed
5. John Anthony Quayle
6. Johan Jordi Cruyff
7. James Harold Wilson
8. Marie Dionne Warwick
9. Michael Vincent O'Brien
10. Marie Debra Winger
11. Richard Edward Geoffrey Howe
12. Ernestine Jane Russell
13. John Enoch Powell
14. Marvin Neil Simon
15. Ruth Bette Davis
16. Alfred Alistair Cooke
17. Norvell Oliver Hardy
18. Isaac Vivian Richards
19. Ruz Fidel Castro
20. Sir Peter Norman Fowler
21. Desmond John Humphrys
22. Georgina Davinia Murphy
23. Olive Marie Osmond
24. Walter Bruce Willis
25. Charles Robert Redford
26. Leonard James Callaghan
27. Roberta Joan (i.e. Joni) Mitchell
28. William Bradley Pitt
29. George Ivan (i.e. Van) Morrison
30. Robert Edward (i.e. Ted) Turner
31. Eldred Gregory Peck
32. Alexander James Naughtie
33. Mary Sean Young
34. Daniel Patrick Macnee
35. Gordon Angus Deayton
36. James Gordon Brown MP
37. George Anthony Newley
38. Sir Edwin Hardy Amies
39. Arthur Nigel Davenport
40. Mark Trevor Phillips
41. Alastair Brian Walden
42. Thomas Richard Dunwoody
43. David Paul Scofield
44. Christopher Nicholas Parsons

22 CELEBRITIES WHO USE THREE NAMES

1. Andrew Lloyd Webber
2. Griff Rhys Jones
3. Harry Dean Stanton
4. David Lee Roth
5. Catherine Zeta Jones
6. Dave Lee Travis
7. Jonny Lee Miller
8. Andreas Whittam Smith
9. Mary Tyler Moore
10. Barbara Taylor Bradford
11. Klaus Maria Brandauer
12. Carole Bayer Sager
13. Joe Don Baker
14. John Lee Hooker
15. George MacDonald Fraser
16. Paul Michael Glaser
17. Nyree Dawn Porter
18. Jennifer Jason Leigh
19. Rachael Heyhoe Flint
20. Mary Elizabeth Mastrantonio
21. Roger Lloyd Pack
22. John Cooper Clarke

55 CELEBRITIES WHO FOUND FAME WITH A SINGLE NAME

1. Caprice
2. Bono
3. Marilyn
4. Capucine
5. Dion
6. Mantovani
7. Sinitta
8. Whigfield
9. RuPaul
10. Sting
11. Pelé
12. Morrissey
13. Twiggy
14. Dana
15. Topol
16. Donovan
17. Prince
18. Massiel
19. Enya
20. Sade
21. Melanie
22. Nicole
23. Madonna
24. Björk
25. Seal
26. Taki
27. Arletty
28. Suggs
29. Eusebio
30. Martika
31. Fish
32. Toyah
33. Nena
34. Lulu
35. Jethro
36. Cher
37. Yazz
38. Heinz
39. Twinkle
40. Fernandel
41. Aneka
42. Limahl
43. Sylvia
44. Nilsson
45. Charlene
46. Hammer
47. Regine
48. Des'ree
49. Fabian
50. Falco
51. Sabrina
52. Louise
53. Tiffany
54. Vangelis
55. Fabio

Chapter 5

Health

3 CELEBRITIES WHO HAVE OVERCOME DEAFNESS

1. Marlee Matlin (The Oscar-winning actress has been deaf since the age of 18 months)
2. Leslie Nielsen (The star of the *Naked Gun* films is legally deaf)
3. Lord Jack Ashley (The politician lost his hearing but now, thanks to a cochlear implant, can hear again)

2 CELEBRITIES WHO EACH HAVE ONLY ONE KIDNEY

1. Bruce Forsyth
2. Brenda Fricker

5 CELEBRITIES WHO HAVE DRUNK THEIR OWN URINE FOR HEALTH REASONS

1. Sarah Miles
2. Rolf Harris
3. Demi Moore
4. Michael Jackson
5. George Harrison

9 CELEBRITIES WHO WEAR/WORE MONOCLES

1. Chris Eubank
2. Patrick Moore
3. A.A. Gill
4. Darius Guppy
5. Leslie Charteris
6. Marlene Dietrich
7. Johnny Craddock
8. Kenneth Tynan
9. Terry-Thomas

10 CELEBRITIES WHO LOST A LUNG

1. Malcolm Allison
2. Auberon Waugh
3. Hughie Green
4. Vaclav Havel
5. Doug Mountjoy
6. Link Wray
7. Stewart Granger
8. King George VI
9. Robert Maxwell
10. Viscount Bernard Montgomery

10 CELEBRITIES WHO SUFFERED FROM PERSISTENT CONSTIPATION

1. Elvis Presley
2. King George III
3. Napoleon
4. Sigmund Freud
5. Marcel Proust
6. Judy Garland
7. George Gershwin
8. Mahatma Gandhi
9. Howard Hughes
10. Abraham Lincoln

16 CELEBRITIES WHO ARE TEETOTALLERS

1. Bruce Willis
2. Tony Benn
3. Griff Rhys Jones
4. Chris Eubank
5. David Bailey
6. Elizabeth Taylor
7. Brendan Powell
8. Bernard Manning
9. Sol Campbell
10. Sir Jimmy Savile
11. Lenny Henry
12. Alastair Campbell
13. Frank Skinner
14. Michael York
15. Tracey Ullman
16. Richard E Grant

10 CELEBRITIES BORN WITH A CLUB FOOT

1. Dudley Moore
2. Josef Goebbels
3. Dr David Starkey
4. Mother Teresa
5. Emperor Claudius
6. Ken Bates
7. Eric Richard
8. Lord Byron
9. Callan Pinckney
10. Roger Dervish

10 CELEBRITIES WHO USE HOMOEOPATHIC MEDICINE

1. The Queen
2. Susan Hampshire
3. Dame Vera Lynn
4. Frank Delaney
5. Montserrat Caballe
6. Wayne Sleep
7. Twiggy
8. Julie Walters
9. Sir Yehudi Menuhin
10. Caron Keating

17 CELEBRITIES WHO SURVIVED SUICIDE ATTEMPTS

1. Drew Barrymore
2. Sir Elton John
3. Marianne Faithfull
4. Frank Sinatra
5. Tom Baker
6. Angie Bowie
7. Tuesday Weld
8. Daniella Westbrook
9. Billy Joel
10. Brenda Fricker
11. Sinead O'Connor
12. Vanilla Ice
13. Gary Glitter
14. Mickey Rooney
15. Yannick Noah
16. Brigitte Bardot
17. Tessa Dahl

26 CELEBRITIES WHO ARE RECOVERING ALCOHOLICS

1. Mel Gibson
2. Barry Humphries
3. Sir Anthony Hopkins
4. Eric Clapton
5. Jimmy Greaves
6. Dick Van Dyke
7. Buzz Aldrin
8. Mike Yarwood
9. Tony Adams
10. Countess Spencer
11. Paul Merson
12. John Daly
13. Jim Davidson
14. Maurice Gibb
15. Terry Biddlecombe
16. Anthony Booth
17. Brian Barnes
18. Keith Chegwin
19. Roseanne
20. Dennis Quaid
21. Paula Hamilton
22. Drew Barrymore
23. Ken Kercheval
24. Elizabeth Taylor
25. Ringo Starr
26. Sharon Gless

45 CELEBRITIES WHO HAD NERVOUS BREAKDOWNS

1. Ken Russell
2. Rupert Brooke
3. Nicola Pagett
4. Sir Isaac Newton
5. John Lennon
6. Emily Lloyd
7. David Helfgott
8. Charlotte Cornwell
9. Honor Blackman
10. Bob Hoskins
11. Jon Pertwee
12. Michael Barrymore
13. Leslie Phillips
14. Sir Denis Thatcher
15. The Duchess of Kent
16. Yitzhak Rabin
17. Sir Peter Hall
18. Leslie Caron
19. Brian Wilson
20. Vivian Stanshall
21. Vince Hill
22. Fiona Fullerton
23. Terry Scott
24. Dame Catherine Cookson
25. Daniel Day-Lewis
26. Brian Blessed
27. Frankie Howerd
28. Yves St Laurent
29. Dora Bryan
30. Sir Richard Hadlee
31. Alastair Campbell
32. Kylie Minogue
33. James Herriot
34. Rex Williams
35. Samantha Janus
36. Lee Evans
37. Jeremy Brett
38. Eric Porter
39. Roseanne
40. Mike Yarwood
41. Spike Milligan
42. Donny Osmond
43. Tony Slattery
44. Jeffrey Rush
45. Enrico Caruso

4 CELEBRITIES WHO HAVE SUFFERED FROM ALZHEIMER'S DISEASE

1. Ronald Reagan
2. Danny Blanchflower
3. Dame Iris Murdoch
4. Jack Lord

13 CELEBRITIES WHO EXPERIENCED BAD STAGE FRIGHT

1. Sir Derek Jacobi avoided the theatre for two years after his drying as Hamlet in 1980.

2. Sir Laurence Olivier went through a bout of terrible stage fright when he was running the National Theatre and playing Othello. Olivier said, 'all I could see were the exit signs and all I wanted to do was run off the stage each night towards them'.

3. Freddie Starr became addicted to Valium because of his stage fright.

4. The first time the Irish singer Enya appeared onstage she took fright, fled and had to be coaxed back by a psychologist.

5. John Sessions fled the stage during a performance of *My Night With Reg* in 1995 because of stage fright although he did eventually return.

6. Carly Simon gave up performing live for 14 years because of stage fright. She had a stutter as a teenager which brought on attacks of nerves.

7. Barry Humphries suffers from stage fright "every night and had to overcome a tremendous reluctance to get on stage."

8. Tim Roth started out as a stage actor on the fringe. Now he sticks to films as his stage fright leads him to having "nightmares" about the stage.

9. Marvin Gaye had such bad stage fright that he once tried climbing out of his dressing-room.

10. Stephen Fry suffered such bad stage fright in *Cell Mates* (as well as other problems) that he left the country.

11. Dawn French was sick every night when she starred in *Then Again* in the West End. "Every night I go on I'm knocking a couple of weeks off my life because of the stress."

12. Barbra Streisand returned to the stage after stage fright put her off. On her return she said, "It has taken me 2,700 hours and $360,000 worth of psychotherapy to be able to sing." Streisand puts her well-known stage fright partly down to a PLO death threat in 1967 which caused her to forget her lines on stage.

13. Elvis Presley's hip-wiggling started out as stage fright. According to Carl Perkins: "Elvis was so nervous his legs would shake. One day he did it and the crowd went wild. He asked guitarist Scotty Moore, 'What'd I do?' and Moore replied, 'I don't know but do it again.'"

10 CELEBRITIES WHO HAVE USED SHIATSU

1. Jenny Seagrove
2. Bjorn Borg
3. Cindy Crawford
4. Dame Shirley Porter
5. Gorden Kaye
6. James Coburn
7. Princess Ira von Furstenburg
8. Michaela Strachan
9. Jeremy Lloyd
10. Jane Lapotaire

3 CELEBRITIES WHO ARE SELF-CONFESSED NEUROTICS

1. Carrie Fisher
2. Andre Agassi
3. Woody Allen

22 CELEBRITIES WHO ARE SELF-CONFESSED WORKAHOLICS

1. Vidal Sassoon
2. Carol Vorderman
3. John Barrowman
4. Jenni Murray
5. Jilly Cooper
6. Anthony Sher
7. Lynda La Plante
8. Sir Derek Jacobi
9. Zandra Rhodes
10. Esther Rantzen
11. Gina G
12. Steven Norris
13. Jill Dando
14. Carol Smillie
15. Rolf Harris
16. Cilla Black
17. David Hasselhoff
18. Eamonn Holmes
19. Faye Dunaway
20. Jackie Collins
21. John Thaw
22. Sir Anthony Hopkins

10 CELEBRITIES WHO ARE SELF-CONFESSED HYPOCHONDRIACS

1. Woody Allen
2. Sir Tim Rice
3. Alan Bleasdale
4. Oliver Sacks
5. David 'Kid' Jensen
6. Dave Stewart
7. Tony Blackburn
8. Roger Moore
9. Steve Wright
10. Ian Broudie

12 CELEBRITIES WHO OVERCAME STAMMERS

1. Bruce Willis
2. Carly Simon
3. Sir Winston Churchill
4. Harvey Keitel
5. King George VI
6. Sam Neill
7. Ben Johnson
8. Jimmy McGovern
9. Frankie Howerd
10. James Earl Jones
11. Martyn Lewis
12. Paul Young

13 CELEBRITIES WHO SUFFERED EPILEPTIC FITS

1. Julius Caesar
2. Alexander The Great
3. Cameron Sharp
4. Francois Pienaar
5. Lord Byron
6. Michael Miles
7. Vincent Van Gogh
8. Julia Somerville
9. Edward Lear
10. Derek Bentley
11. Peter The Great
12. Max Clifford
13. Billy Idol

10 CELEBRITIES WHO ARE/WERE MANIC DEPRESSIVES

1. Spike Milligan
2. Nicola Pagett
3. Sir James Goldsmith
4. Vincent Van Gogh
5. Ted Turner
6. Vivien Leigh
7. Jeremy Brett
8. Freddie Starr
9. Jess 'The Bishop' Yates
10. Robert Schumann

10 CELEBRITIES WHO ARE SELF-CONFESSED SHOPAHOLICS

1. Cher
2. Zoë Ball
3. Paula Hamilton
4. Andi Peters
5. Yasmine Bleeth
6. Elizabeth Taylor
7. The Duchess of York
8. Kimberley Davies
9. Lisa Snowdon
10. Penny Morrell

10 CELEBRITIES WHO HAVE SUFFERED FROM AGORAPHOBIA

1. Liam Gallagher
2. Stephanie Cole
3. Aretha Franklin
4. Kim Basinger
5. Alice Thomas Ellis
6. Olivia Hussey
7. Monica Seles
8. Sandra Gough
9. Tom Kempinski
10. Alison Moyet

105 CELEBRITIES WHO ARE VEGETARIANS

1. Bryan Adams
2. Leonardo DiCaprio
3. Danny De Vito
4. Kathy Lloyd
5. Jason Orange
6. Charlie Watts
7. Sara Crowe
8. Belinda Carlisle
9. Dustin Hoffman
10. Lindi St Clair
11. Christie Brinkley
12. Billy Idol
13. Kim Basinger
14. Damon Albarn
15. Jerome Flynn
16. Seal
17. Billy Connolly
18. Woody Harrelson
19. Tony Banks MP
20. Ted Danson
21. Daryl Hannah
22. Richard Gere
23. Joan Armatrading
24. Julie Christie
25. Candice Bergen
26. Rosanna Arquette
27. Brooke Shields
28. Paul Newman
29. Wendy James
30. Peter Gabriel
31. Sinitta
32. Boy George
33. William Wollard
34. Martina Navratilova
35. Sir Ian McKellen
36. Brigid Brophy
37. Sean Hughes
38. Piers Merchant
39. Martin Kemp
40. Gary Kemp
41. Paul McGann
42. LaToya Jackson
43. Martin Shaw
44. Virginia McKenna
45. Nik Kershaw
46. Sandie Shaw
47. Jenny Seagrove
48. Siouxsie Sioux
49. Kevin Godley
50. Kirsty Wade
51. (The Artist Formerly Known As) Prince
52. Bill Maynard
53. Rhea Perlman
54. John Peel
55. Howard Jones
56. Hayley Mills
57. Penny Junor
58. Jeff Beck
59. Benazir Bhutto
60. Ringo Starr
61. Terence Stamp
62. Michael Jackson
63. Gladys Knight
64. Whitney Houston
65. Catherine Oxenberg
66. Louise Jameson
67. Michael Bolton
68. Imelda Staunton
69. Carol Decker
70. Dennis Weaver
71. Elkie Brooks
72. Nigel Hawthorne
73. Phil Cool
74. Tanita Tikaram
75. Morrissey
76. Ed Moses
77. Chrissie Hynde
78. Lenny Kravitz
79. Ricki Lake
80. Rita Tushingham
81. Pamella Bordes
82. Vanessa Williams
83. Johnny Dankworth
84. Charlotte Cornwell
85. Don McLean
86. Pamela Armstrong
87. Ozzy Osbourne
88. Joe Jackson
89. Kirsty McDermott
90. Margi Clarke
91. Tony Benn
92. Janice Long
93. Barry Fantoni
94. Faith Brown
95. Sir Peter Hall
96. Howard Goodall
97. Yasmin Le Bon
98. Stevie Nicks
99. Judi Spiers
100. Sir Paul McCartney
101. Kenneth Kaunda
102. Carla Lane
103. Molly Parkin
104. Tracy Ward
105. Ruth Rendell

13 CELEBRITIES WHO'VE SUFFERED FROM ASTHMA

1. Nick Hancock
2. Adam Woodyatt
3. Tony Robinson
4. Edwina Currie
5. Liz McColgan
6. Lee Hurst
7. Dewi Morris
8. Gerald Scarfe
9. Rodney Bewes
10. Ian Wright
11. Jason Donovan
12. Steven Seagal
13. Alan Freeman

14 CELEBRITIES AND WHAT THEY'RE ALLERGIC TO

1. Roger Cook: Cucumbers
2. Steve Wright: Feathers
3. Gaby Roslin: Wheat
4. Honor Blackman: Cats
5. Beverley Callard: Avocados
6. Andi Peters: Chocolate
7. Sue Townsend: Monosodium Glutamate
8. Clint Eastwood: Horses
9. Susan Hill: Wasps
10. Nick Hancock: Cats and dogs
11. Ian Kelsey: Wood
12. Bill Clinton: Flowers
13. Richard E. Grant: Alcohol
14. Donald Sutherland: Cigarette smoke

12 CELEBRITIES WHO USE AROMATHERAPY

1. Toyah Willcox
2. Pamela Anderson
3. Eric Cantona
4. David Baddiel
5. Martine McCutcheon
6. Debbie Moore
7. Mandy Smith
8. The Duchess of York
9. Nick Owen
10. Jenny Seagrove
11. Gloria Hunniford
12. Anita Harris

15 CELEBRITIES WHO SUFFERED FROM POLIO AS CHILDREN

1. Alan Alda
2. Ian Dury
3. Lord Snowdon
4. Kerry Packer
5. Sir Walter Scott
6. Joni Mitchell
7. Sir Julian Critchley
8. Neil Young
9. Itzhak Perlman
10. Steve Harley
11. Joe Coral
12. Harold Hobson
13. Sylvia Syms
14. Wilma Rudolph
15. Ruskin Spear

17 CELEBRITIES WHO WEAR CONTACT LENSES

1. Jesper Parnevik
2. Jill Dando
3. Cilla Black
4. Rob Andrew
5. Robert Redford
6. Devon Malcolm
7. Hillary Clinton
8. Michael Buerk
9. George Michael
10. Barbara Windsor
11. Dickie Davies
12. Sophie Dahl
13. Paul Kaye (aka Dennis Pennis)
14. Steve Cram
15. Marie Helvin
16. Geoffrey Boycott
17. Jennifer Capriati

11 CELEBRITIES WHO LOST THEIR SPLEENS

1. Auberon Waugh
2. Dale Gibson
3. Lord Longford
4. Billy Pearce
5. Keanu Reeves
6. Bob Hawke
7. Sidney Gilliat
8. Eamon Murphy
9. David Hunter
10. Andrew Knight
11. Burt Reynolds

12 CELEBRITIES WHO OVERCAME TUBERCULOSIS

1. Nelson Mandela
2. Paul Eddington
3. Stewart Granger
4. Sir Leonard Cheshire
5. Bill McLaren
6. Engelbert Humperdinck
7. Richard Harris
8. Alan Sillitoe
9. Sir Gordon Richards
10. Sir Roger Hollis
11. Ray Galton
12. Alan Simpson

11 CELEBRITIES WHO SUFFER FROM HAY FEVER

1. Michael Fish
2. Simon Mayo
3. Chris Evans
4. Suzanne Charlton
5. John Major
6. Steffi Graf
7. Nigel Mansell
8. Laura Greene
9. Richey Renenberg
10. Stuart Miles
11. Hugh Lloyd

17 CELEBRITY GOUT SUFFERERS

1. Jonathan King
2. Ronnie Biggs
3. Terry Wogan
4. Fran Cotton
5. Tony Robinson
6. Sam Torrance
7. Antonio Carluccio
8. Sam Mendes
9. Carl Wilson
10. Nicholas Coleridge
11. Spike Milligan
12. John Poulson
13. Matthew Harding
14. Joseph Conrad
15. Julius Caesar
16. John Milton
17. Dr Samuel Johnson

8 CELEBRITIES WHO'VE SUFFERED FROM MIGRAINES

1. Princess Margaret
2. Sir Elton John
3. Maureen Lipman
4. Bill Maynard
5. Cathy McGowan
6. Roger Black
7. Michael Aspel
8. Pam Ayres

11 CELEBRITIES WHO SUFFER FROM DIABETES

1. Gary Mabbutt
2. Sir Harry Secombe
3. Leo McKern
4. Bill Maynard
5. Kevin Lloyd
6. Bernard Manning
7. Lisa Harrow
8. Michael Barry
9. Luther Vandross
10. Mary Tyler Moore
11. Jonathan Lower

9 CELEBRITIES WHO USE GINSENG

1. Linford Christie
2. Lord Nigel Lawson
3. George Hamilton
4. Dame Barbara Cartland
5. Michael Caine
6. Sir Cliff Richard
7. Baroness Thatcher
8. The Duchess of York
9. Ben Johnson

21 CELEBRITIES WHO'VE BEEN IN THE BETTY FORD CLINIC

1. Elizabeth Taylor
2. Liza Minnelli
3. Ali MacGraw
4. Don Johnson
5. Oprah Winfrey
6. Tony Curtis
7. William Hurt
8. Richard Pryor
9. Chevy Chase
10. Charlie Sheen
11. Johnny Cash
12. Kelsey Grammer
13. John Daly
14. Stevie Nicks
15. Bobby Brown
16. Tammy Wynette
17. Laura Baugh
18. Anna Nicole Smith
19. Ozzy Osbourne
20. Jean Simmons
21. Mary Tyler Moore

10 CELEBRITIES WHO USE REFLEXOLOGY

1. Anthea Turner
2. Liza Goddard
3. Kate O'Mara
4. Suzanne Mizzi
5. Gloria Hunniford
6. Anita Harris
7. Amanda Burton
8. Caron Keating
9. Abigail McKern
10. Jane Lapotaire

10 CELEBRITIES WHO'VE SUFFERED FROM HAEMORRHOIDS

1. Jimmy McGovern
2. Vanessa Feltz
3. Greg Norman
4. Jimmy Carter
5. Leo McKern
6. Madonna
7. Jon Ridgeon
8. Viv Richards
9. Elizabeth Taylor
10. Gerald Ford

10 CELEBRITIES WHO SUFFERED FROM GALLSTONES

1. Aristotle Onassis
2. Alexandra Bastedo
3. Larry Hagman
4. Linda Robson
5. Rosemary Conley
6. Pam Ferris
7. Benazir Bhutto
8. Claire Rayner
9. Pope John Paul II
10. Harold Macmillan

7 CELEBRITIES WHO HAD A PERFORATED EAR DRUM

1. Retief Goosen
2. Duke McKenzie
3. Nigel Benn
4. Doddie Weir
5. Fulton Mackay
6. Ronnie Kray
7. Stephen King (punctured rather than perforated)

13 CELEBRITIES WHO'VE SUFFERED FROM HIGH BLOOD PRESSURE

1. Ronnie Barker
2. Frank Sinatra
3. Stephen King
4. Bryan Mosley
5. Francis Lee
6. Peter Baldwin
7. Dickie Davies
8. Terry O'Neill
9. Diego Maradona
10. Elizabeth Taylor
11. Kevin Lloyd
12. Paul McGuigan
13. Reg Varney

10 CELEBRITIES WHO SUFFERED FROM TINNITUS

1. Russell Grant
2. Pete Townshend
3. Barbra Streisand
4. Peter Adamson
5. Julia McKenzie
6. Oliver Reed
7. Alan Bleasdale
8. Lord Jack Ashley
9. Julian Wilson
10. Vincent Van Gogh (which is why, it is now thought, he cut his ear off)

10 CELEBRITIES WHO HAVE HAD HEART MURMURS

1. Judy Finnigan
2. Arnold Schwarzenegger
3. Bridget Fonda
4. Gareth Hale
5. Jill Dando
6. Retief Goosen
7. Pat Coombs
8. Rachel Hunter
9. Evander Holyfield
10. Elizabeth Taylor

14 CELEBRITIES WHO'VE BEATEN CANCER

1. Wendy Richard
2. Olivia Newton-John
3. Joe Longthorne
4. Liza Goddard
5. Jonjo O'Neill
6. Tom Lehman
7. Bob Champion
8. King Hussein of Jordan
9. Paul Azinger
10. Anne Kirkbride
11. Lynne Perrie
12. Lynn Faulds-Wood
13. George Cohen
14. Timothy Spall

27 CELEBRITIES WHO HAD THEIR TONSILS REMOVED (*= As an adult)

1. David Coulthard*
2. Isla Blair
3. Ringo Starr*
4. Bryan Ferry*
5. Robert Powell
6. Jancis Robinson
7. Don Maclean (twice: as a child and as an adult when they'd grown back)
8. Kelly Holmes*
9. Kyran Bracken*
10. Judy Simpson (Nightshade)*
11. Darren Day
12. Max Clifford
13. Paul Way*
14. Chelsea Clinton
15. Roger Cook*
16. Drew Barrymore*
17. Rabbi Julia Neuberger*
18. Michael Parkinson
19. Raymond Blanc
20. Russell Grant
21. Joseph Heller
22. Niamh Cusack
23. Wolfgang Mozart
24. Judith Hann
25. Ben Okri*
26. Rudolf Nureyev*
27. Catherine Zeta Jones

15 CELEBRITIES WHO HAD THEIR APPENDIX REMOVED

1. Dave Stewart (unnecessarily so – it was just wind)
2. Dian Fossey (as a precaution before being allowed to go into the jungle)
3. Mel Gibson
4. Stephen Redgrave
5. Pope John Paul II
6. Isla Blair
7. Mika Hakkinen
8. Patsy Palmer
9. Dan Quayle
10. Sue Barker
11. Gregory Peck
12. Ann Widdecombe
13. Robert Powell
14. Steven Norris
15. Jeremy Beadle

18 CELEBRITIES WHO HAD KIDNEY STONES

1. Michael Heseltine
2. Edward Stourton
3. Sir Gary Sobers
4. Anne Diamond
5. Sir Ranulph Fiennes
6. Bob Dole
7. Letitia Dean
8. David Coleman
9. John Reid
10. Montserrat Caballe
11. Eduardo Romero
12. Henry Kelly
13. Michael Crawford
14. Lord David Steel
15. Gerry Francis
16. Charles Haughey
17. Lord Richard Attenborough
18. Steve Cram

12 CELEBRITIES WHO SURVIVED STROKES

1. Dickie Davies
2. Robert McCrum
3. Raymond Blanc
4. Bill Maynard
5. Kirk Douglas
6. Sir Dirk Bogarde
7. Charlie Drake
8. Sir John Harvey-Jones
9. Barbara Windsor
10. Boris Yeltsin
11. King Fahd of Saudi Arabia
12. Lonnie Donegan

10 CELEBRITIES WHO SUFFERED FROM LOW BLOOD PRESSURE

1. Sir Stanley Matthews
2. Michael Jackson
3. Jane Austen
4. John F. Kennedy
5. Christopher Reeve
6. Sir Michael Redgrave
7. Richie Richardson
8. Jeremy Bates
9. Danny Morrison
10. Jahangir Khan

11 CELEBRITIES WHO HAD HIPS REPLACED

1. Murray Walker
2. Maeve Binchy
3. The Queen Mother
4. Dave Prowse
5. Elizabeth Taylor
6. Mary Wesley
7. Oscar Peterson
8. Peter Vaughan
9. Anita Pallenberg
10. Charlton Heston
11. Jimmy Young

16 CELEBRITIES WHO SUFFER FROM ARTHRITIS

1. John Cleese
2. The Queen
3. Claire King
4. Tommy Smith
5. Jose Maria Olazabal
6. Elizabeth Taylor
7. Prince Philip
8. Simon Geoghegan
9. Dermot Reeve
10. Jack Nicklaus
11. Lord Nigel Lawson
12. Malcolm Allison
13. Chris Broad
14. Joe Royle
15. Julie Neuberger
16. Jo Durie

14 CELEBRITIES WHO ARE HARD OF HEARING

1. George Melly
2. John Entwhistle
3. David Hockney
4. Eric Sykes
5. Lester Piggott
6. Bill Clinton
7. Norman Mailer
8. King Juan Carlos
9. Desmond Wilcox
10. Luciano Pavarotti
11. Dominick Dunne
12. Sir John Mills
13. Stephanie Beacham
14. Sir Georgre Martin

5 CELEBRITIES WHO'VE SUFFERED FROM ECZEMA

1. Liz Earle
2. Liam Gallagher
3. Trudie Goodwin
4. Brett Anderson
5. Michaela Strachan

14 CELEBRITIES AND THEIR PHOBIAS

1. Howard Hughes (Germs)
2. George Peppard (Being alone)
3. Johnny Depp (Clowns)
4. Queen Elizabeth I (Roses)
5. Madonna (Thunder)
6. Joan Collins (The dark)
7. Natalie Wood (Water. Ironically, she died by drowning)
8. (The Artist Formerly Known As) Prince (Heights and dirt)
9. The Duchess of York (Snakes)
10. Sir James Goldsmith (Scorpions)
11. Sean Connery (Needles)
12. Margaret Thatcher (The dark)
13. David Bowie (Death)
14. Glenda Jackson (Enclosed spaces)

15 CELEBRITIES WHO SUFFERED FROM INSOMNIA

1. David Baddiel
2. Mia Farrow
3. Sir Magdi Yacoub
4. Elizabeth Taylor
5. Samuel Beckett
6. Una Stubbs
7. Andy de la Tour
8. Winona Ryder
9. Damon Albarn
10. Eileen Atkins
11. Lord Robert Runcie
12. Dulcie Gray
13. Abraham Lincoln
14. Marilyn Monroe
15. Spencer Tracy

19 CELEBRITIES WHO ARE SELF-CONFESSED CHOCAHOLICS

1. Zoë Ball
2. John Daly
3. Peter Beardsley
4. Benazir Bhutto
5. Cher
6. Michael Schumacher
7. Toyah Willcox
8. Stephanie Cole
9. Gabrielle
10. Joe McGann
11. Robert Lee
12. Vanessa Feltz
13. Dame Shirley Porter
14. Nina Myskow
15. Daniella Westbrook
16. Rachael Lindsay
17. David Sullivan
18. Katharine Hepburn
19. Elizabeth Taylor

14 CELEBRITIES WHO HAVE USED PROZAC

1. Elizabeth Taylor
2. Libby Purves
3. Mariella Frostrup
4. The Duchess of York
5. P.J. Proby
6. Jim Carrey
7. Jill Gascoine
8. Shaun Ryder
9. Cher
10. Burt Reynolds
11. Flora Fraser
12. Fiona Wright
13. Richard Fairbrass
14. Denise Welch

22 CELEBRITIES WHO HAVE HAD A FEAR OF FLYING

1. Dennis Bergkamp
2. Whitney Houston
3. Aaron Spelling
4. Phil Tufnell
5. Whigfield
6. John Daly
7. Richard Briers
8. The Dalai Lama
9. Lenny Kravitz
10. Mike Oldfield
11. Dina Carroll
12. David Bowie
13. Lesley Joseph
14. Bret Easton Ellis
15. Paul Newlove
16. Alan Price
17. Bob Newhart
18. Muhammad Ali
19. Nigel Benn
20. Colin Montgomerie
21. Joan Baez
22. Eric Hall

Chapter 6

Sport

10 CELEBRITIES WHO ARE ADEPT AT JUDO

1. Tony Slattery (Actor – Black belt)
2. Honor Blackman (Actress – Brown belt)
3. Tony Bullimore (Lone Yachtsman – Black belt)
4. David Lee Roth (Rock star – Black belt)
5. Jak (Cartoonist – Black belt)
6. Kelly Holmes (Athlete – Blue belt)
7. Manuel Noriega (Former leader of Panama – Black belt)
8. Buddy Rich (Jazz musician – Black belt)
9. Terence Donovan (Photographer – Black belt)
10. Nigel Mansell (Racing driver – Black belt

12 CELEBRITIES WHO LEARNED TO SWIM AS ADULTS

1. Norma Major
2. Shirley Bassey
3. Sir Paul McCartney
4. Tina Turner
5. Pablo Picasso
6. Peter O'Sullevan
7. Donna D'Errico
8. Robin Williams
9. Sir David Frost
10. Sir John Nott
11. Adam Faith
12. Steve Wright (Taught by his son)

37 CELEBRITIES AND THE SPORTS AT WHICH THEY EXCELLED

1. Paul Shane (Table-tennis). The comic actor won a junior table-tennis championship at the age of 16.

2. Pope John Paul II (Soccer). The Pontiff played in goal for the amateur Polish team, Wotsyla.

3. Gary Webster (Badminton). *The Minder* star is a former Essex county badminton player.

4. Dr Benjamin Spock (Rowing). The childcare expert won a rowing gold medal at the 1924 Olympic Games.

5. Tommy Lee Jones (Polo). The Oscar-winning actor is a champion polo player.

6. Chevy Chase (Tennis). The American film comedian used to work as a tennis professional at a club.

7. Paul Newman (Motor Racing). The blue-eyed actor is a keen driver and once achieved second place in the gruelling 24 Hours At Le Mans race.

8. Richard Harris (Rugby Union). The actor won a Munster Cup medal playing in the second row for Garryowen in 1952 and might well have gone on to play for Ireland had he not contracted TB.

9. Richard Gere (Gymnastics). The actor won a gymnastics scholarship to the University of Massachusetts.

10. Keanu Reeves (Ice Hockey). The actor was the goalkeeper in his high school team where he earned the nickname 'The Wall' and where he was voted MVP (Most Valuable Player)

11. Arnold Schwarzenegger (Weightlifting). The actor was not only a bodybuilding champion but also won the Austrian Junior Olympic Weightlifting Championship.

12. James Whale (Archery). The broadcaster was Surrey Junior Archery Champion in 1965.

13. Charles Palmer-Tomkinson (Skiing). The pal of the Prince of Wales – and the father of Tara – was in the 1964 British Olympic Ski team.

14. Julio Iglesias (Soccer). The smoothie singer used to play in goal for Real Madrid's second team.

15. Robert De Niro (Boxing). The actor learned to box for his Oscar-winning role as Jake La Motta in *Raging Bull* and was so good that La Motta himself said that he could have taken it up professionally.

16. Bill Cosby (American Football). The billionaire actor and comedian was good enough to be offered a trial with the Green Bay Packers – this year's Super Bowl winners.

17. Suzanne Dando (Gymnastics). The TV presenter used to represent Britain at her sport and was known as 'The Golden Girl of Gymnastics'.

18. Mike Yarwood (Soccer). The impressionist had trials with Stockport County and Oldham Athletic.

19. William Baldwin (Baseball). The actor was a good enough player to have originally considered a professional career with the New York Yankees.

20. David Storey (Rugby League). The playwright and novelist financed his studies at the Slade by playing professionally for Leeds.

21. Kirk Douglas (Wrestling). At the start of his career, the actor supplemented his meagre earnings with professional appearances in the ring.

22. Billy Crystal (Baseball). The American actor attended college on a full baseball scholarship but decided not to pursue a career in the sport.

23. Peter O'Toole (Rugby Union). When the actor served in the Navy (from 1950-52), he is said to have 'distinguished himself on the rugby field'.

24. David Suchet (Rugby Union). The *Poirot* actor played on the wing for Richmond RFC.

25. Jim Brown (American Football). Like O.J. Simpson, the actor only embarked on an acting career after having been a star at American Football.

26. Davy Jones (Horseracing). Before joining The Monkees, the singer was an apprentice jockey. However, it was only after he retired from singing and made a racing comeback that he had his first win as a jockey.

27. David Coleman (Athletics). The commentator was a fine athlete himself – winning the Manchester Mile in 1949.

28. Warren Beatty (American Football). The actor was offered scholarships as an American Football player from several universities but turned them all down to concentrate on acting.

29. Tom Cruise (Wrestling). The actor was an all-round sporting star at school but it was his wrestling that led to his acting career. He was in the school wrestling team but injured his knee and so turned to acting.

30. Pat Roach (Wrestling). *The Auf Wiedersehen, Pet* actor used to work as a professional wrestler.

31. Ian McShane (Soccer). The actor, a left-back, could have followed his father into a career with Manchester United but he turned down the opportunity to pursue an acting career.

32. Jack Palance (Boxing). Before becoming an actor, he worked as a professional boxer – thereby suffering the broken nose which helped him to earn parts playing the heavy!

33. Mickey Rourke (Boxing). The actor had 26 amateur fights in the 1970s and then quit when his acting career took off. In recent years, he has returned to the ring with some success.

34. Liam Neeson (Boxing). The actor boxed for a local team from the age of nine until the age of 17. In one early match, his nose was broken and he had it set on the spot by his manager.

35. Dick Francis (Horseracing). The novelist was champion jockey 1953-54 and so very nearly won the Grand National on Devon Loch.

36. Brian Glover (Wrestling). Before finding fame as an actor, he worked as a professional wrestler.

37. Jonathan Dimbleby (Showjumping). In 1964, he was showjumping champion of the South of England.

20 CELEBRITIES WHO ARE MEMBERS OF THE MCC (Marylebone Cricket Club)

1. Sir Tim Rice
2. Lord Robert Runcie
3. Gary Lineker
4. Michael Denison
5. Sir Leon Brittan
6. Ian Carmichael
7. William Franklyn
8. Leslie Thomas
9. Sir David Puttnam
10. Sir Clement Freud
11. Barry Took
12. Eric Morley
13. Ronald Harwood
14. Michael Jayston
15. Sir Donald Sinden
16. Lord Brian Rix
17. Christopher Lee
18. John Hurt
19. Sir David Frost
20. Lord Jeffrey Archer

9 CELEBRITIES WHO ARE KARATE BLACK BELTS

1. John Fashanu
2. Sharon Stone
3. Chris Silverwood
4. Nigel Mansell
5. Taki
6. Phil Spector
7. Jean Jacques Burnel
8. Chuck Norris
9. Glen Murphy

55 CELEBRITIES WHO ARE KEEN GOLFERS

1. Matt Le Tissier
2. Nasser Hussain
3. Gordon Brown MP
4. Gary Webster
5. Bill Clinton
6. Mike Catt
7. Eddie Irvine
8. Gary Pallister
9. Paul Daniels
10. Joel Cadbury (once hit a hole-in-one on a par 4 hole)
11. Carol Barnes
12. Trevor Eve
13. Dame Kiri Te Kanawa
14. Jeremy Guscott
15. Gavin Hastings
16. Vinnie Jones
17. Les Dennis
18. Bruce Grobbelaar
19. Matthew Pinsent
20. Mary Parkinson
21. Jonathan Agnew
22. Linus Roache
23. Rula Lenska
24. Steve Cram
25. Martin Brundle
26. Richard Dunwoody
27. Terry Wogan
28. Kevin Whateley
29. Kelvin Mackenzie
30. Stephen Hendry
31. David Gower
32. Jo Durie
33. Mark Blundell
34. Nick Gillingham
35. Rachael Heyhoe Flint
36. Shaun Edwards
37. Damon Hill
38. Mike Gatting
39. Will Smith
40. Mike Atherton
41. Glenn Hoddle
42. Nicholas Parsons
43. Moira Lister
44. Jimmy Greaves
45. Dennis Waterman
46. Dame Naomi James
47. Mike Yarwood
48. Sandy Gall
49. Jackie Stewart
50. Pat Eddery
51. Wayne Eagling
52. Osvaldo Ardiles
53. Dennis Wise
54. Trevor Brooking
55. John Regis

11 CELEBRITIES WHO WON OXBRIDGE BLUES

1. Hugh Laurie (rowing)

2. Lord Jeffrey Archer (athletics and gymnastics)

3. Kris Kristofferson (boxing)

4. Howard Jacobson (table-tennis). Note: 'minor' sports like Table-tennis attract Half Blues rather than Full Blues

5. Frank Bough (soccer)

6. Colin Moynihan (rowing and boxing)

7. Lord Snowdon (rowing)

8. Lord James Douglas-Hamilton (boxing)

9. Ian Balding (Rugby Union)

10. Sir Adrian Cadbury rowing)

11. John Gosden (athletics)

20 CELEBRITIES WHO ARE KEEN SNOOKER PLAYERS

1. Steve Cram
2. Don Black
3. Bob Hawke
4. Ian Woosnam
5. Barry Hearn
6. Graham Bradley
7. Pat Eddery
8. George MacDonald Fraser
9. Alex Ferguson
10. Matt Le Tissier
11. Robert Harris
12. Mordecai Richler
13. Gary Lineker
14. Saeed Jaffrey
15. Gary Speed
16. Rula Lenska
17. Alan Plater
18. Sam Torrance
19. Nick Faldo
20. Craig Chalmers

34 CELEBRITIES WHO ARE KEEN SKIERS

1. Ruthie Henshall
2. Michel Roux
3. Andrew Neil
4. Jane Asher
5. Jeremy Irons
6. Tim Brooke-Taylor
7. Bernard Hill
8. Melanie Griffith
9. Angus Deayton
10. Sandi Toksvig
11. Sir Chris Bonington
12. Bobby Robson
13. Michael Kitchen
14. Lord John Oaksey
15. Patsy Kensit
16. Ian Balding
17. Peter Powell
18. Jo Durie
19. The Duchess of York
20. Chay Blyth
21. Michael Brandon
22. Carol Barnes
23. Sue MacGregor
24. Mike Oldfield
25. Richard Branson
26. Frederic Raphael
27. Mark Todd
28. Dr Miriam Stoppard
29. Elaine Paige
30. Gavin Esler
31. Prince Charles
32. Bruce Beresford
33. David Gower
34. Peter Snow

17 CELEBRITIES WHO ARE KEEN ON SAILING

1. Jonathan Dimbleby
2. John Major
3. Peter Jay
4. Rupert Allason
5. Michael Grade
6. Sir John Harvey-Jones
7. Robbie Coltrane
8. Sir Peter Ustinov
9. Annabel Croft
10. Charles Haughey
11. Rabbi Julia Neuberger
12. Bill Treacher
13. Jeremy Irons
14. Valerie Singleton
15. Brent Sadler
16. Leo McKern
17. Peter Skellern

5 CELEBRITY POLO PLAYERS

1. Kenny Jones
2. Prince Charles
3. Ted Rogers
4. Kerry Packer
5. Trevor Eve

12 CELEBRITIES WHO ARE KEEN WATER-SKIERS

1. Ruthie Henshall
2. Barry Davies
3. Gus Dudgeon
4. Richard Dunwoody
5. David Emanuel
6. Tess Stimson
7. Roger Twose
8. Ian Woosnam
9. John Jeffrey
10. Stirling Moss
11. Susan Hampshire
12. Mark Pitman

31 CELEBRITIES WHO ARE KEEN HORSERIDERS

1. Kylie Minogue
2. Frazer Hines
3. Liza Goddard
4. Keith Chegwin
5. Jimmy Hill
6. Cybill Shepherd
7. Jane Seymour
8. Dickie Davies
9. Janet Jackson
10. Angela Rippon
11. William Roache
12. Alan Bates
13. Tracy Edwards
14. Prue Leith
15. Rosie Boycott
16. Alan Coren
17. Lynn Redgrave
18. Sir Paul Condon
19. Alan Titchmarsh
20. Joe Brown
21. Michael Kitchen
22. Chay Blyth
23. Patsy Kensit
24. Gerry Cottle
25. Tracey Ullman
26. Peter De Savary
27. Desmond Wilcox
28. David Emanuel
29. Michael Brandon
30. Jeremy Irons
31. Sue Carpenter

15 CELEBRITIES WHO HAVE DONE FITNESS VIDEOS

1. Marky Mark: *The Marky Mark Workout*
2. Cindy Crawford: *The Next Challenge Workout*
3. Cher: Cher Fitness: *A New Attitude*
4. Joan Collins: *Secrets of Fitness & Beauty*
5. Jane Fonda: *Sports Aid*
6. Raquel Welch: *Total Beauty & Fitness*
7. Mr. Motivator: *BLT Workout*
8. Gloria Hunniford: *Fit For Life*
9. Richard Wilson: *Let's Dance*
10. Paula Hamilton: *Step Into Shape*
11. Rosemary Conley: *Ultimate Fat Burner*
12. Elle Macpherson: *The Body Workout*
13. Beverley Callard: *Rapid Results*
14. Jet (Diane Youdale): *Summer Circuit*
15. Claudia Schiffer: *Perfectly Fit*

5 CELEBRITIES WHOSE FATHERS WERE PROFESSIONAL FOOTBALLERS

1. Jason Weaver
2. Gil Scott-Heron
3. Ian McShane
4. Steve Harley
5. Donald Houston

10 OLYMPIC CELEBRITIES WHO BECAME ACTORS

1. Bob Mathias (decathlon, Gold, 1948 and 1952). Played himself in *The Bob Mathias Story*
2. Charley Paddock (100 metres, Gold 1920). Played the title role in *The Olympic Hero*
3. Sonja Henie (skating, Gold, 1928, 1932 and 1936). After her skating career, she went to Hollywood and starred in films like *One In A Million* and *Thin Ice*
4. Johnny Weissmuller (swimming, Gold, 1924 and 1928). Starred in *Tarzan, The Ape Man* and went on to become the most famous Tarzan actor of them all.
5. Muhammad Ali (boxing, Gold, 1960) Played himself in *The Greatest* and also acted in the film *Freedom Road*
6. Helene Madison (swimming, Gold, 1932). Played an Amazon in the 1933 film *The Warrior's Husband*
7. Jim Thorpe (decathlon and pentathlon, Gold, 1912) Played the Captain of the Guard in *She* and played a prisoner in the James Cagney film *White Heat*
8. Glenn Morris (decathlon, Gold, 1936). Co-starred with 1932 Olympic gold medallist Eleanor Holm in the film *Tarzan's Revenge*
9. Bruce Jenner (decathlon, Gold, 1976). Appeared in the film *Can't Stop The Music* before gaining a role in the TV series *CHiPs*.
10. Buster Crabbe (swimming, Gold, 1932). Became Flash Gordon in the cinema serials and also appeared in films like *Buck Rogers* and *Gunfighters in Abilene*

THE ONLY 10 WOMEN CELEBRITIES EVER TO HAVE WON THE BBC SPORTS PERSONALITY OF THE YEAR AWARD

1. Anita Lonsborough (1962)
2. Dorothy Hyman (1963)
3. Mary Rand (1964)
4. Ann Jones (1969)
5. Princess Anne (1971)
6. Mary Peters (1972)
7. Virginia Wade (1977)
8. Jayne Torvill (with Christopher Dean) (1984)
9. Fatima Whitbread (1987)
10. Liz McColgan (1991)

15 CELEBRITIES WHO ARE KEEN SQUASH PLAYERS

1. Tommy Steele
2. Mary Archer
3. Bernard Hill
4. Gordon Burns
5. Richard Dunwoody
6. Richard Wilson
7. Mike Atherton
8. David Essex
9. Anton Mosimann
10. Nick Owen
11. Nigel Dempster
12. Ian Balding
13. Bruce Grobelaar
14. Bobby Robson
15. John Tusa

20 CELEBRITIES WHO ARE ACCOMPLISHED ROLLER-BLADERS

1. Tom Cruise
2. Lady Helen Taylor
3. Janet Jackson
4. Caroline Waldegrave
5. Dustin Hoffman
6. Amanda de Cadenet
7. Warren Beatty
8. Tiggy Legge-Bourke
9. Peter Gabriel
10. Emilio Estevez
11. Nicole Kidman
12. Adam Faith
13. Annabel Croft
14. Paula Yates
15. Phillip Schofield
16. Cher
17. Viscount Linley
18. Daryl Hannah
19. Bruce Willis
20. Madonna

13 CELEBRITIES WHO ARE KEEN DIVERS

1. Nick Ross
2. Nicholas Lyndhurst
3. Loyd Grossman
4. John Simpson
5. Douglas Adams
6. Wayne Eagling
7. Richard E. Grant
8. David Jason
9. Jeff Probyn
10. Chris De Burgh
11. John Prescott
12. Derek Bell
13. Duke of Westminster

13 CELEBRITIES AND THEIR GOLFING HANDICAPS

1. Geoffrey Boycott (10)
2. Ian Botham (10)
3. Alan Hansen (3)
4. Kenny Dalglish (11)
5. Jasper Carrott (11)
6. Bruce Forsyth (11)
7. Henry Cooper (10)
8. Don Johnson (4)
9. Sean Connery (12)
10. Ronnie Corbett (16)
11. Prince Andrew (7)
12. Jimmy Tarbuck (6)
13. Gary Lineker (11)

14 CELEBRITIES WHO HAVE DONE BUNGEE JUMPS

1. Andre Agassi
2. Ian Wright
3. Lord John Oaksey
4. Jeremy Guscott
5. Chris Lewis
6. Julian Lennon
7. Anna Walker
8. Chris Eubank
9. Debbie Harry
10. Jonathan Davies
11. Renny Harlin
12. Anders Limpar
13. Stuart Barnes
14. Joe McGann

10 CELEBRITIES WHO ARE NON-SWIMMERS

1. Eamonn Holmes
2. Lindsay Duncan
3. Alex 'Hurricane' Higgins
4. David Mellor
5. Sir Elton John
6. & 7. Andy Bell and Vince Clarke (of Erasure)
8. Edna O'Brien
9. Sheena Easton
10. Peter McKay

134 CELEBRITIES AND THE SOCCER TEAMS THEY SUPPORT

1. Jarvis Cocker: Sheffield Wednesday
2. June Whitfield: Wimbledon
3. Alison Moyet: Southend United
4. Clive Anderson: Arsenal
5. Tessa Sanderson: Fulham
6. Zoë Ball: Manchester United
7. Danny Baker: Millwall
8. Timmy Mallett: Wycombe Wanderers
9. Les Dennis: Liverpool
10. Jimmy Nail: Newcastle United
11. Simon Mayo: Tottenham Hotspur
12. Robert Lindsay: Derby County
13. Bernard Manning: Manchester City
14. Mick Hucknall: Manchester United
15. Roger Whittaker: Hereford United
16. Nick Owen: Luton Town
17. Sir Alastair Burnet: Partick Thistle
18. Marti Pellow: Rangers
19. Uri Geller: Reading
20. Elizabeth Dawn: Leeds United
21. Sebastian Coe: Chelsea
22. Windsor Davies: Crystal Palace
23. Hugh Grant: Fulham
24. Stephen Hendry: Heart of Midlothian
25. Kriss Akabusi: West Ham
26. Jim Rosenthal: Oxford United
27. Freddie Starr: Everton
28. John Alderton: Hull City
29. Nigel Kennedy: Aston Villa
30. Hugh Lloyd: Chester
31. Jimmy Cricket: Rochdale
32. Rod Hull: Gillingham
33. Jim Bowen: Blackburn Rovers
34. Michelle Gayle: Arsenal
35. Desmond Lynam: Brighton & Hove Albion
36. Rod Stewart: Celtic
37. Nigel Havers: Ipswich Town
38. John Motson: Barnet
39. Robson Green: Newcastle United
40. Shane Ritchie: Manchester United
41. Sean Connery: Rangers
42. Mikhail Gorbachev: Wigan Athletic
43. Robert Plant: Wolverhampton Wanderers
44. Wolf (Gladiators): Wimbledon
45. John Parrott: Everton
46. Brian Moore: Gillingham
47. Mel C.: Liverpool
48. Michael Palin: Sheffield United
49. Julian Wilson: Swindon Town
50. Jasper Carrott: Birmingham City
51. Tony Robinson: Bristol City
52. Tim Brooke-Taylor: Wycombe Wanderers
53. Michael Parkinson: Barnsley
54. Roy Walker: Blackpool
55. Sean Bean: Sheffield United
56. Russell Grant: Brentford
57. Jim Kerr: Celtic
58. Dean Reynolds: Grimsby Town
59. Melvyn Bragg: Carlisle United
60. Rory McGrath: Arsenal
61. Johnny Briggs: Burnley
62. David Baddiel: Chelsea
63. Jo Brand: Crystal Palace
64. Cheryl Baker: Charlton Athletic
65. Sir Elton John: Watford
66. Michael Foot: Plymouth Argyle

67. Billy Connolly: Celtic

68. Desmond Morris: Oxford United

69. John Stapleton: Oldham Athletic

70. Catherine Zeta Jones: Swansea City

71. John Major: Chelsea

72. Warren Mitchell: Tottenham Hotspur

73. Terry Christian: Manchester United

74. Robbie Williams: Port Vale

75. Noel and Liam Gallagher: Manchester City

76. Leslie Thomas: Queens Park Rangers

77. Steve Davis: Charlton Athletic

78. John Virgo: Manchester United

79. Frank Skinner: West Bromwich Albion

80. Jimmy Tarbuck: Liverpool

81. Julia Somerville: Arsenal

82. Linda Nolan: Blackpool

83. Bill Wyman: Crystal Palace

84. Elvis Costello: Tranmere Rovers

85. Richard Branson: Oxford United

86. Sean Hughes: Crystal Palace

87. Leslie Grantham: West Ham

88. Julian Lloyd Webber: Leyton Orient

89. Willie Thorne: Leicester City

90. Cardinal Hume: Newcastle United

91. Bruce Forsyth: Tottenham Hotspur

92. Steve Cram: Sunderland

93. Richard Digance: West Ham

94. Daley Thompson: Wimbledon

95. Nick Hancock: Stoke City

96. Chris Evans: Sheffield Wednesday

97. Bob Mortimer: Middlesbrough

98. Damon Albarn: Chelsea

99. Sir Harry Secombe: Swansea City

100. Frankie Dettori: Arsenal

101. David Essex: West Ham

102. Syd Little: Newcastle United

103. Tony Banks: Chelsea

104. Roger de Courcey: Crystal Palace

105. Stephen Fry: Norwich City

106. Paul Shane: Rotherham United

107. Tommy Cannon: Rochdale

108. Richard Littlejohn: Tottenham Hotspur

109. Roger Daltrey: Arsenal

110. Henry Kelly: Tottenham Hotspur

111. Nick Berry: West Ham

112. Rachael Heyhoe Flint: Wolverhampton Wanderers

113. Kenneth Clarke: Notts Forest

114. Bonnie Tyler: Swansea City

115. Sharon Duce: Fulham

116. Bobby Davro: Tottenham Hotspur

117. Noel Edmonds: West Ham

118. John Leslie: Hibernian

119. Eamonn Holmes: Manchester United

120. Ken Dodd: Liverpool

121. Susan Tully: Arsenal

123. Roy 'Chubby' Brown: Middlesbrough

124. Michael Barrymore: Tottenham Hotspur

125. Graham Gooch: West Ham

126. Lulu: Tottenham Hotspur

127. Jonathan Edwards: Newcastle United

128. Reece Dinsdale: Huddersfield Town

129. Nigel Benn: West Ham

130. Lord Roy Hattersley: Sheffield Wednesday

131. Chesney Hawkes: Tottenham Hotspur

132. Lee Hurst: West Ham

133. John Cole: West Ham

134. Sting: Tottenham

Chapter 7

Trials and Tribulations

▬▬ ▬▬ ▬▬ ▬▬ ▬▬ ▬▬ ▬▬ ▬▬ ▬▬ ▬▬ ▬▬ ▬▬ ▬▬

112 CELEBRITIES AND WHAT THEY DID IN WORLD WAR 2

1. Sir Dirk Bogarde. The actor and writer served as a Captain in the Queen's Royal Regiment and saw action in France, Germany and the Far East. He also helped to liberate the Nazi concentration camp of Belsen.

2. Denholm Elliott. The actor served in the RAF until being shot down in a bombing mission over Denmark. He was captured and sent to a POW camp in Silesia for the last three years of the war. He gave a hugely praised performance as Eliza Doolittle in the camp (no pun intended) production of *Pygmalion*.

3. Lord Denis Healey. The retired politician was a Major in the Army and was the Beachmaster in the Anzio landings in Italy for which he was mentioned in despatches. He was also awarded a military MBE.

4. Tony Benn. The politician joined the RAF in 1943 at the age of 18 and and got his wings just as Germany surrendered and so he switched to the Fleet Air Arm to fight against Japan.

5. Kirk Douglas. The actor was a Lieutenant in the US Navy and saw action in the Pacific before internal injuries suffered in combat led to an early discharge.

6. Jimmy Young. The broadcaster served in the RAF as a physical training instructor with the rank of Sergeant.

7. Paul Eddington. The *Yes, Prime Minister* actor joined ENSA but, when he was called up, he registered as a conscientious objector. He was duly dismissed from ENSA but the war ended before his case (for being a conscientious objector) could be heard.

8. Baroness Barbara Castle. The former politician was an administration officer in the Ministry of Food and served as an Air Raid Warden.

9. Sam Kydd. The character actor was a private in the army but was captured and sent to a German POW camp. His book about his time there – *For You, The War is Over* – illustrated just how different POW camps were for officers than for non-officers. He was also the POW adviser on the POW movie *The Captive Heart*.

10. Sir Peter Ustinov. The actor, writer and raconteur served as a private in the Royal Sussex Regiment before being transferred to the position of David Niven's batman so that they could collaborate on the film *The Way Ahead*.

11. Hughie Green. The TV presenter tried unsuccessfully to get into the RAF and so joined the Royal Canadian Air Force.

12. Richard Todd. The actor who went on to portray Guy Gibson in *The Dam Busters* served with the Light Infantry, the Parachute Regiment and the 6th Airborne Division seeing action on (among others) D Day and in the Battle of the Bulge.

13. Billy Wright. The former England soccer captain was a corporal in the Shropshire Light Infantry and also made his debut for Wolves (as a winger) and for England (at right-half) in an 'unofficial' wartime international.

14. E.W. "Jim" Swanton. The doyen of cricket writers served as an acting Major in the Royal Artillery before being captured in Singapore in 1942 and spending the rest of the war in a Japanese POW camp.

15. Earl of Harewood. The Queen's cousin was a Captain in the Grenadier Guards before being wounded and captured and spending the rest of the war in a POW camp.

16. Lord Robert Runcie. The former Archbishop of Canterbury served with the Scots Guards and was a tank officer seeing action in Normandy and being awarded the Military Cross.

17. Lord Brian Rix. The farceur served in the RAF and also down the mines as a Bevin Boy (N.B. One in ten conscripts in the latter stages of WW2 were sent down the mines as Bevin Boys – named after the Cabinet Minister, Ernest Bevin).

18. Enoch Powell. The retired politician rose through the ranks from Private in the Royal Warwickshire Regiment to become a Brigadier.

19. Sammy Davis Jnr. The entertainer served in the US Army but was bullied by white southerners – five of whom once painted him white. However, he was taught to read by a black sergeant.

20. Ray Lindwall. The legendary Australian fast bowler served with the Australian army in New Guinea and in the Solomon Islands.

21. Patrick Moore. The astronomer served in the RAF as a navigator with Bomber Command reaching the rank of Flight Lieutenant.

22. Eli Wallach. The actor served in the US Army Medical Corps and helped battle casualties in Europe.

23. Sheila Mercier. The actress who plays Annie Sugden in *Emmerdale* (and sister of Brian Rix) served in the WAAF Signals rising from section officer to adjutant.

24. Lord Bob Mellish. The former politician rose through the ranks to become a Major in the Royal Engineers serving in South-East Asia.

25. Patrick Macnee. The actor who starred as John Steed in *The Avengers* served in the Royal Navy as a Lieutenant, winning the Atlantic Medal.

26. Peter Sellers. The actor and comedian was in the Entertainments Division of the RAF and was attached to the Ralph Reader Gang Show.

27. Dame Vera Lynn. The singer raised morale for Britons everywhere with concerts and radio performances at home and abroad in Egypt, India and Burma.

28. Sir Ludovic Kennedy. The writer and broadcaster served in the Royal Navy (Volunteer Reserve) as a Lieutenant and was also private secretary and ADC to the Governor of Newfoundland.

29. Sir Edmund Hillary. The mountaineer who went on to conquer Mount Everest served as a navigator in the Royal New Zealand Air Force in the Pacific.

30. Leslie Nielsen. The actor who starred in the *Naked Gun* films joined the Royal Canadian Air Force and trained as an air gunner but the war ended before he could see combat.

31. Michael Bentine. The comedian served in the RAF as an Intelligence Officer.

32. Burt Lancaster. The actor served as a private in the American Fifth Army having enlisted immediately after Pearl Harbor.

33. Brian Johnston. The broadcaster and cricket commentator known as 'Johnners' was a Grenadier Guards officer who was awarded the Military Cross for, among other reasons, his "cheerfulness under fire" in Normandy.

34. Lord Hailsham. The former Lord Chancellor was an MP at the outbreak of war but also served in the Rifle Brigade before becoming a junior minister for Air in 1945.

35. David Croft. The writer and producer who co-created *Dad's Army, It Ain't Half Hot Mum, Are You Being Served?* and *Hi De Hi!* served in the Royal Artillery and the Dorset Regiment in North Africa, India and Malaya ending up as a Major.

36. Donald Swann. The entertainer (Flanders & Swann) had become a Quaker and so registered as a conscientious objector but he still joined the Friends Ambulance Unit working with refugees in Greece and the Middle East.

37. Dora Bryan. The actress served with the army entertainment organisation ENSA at home and abroad (Italy).

38. Ian Fleming. The creator of James Bond served as assistant to the director of Naval Intelligence. After D Day, he was put in charge of Assault Unit No 30 which was known as Fleming's Private Navy.

39. Kenneth Wolstenholme. The football commentator served as a bomber pilot in the RAF. He flew 100 missions over Germany and won the Distinguished Flying Cross (DFC) and Bar.

40. Lord Carrington. The retired politician was an officer in the Grenadiers and won the Military Cross.

41. Walter Matthau. The actor served in the US Army in France (where he lost his virginity!).

42. David Tomlinson. The *Mary Poppins* actor served as a Flight Lieutenant in the RAF.

43. Alfred Marks. The comedian and comic actor served in the RAF in the Middle East where, as a Flight Sergeant, he organised concerts for servicemen in remote areas which were beyond the reach of ENSA.

44. Tony Curtis. The actor served in the US Navy in the Pacific where he witnessed the Japanese surrender.

45. Alan Weeks. The sports commentator served in the Royal Navy - having been in the Merchant Navy since school – and rose to the rank of Lieutenant.

46. Larry Adler. The mouth organist gave recitals for the allied troops in Europe.

47. Patrick Cargill. The comic actor served in the army in India as an entertainments officer.

48. Aaron Spelling. The TV mini-series producer served in the US Army Air Force and was awarded the Bronze Star and Purple Heart with Oak Leaf Cluster.

49. Jon Pertwee. The actor who played *Doctor Who* served as an officer in the Royal Navy (Volunteer Reserve). He served on HMS Hood and was lucky to be on shore leave when his ship was sunk by the *Bismarck* with only three survivors.

50. Ronald Searle. The artist and illustrator was captured by the Japanese and was sent to the infamous Changi POW camp. He was also forced to work on the Burma-Siam railway. His drawings from that time are on display at the Imperial War Museum.

51. Lord Woodrow Wyatt. The late politician served as an Army Major and was mentioned in despatches.

52. Sir Kingsley Amis. The late novelist served as an officer in the Royal Corps of Signals and landed in Normandy three weeks after D Day.

53. Lord Home. The former Prime Minister was an MP throughout the war but also saw active service as a Major in the Lanarkshire Yeomanry before being invalided out with tuberculosis of the spine.

54. Carl Giles. The cartoonist – known as Giles – served as a war correspondent and sent back sketches from the battlefields of Europe.

55. Sir Michael Hordern. The actor was a Royal Navy officer and spent much of the war aboard the aircraft carrier Illustrious where he was also in charge of "ship's entertainments".

56. Arthur English. The comic actor served in the Army for six years, ending the war as a Sergeant

57. James Herriot. The vet and author served in the RAF.

58. Donald Pleasence. The actor declared himself to be a conscientious objector at the start of the war and was sent to the Lake District to work as a forester. However, he had a change of heart and joined the RAF. He was shot down in France and spent the last year of the war in a German POW camp.

59. Sir Alec Guinness. The actor served in the Royal Navy in Combined Operations and captained a ship.

60. Lord Bernard Weatherill. The former Speaker of the House of Commons served in the 4/7 Royal Dragoon Guards & Indian Army and the 19th KGVO Lancers.

61. Marilyn Monroe. The actress worked in a Defense Plant while her then husband (James Dougherty) went into the Merchant Marines.

62. Rod Steiger. The actor lied about his age to join the US Navy as a torpedoman on a destroyer in the South Pacific and saw action at Iwo Jima.

63. Lord Bernard Delfont. The theatrical impresario tried to join the forces but, as a stateless person (his lawyer had disappeared with the £15 he had paid for his naturalisation papers), he was forbidden and so he staged shows instead.

64. Sir Edward Heath. The former Prime Minister served in the Royal Artillery rising to the rank of Major and getting a Mention in Despatches as well as being awarded a military MBE.

65. Bill Travers. The *Born Free* actor was dispatched to India's North-West Frontier to join a Gurkha regiment which was operating behind enemy lines alongside General Wingate's Chindits. He parachuted into the Malayan jungle in command of a small group of men to harass the Japanese.

66. Ian Carmichael. The actor who starred as Bertie Wooster on TV and in most of the Boulting Brothers films served as a Major in the 22 Dragoons in North-West Europe gaining a Mention in Despatches.

67. Telly Savalas. The *Kojak* actor served with the US Army towards the end of the war and was injured in action.

68. Spike Milligan. As readers of all his wartime memoirs will know, the humorist served with the Royal Artillery in Italy and North Africa.

69. James Stewart. The actor saw active service as a pilot in the US Air Force with the rank of Colonel.

70. Rossano Brazzi. The *South Pacific* actor joined the Italian Resistance after his parents were murdered by the Fascists. He also continued to make films during the war.

71. Michael Foot. The retired politician was appointed acting editor of the London *Evening Standard*.

72. Sir Denis Thatcher. The former Prime Minister's husband served as a Major in the Royal Artillery.

73. Sir Laurens Van Der Post. The writer and friend of Prince Charles served with the Commandos and led guerrilla groups behind enemy lines in Ethiopia and the Dutch East Indies before being captured in Java and spending three years in a Japanese POW camp.

74. Dick Francis. The jockey turned novelist served as a Pilot Officer in the RAF flying Lancaster and Wellington bombers.

75. Audrey Hepburn. The actress starved in occupied Holland living on two loaves of bread for one month.

76. Jimmy Perry. The writer who co-created *Dad's Army*, *It Ain't Half Hot Mum* and *Hi De Hi!* served in the Home Guard (where he got the inspiration for *Dad's Army*).

77. Lord Roy Jenkins. The politician served in the Royal Artillery and then in special intelligence where he reached the rank of Captain.

78. Nicholas Parsons. The broadcaster was too young to join the forces but still served in the Home Guard.

79. George Cole. The *Minder* actor served in the RAF but spent most of his time making films.

80. Dinah Shore. The singer travelled more miles than any other American entertainer to entertain the troops.

81. Jean Borotra. The former Wimbledon champion was Sports Minister in the Vichy (pro-Nazi) French Government.

82. Clive Dunn. The *Dad's Army* actor was captured and spent some of the war in a German POW camp.

83. Dr Timothy Leary. The man who encouraged a whole generation of American youth to try LSD was expelled from West Point after a drinking incident which led to a court-martial. However, he went on to become an army psychologist.

84. Robert Kee. The broadcaster spent much of the war in a German POW camp. His book on his experiences – *A Crowd Is Not Company* – was described by *The Times* as "arguably the best POW book ever written".

85. Christopher Lee. The horror film actor served in the RAF as a Flight Lieutenant and with Intelligence and Special Forces in the Western Desert, Malta, Sicily, Italy and Central Europe. He was Mentioned in Despatches in 1944.

86. Bill Edrich. The England cricketer was an RAF pilot who won the DFC for taking part in a daylight attack on Cologne in 1941. In one 48-hour period, he claims to have flown two bombing missions over occupied Europe, scored a century for Norfolk and made love to a local lass!

87. Roy Dotrice. The actor (and father of the actresses Michele and Karen) was a POW in Germany.

88. Viscount Whitelaw. The retired politician served as a Major in the Scots Guards, winning the Military Cross.

89. Leo Abse. The retired politician served in the RAF but was arrested for 'political activities' in 1944 which gave rise to a debate in Parliament.

90. Bob Paisley. The former Liverpool manager served in the Royal Artillery and fought in the North African and Italian campaigns, taking part in the liberation of Rome.

91. Tony Bennett. The singer served with the American army in Europe as an infantryman.

92. John Profumo. The former politician whose career was sensationally cut short by his affair with Christine Keeler served as a Brigadier in the Army and was Mentioned in Despatches. He also found the time to win Kettering in the 1940 by-election.

93. Sir Jimmy Savile. The broadcaster and charity worker was sent down the mines as a Bevin Boy.

94. Robert Maxwell. The disgraced publisher went from being a private in the Pioneer Corps to being a Captain in the Infantry. A marksman, he was awarded the Military Cross for storming an enemy pillbox in Brussels in 1945.

95. Jeff Chandler. The actor served in the army in the Pacific, rising from infantryman to First Lieutenant.

96. Raymond Baxter. The broadcaster was an officer in the RAF, flying Spitfires.

97. Rabbi Hugo Gryn. The late broadcaster was in Auschwitz extermination camp where he worked as a slave labourer.

98. George Bush. The former US President was the US Navy's youngest ever fighter pilot. He flew 58 missions and was once shot down (and rescued). He won five medals.

99. Baroness Sue Ryder. The charity worker and founder of the Sue Ryder Foundation (and therefore the inspiration behind all the Sue Ryder charity shops) worked in the Special Operation Executive (SOE).

100. Ian Smith. The former Prime Minister of Rhodesia (now Zimbabwe) served as a pilot in the RAF.

101. Sir Hardy Amies. The Queen's dressmaker served in the Intelligence Corps and was head of the 1944 Special Forces Mission to Belgium. He rose to the rank of Lieutenant-Colonel.

102. Sir Fred Pontin. The holiday camp founder worked for the Admiralty in catering and welfare.

103. Prince Philip. The Queen's husband served in the Royal Navy and captained a ship.

104. Anthony Powell. The novelist of the twelve-volume *A Dance To The Music of Time* served in the Welch Regiment and the Intelligence Corps as a Major.

105. Lord George Weidenfeld. The publisher worked for the BBC in the Monitoring Service before becoming a news commentator.

106. Terry Scott. The comic actor served in the Royal Navy.

107. Humphrey Lyttelton. The jazz trumpeter and bandleader served with the Grenadier Guards

108. Richard Baker. The newsreader and broadcaster was in the Royal Navy.

109. Lorne Greene. The *Bonanza* actor served in the Royal Canadian Air Force.

110. Martin Balsam. The actor served in the US Army Combat Engineers before transferring to the US Army Air Force.

111. George MacDonald Fraser. The Flashman author served in the British army in Burma.

112. Robert Altman. The director was a bomber pilot in the Pacific.

3 CELEBRITIES WHO SERVED IN THE ISRAELI ARMY

1. Dr Ruth Westheimer

2. Uri Geller

3. Debra Winger

30 CELEBRITIES TAKEN APART BY OTHER CELEBRITIES

1. "Olivia looks as antiseptic as an intensive care unit in a maternity hospital" (Clive James on Olivia Newton-John)

2. "I acted vulgar, Madonna IS vulgar" (Marlene Dietrich)

3. "Elizabeth Taylor's so fat, she puts mayonnaise on an aspirin" (Joan Rivers)

4. "She looked like a bag lady" (Lenny Henry on Joan Collins)

5. "In real life, Diane Keaton believes in God. But she also believes that the radio works because there are tiny people inside it" (Woody Allen)

6. "This arrogant, sour, ceremonial, pious, chauvinistic egomaniac" (Elliot Gould on Jerry Lewis)

7. "Who could take that scruffy, arrogant buffoon seriously?" (Eddie Fisher on Richard Burton - just before Burton ran off with Elizabeth Taylor, Fisher's wife)

8. "All I could think about her (Patti Smith) was B.O. She wouldn't be bad-looking if she would wash up and glue herself together a little bit" (Andy Warhol)

9. "Somebody should clip Sting around the head and tell him to stop singing in that ridiculous Jamaican accent" (Elvis Costello)

10. "I can imagine him (Johnny Rotten) becoming a successful hairdresser: a singing Vidal Sassoon" (Malcolm McLaren)

11. "He (Roger Daltrey) has a face like a police identikit photograph" (Richard Baker)

12. "I may be ugly but I'm a much better songwriter than Take That's Gary Barlow" (Tony Mortimer of East 17)

13. "I think for the life span he's lasted, Chuck Berry's productivity has been nil, more or less" (Sir Elton John)

14. He (Morrissey) sometimes brings out records with the greatest titles in the world which, somewhere along the line, he neglects to write songs for" (Elvis Costello)

15. "If I found her (Yoko Ono) floating in my pool, I'd punish my dog" (Joan Rivers)

16. "Elvis Presley had nothing to do with excellence, just myth" (Marlon Brando)

17. "(Diana Ross) is a piece of liquorice in shoes. She walks into a pool hall and they chalk her head" (Joan Rivers)

18. "I'll wear anything as long as it hasn't been on George Michael's back" (Boy George)

19. "Who's going to tell him (Stevie Wonder) that he's got a macramé plant holder on his head" (Joan Rivers)

20. "(The Artist Formerly Known As Prince) looks like a dwarf who's been dipped in a bucket of pubic hair" (Boy George)

21. "Billy Idol: The Perry Como of punk" (Johnny Rotten)

22. "He (Bryan Ferry) sings like he's throwing up" (Andrew O'Connor)

23. "Rock critics like Elvis Costello because rock critics look like Elvis Costello" (David Lee Roth)

24. "Barry (Manilow) is bringing out a new range of nose-clippers. To the rest of us, they'll be more recognisable as shears" (Angus Deayton)

25. "Comparing Madonna with Marilyn Monroe is like comparing Raquel Welch with the back end of a bus" (Boy George)

26. "He's (Bruce Springsteen) the Walt Disney of street poets - as useful a social commentator as Donald Duck" (Chris Rea)

27. "He (Mick Hucknall) looks like Charlie Drake and he's a midget" (Carol Decker)

28. "He (Jimmy Somerville) isn't very attractive. He looks not quite finished - as if there's still a lot of work to be done on him" (Richard Fairbrass)

29. "Alice Cooper is the worst, most disgusting side of rock music" (Lou Reed)

30. "He (Pete Townshend) is so talentless, and as a lyricist he's so profoundly untalented and philosophically boring to say the least" (Lou Reed)

70 CELEBRITIES WHO HAVE BEEN IMMORTALISED IN WAX AT MADAME TUSSAUD'S

1. Oscar Wilde (added to the collection in 1997)
2. Mary, Queen of Scots (1997)
3. Darcey Bussell (1997)
4. Brad Pitt (1997)
5. Pelé (1997)
6. Jesse Owens (1997)
7. William Hague (1997)
8. Jacques Santer (1996)
9. Jean-Paul Gaultier (1996)
10. Eric Cantona (1996)
11. Naomi Campbell (1996)
12. Jacques Chirac (1996)
13. King Baudouin of Belgium (1996)
14. Helen Sharman (1996)
15. Jayne Torvill (1996)
16. Christopher Dean (1996)
17. Olga Korbut (1996)
18. Daley Thompson (1996)
19. Ayrton Senna (1995)
20. Pierce Brosnan (1995)
21. Mel Gibson (1995)
22. Jurgen Klinsmann (1995)
23. Hugh Grant (1995)
24. David Copperfield (1995)
25. Terry Venables (1995)
26. Linford Christie (1995)
27. Brian Lara (1995)
28. Tony Blair (1995)
29. Stephen Hawking (1995)
30. Oprah Winfrey (1995)
31. Henry Moore (1995)
32. Chris Evans (1994)
33. Joanna Lumley (1994)
34. Paul Keating (1994)
35. Mary Robinson (1994)
36. Keith Floyd (1994)
37. Kenneth Clarke (1994)
38. Bill Clinton (1993)
39. Boris Yeltsin (1993)
40. Sir Anthony Hopkins (1993)
41. John Smith MP (1993)
42. Saddam Hussein (1993)
43. Nigel Mansell (1993)
44. Gerard Depardieu (1993)
45. The Dalai Lama (1993)
46. Yitzhak Rabin (1993)
47. Harrison Ford (1993)
48. Sir David Attenborough (1992)
49. Patrick Moore (1992)
50. Nigel Kennedy (1992)
51. Francois Mitterrand (1992)
52. George Bush (1992)
53. F.W. de Klerk (1992)
54. Will Carling (1992)
55. Arnold Schwarzenegger (1992)
56. Madonna (1992)
57. Paul Gascoigne (1991)
58. John Major (1991)
59. Nelson Mandela (1991)
60. Nick Faldo (1991)
61. Neil Kinnock (1991)
62. Paddy Ashdown (1991)
63. Dr George Carey (1991)
64. Luciano Pavarotti (1990)
65. Jane Seymour (1990)
66. Dudley Moore (1990)
67. Sir Jimmy Savile (1990)
68. Mikhail Gorbachev (1990)
69. Yasser Arafat (1990)
70. Phillip Schofield (1990)

3 CELEBRITIES WHO SERVED IN VIETNAM

1. Oliver Stone
2. Al Gore
3. Steve Kanaly (Ray Krebbs, *Dallas*) – awarded the Purple Heart for the injuries he suffered there

25 CELEBRITIES WHOSE WAXWORKS HAVE BEEN REMOVED FROM MADAME TUSSAUD'S

1. Steve Davis (removed from the collection in 1997)

2. Anneka Rice (1997)

3. The Duchess of York (1996)

4. Arthur Scargill (1996)

5. Brian Mulroney (1996)

6. Francois Mitterrand (1996)

7. Ken Livingstone (1995)

8. Peter Shilton (1995)

9. Michael Foot (1994)

10. Terry Wogan (1994)

11. Lord Roy Hattersley (1994)

12. Bob Hawke (1994)

13. Lord Carrington (1994)

14. Charles Dance (1993)

15. Jane Seymour (1993)

16. Lord Geoffrey Howe (1992)

17. Lord Nigel Lawson (1992)

18. Sir Robert Menzies (1992)

19. Nastassja Kinski (1992)

20. Michael Heseltine (1992)

21. Lord Norman Tebbit (1992)

22. Lord David Owen (1991)

23. Benny Hill (1990)

24. Fatima Whitbread (1990)

25. John McEnroe (1990)

10 CELEBRITIES WHO WERE STILL ALIVE AT THE START OF WORLD WAR TWO

1. James Joyce

2. Damon Runyon

3. Kaiser Wilhelm II

4. Orville Wright

5. H.G. Wells

6. F. Scott Fitzgerald

7. Beatrix Potter

8. Lord Baden-Powell

9. Virginia Woolf

10. John Logie Baird

25 CELEBRITIES WHO WERE ALIVE IN WORLD WAR TWO

1. Victoria Principal
2. Rod Stewart
3. Jasper Carrott
4. Michael Douglas
5. Raquel Welch
6. Eric Clapton
7. Carol Barnes
8. Freddie Starr
9. Anna Ford
10. Robert De Niro
11. John Thaw
12. Terry Venables
13. Michael Crawford
14. Hannah Gordon
15. Gloria Hunniford
16. Cilla Black
17. Mick Jagger
18. Jonathan Dimbleby
19. Jacqueline Bisset
20. Roger Daltrey
21. Anna Ford
22. Willie Carson
23. Calvin Klein
24. Sir Paul McCartney
25. Brough Scott

12 CELEBRITIES WHO FOUGHT IN THE KOREAN WAR

1. Michael Caine
2. James Garner
3. Jamie Farr (Corporal Klinger in the TV series *M*A*S*H*)
4. Faron Young
5. P.J. Kavanagh
6. Clint Eastwood
7. Charlie Rich
8. Link Wray
9. John Mayall
10. Leonard Nimoy
11. John Wells
12. Richard Ingrams

11 CELEBRITIES WHO WERE EVACUATED IN WORLD WAR TWO

1. Michael Aspel
2. Jack Rosenthal
3. Shirley Williams
4. Michael Caine
5. The Beverley Sisters
6. Bernard Kops
7. Derek Jameson
8. Justin de Villeneuve
9. Jonathan Miller
10. Jeremy Thorpe
11. Phyllida Law

4 CELEBRITIES WHO ENTERED COMPETITIONS TO IMITATE OR IMPERSONATE THEMSELVES AND LOST

1. David Bellamy

2. Dolly Parton

3. Graham Greene

4. Charlie Chaplin

21 CELEBRITIES WHO WERE BULLIED AT SCHOOL

1. Harrison Ford (Because he "liked to hang out with girls")

2. Anthea Turner (Because of her "posh" accent)

3. Martyn Lewis (Because he was fat)

4. Gillian Anderson (Because of her "independent" and "bossy" attitude)

5. Prince Charles (Because he was heir to the throne – was especially bullied during rugby games)

6. Marcella Detroit (Because she was Jewish)

7. Mel Gibson (Because of his Australian accent at his American school)

8. Sandra Bullock (Because she was "ugly")

9. Tom Cruise (Because he "was always the new kid in town")

10. Laura Dern (Because her father – Bruce Dern – was "the only person to kill John Wayne in the movies")

11. Gwyneth Paltrow (Because she was "gawky")

12. Norman Pace (Because he was so small)

13. Michelle Pfeiffer (Because of her "big lips")

14. Damon Albarn (Because the other boys thought he was a "gayboy")

15. Betty Boo (Because she was a bookworm)

16. Patrick Swayze (Because he liked to dance)

17. Whitney Houston (Because her "hair was too straight" and her "skin was too white")

18. Dudley Moore (Because he was short and had a club foot)

19. Dannii Minogue (Because she appeared on an Australian TV variety show at the age of ten)

20. Morrissey (Because of the way he was)

21. Woody Allen

22. Sir Ranulph Fiennes (Because he was "rather pretty")

23. Sir Cliff Richard (Because, having come from India, he "looked different")

24. Tessa Sanderson (Because she's black)

25. Laurie Taylor (Because he's thin and gangly)

26. Martyn Lewis (Because he was born in Wales)

27. Sir John Harvey-Jones (Because he was at a school where bullying thrived)

28. Wayle Sleep (Because he was going to dancing classes)

18 CELEBRITIES AND HOW MUCH THEIR POSSESSIONS FETCHED AT AUCTION

1. Madonna: Black bra - as worn on the 1993 Girlie Show tour - £4,600 (1997)

2. Sir Elton John: *Goodbye Yellow Brick Road* stage costume - £11,500 (1997)

3. John Lennon: 1965 letter to wife Cynthia - £17,250 (1997)

4. Geri Halliwell: Costume worn for the launch of Channel 5 - £6,440 (1997)

5. Ella Fitzgerald: 1959 Mercedes - £50,630 (1997)

6. Marlon Brando: Costume from *Mutiny On The Bounty* - £6,940 (1997)

7. Courtney Love: Fender Jazzmater guitar - £2,990 (1997)

8. Jane Seymour: Dress worn in *Live And Let Die* - £2,530 (1997)

9. Charlton Heston: Loin-cloth from *Ben-Hur* - £6,250 (1997)

10. Mick Jagger: Handwritten lyrics from the mid-1960s - £2,070 (1997)

11. Sir Paul McCartney: Recording notes for *Hey Jude* – £25,300 (1997)

12. Pete Townshend: Gibson Les Paul guitar – £14,950 (1997)

13. Jimi Hendrix: Afghan jacket – £11,270 (1997)

14. Charlie Parker: Saxophone – £93,500 (1994)

15. Bill Clinton (in the sense that it was signed by him): Saxophone - £22,000 (1994)

16. Elvis Presley: Acoustic guitar - £99,000 (1993)

17. Marilyn Monroe: Dress from *Some Like It Hot* – £19,800 (1988)

18. Charlie Chaplin: Boots - £38,500 (1987)

16 CELEBRITIES AWARDED HONORARY KNIGHTHOODS

1. Pelé (1997)

2. Henry Kissinger (1995)

3. Cyrus Vance (1994)

4. George Bush (1993)

5. Norman Schwarzkopf (1991)

7. Perez de Cuellar (1991)

8. Alfred Brendel (1989)

9. Richard Giordano (1989)

10. Caspar Weinberger (1988)

11. Bernard Haitink (1977)

12. Dean Rusk (1976)

13. Chaim Herzog (1971)

14. Kurt Waldheim (1969)

15. J. Edgar Hoover (1947)

16. Bob Hope (1998)

18 CELEBRITIES WHO HAVE THEIR OWN FAN CLUBS

1. Janet Ellis
2. Sharon Gless
3. Joe Pasquale
4. Adrian Paul
5. Rik Mayall
6. David McCallum
7. Jack Wild
8. John Boulter
9. Steve Coogan
10. Julia Sawalha
11. David Soul
12. Kathy Staff
13. Paul Nicholls
14. Linsey Dawn McKenzie
15. Bruce Forsyth
16. Shane Ritchie
17. Terry Wogan
18. John Noakes

10 CELEBRITIES WHO SURVIVED HELICOPTER CRASHES

1. Christy O'Connor Jnr
2. Christie Brinkley
3. Sarah Greene
4. Mike Smith
5. Kirk Douglas
6. Joe Longthorne
7. Brian Duffy (Guinness boss)
8. Barbara McCann (GMTV reporter)
9. Alessandro Nannini (Italian motor-racing driver)
10. Roy of The Rovers

6 CELEBRITIES WHO SURVIVED PLANE CRASHES

1. Clint Eastwood
2. Sir Matt Busby
3. Sir Bobby Charlton
4. Yasser Arafat
5. Elizabeth Taylor
6. Peter de Savary

11 CELEBRITIES WHO WERE MADE COMPANIONS OF HONOUR

1. David Hockney (1997)
2. Eric Hobsbawm (1998)
3. Sir John Gielgud (1977)
4. Jack Jones (1978)
5. Sir David Attenborough (1996)
6. Dame Janet Baker (1994)
7. Sir Alec Guinness (1994)
8. Anthony Powell (1988)
9. Chris Patten (1998)
10. A.L. Rowse (1997)
11. Sir Hugh Casson (1985)

11 CELEBRITIES WHO BECAME PENSIONERS IN 1998 (Women: 60; Men: 65)

1. Eleanor Bron
2. Barry Norman
3. Ann Jones
4. Michael Aspel
5. Dame Diana Rigg
6. Daniel Massey
7. Dickie Davies
8. Victor Spinetti
9. Caryl Churchill
10. Andrea Newman
11. David Bellamy

105 CELEBRITIES AND THE PRICE OF THEIR AUTOGRAPHS

1. Jodie Foster £175
2. Julie Andrews £125
3. David Bowie £250
4. Cameron Diaz £125
5. Winona Ryder £150
6. Nick Nolte £45
7. Mike Tyson £225
8. Glenn Close £65
9. Nicole Kidman £125
10. Kevin Costner £75
11. Clint Eastwood £150
12. George Clooney £85
13. Keanu Reeves £85
14. Sandra Bullock £175
15. Tom Cruise £125
16. Cindy Crawford £85
17. Michelle Pfeiffer £125
18. Björk £175
19. Leonardo DiCaprio £85
20. Val Kilmer £65
21. Kate Moss £100
22. Gillian Anderson £75
23. Gabriel Byrne £45
24. Harrison Ford £175
25. Jamie Lee Curtis £65
26. Julie Christie £95
27. Patrick McGoohan £275
28. Celine Dion £75
29. Jane Fonda £55
30. Jerry Hall £75
31. Nigel Hawthorne £125
32. Eric Cantona £65
33. Kirstie Alley £65
34. Sir Paul McCartney £275
35. Ted Danson £50
36. Jean Shrimpton £150
37. Morgan Freeman £55
38. Richard Dreyfuss £65
39. Stevie Wonder £9,100
40. Robert De Niro £95
41. Arnold Schwarzenegger £95
42. Andy Garcia £65
43. Noel Gallagher £75
44. Honor Blackman £55
45. Mariel Hemingway £60
46. Annette Bening £100
47. Christopher Reeve £150
48. Matt Dillon £65
49. Robert Redford £150
50. Ellen Barkin £45
51. Brad Pitt £75
52. Willem Dafoe £45
53. Cherie Lunghi £45
54. Leonard Nimoy £85
55. Teri Hatcher £100
56. Pamela Anderson £75
57. Madonna £400
58. Wesley Snipes £45
59. Sharon Stone £150
60. Pierce Brosnan £125
61. George Segal £35
62. Uma Thurman £125
63. Liam Gallagher £85
64. Johnny Depp £100
65. Meg Ryan £100
66. Jim Carrey £85
67. Joanna Lumley £75
68. Daniel Day-Lewis £75
69. Alec Baldwin £75
70. Gwyneth Paltrow £125
71. Rebecca De Mornay £45
72. Richard Gere £85
73. Elizabeth Hurley £125
74. Michael Keaton £85
75. Al Pacino £85
76. William Shatner £85
77. Hugh Grant £75
78. Carrie Fisher £175
79. Tom Hanks £95
80. George Cole £45
81. Brigitte Bardot £125
82. David Duchovny £95
83. Charlton Heston £75
84. John Daly £55
85. Patsy Kensit £100
86. Lauren Bacall £85
87. Doris Day £125
88. Jennifer Aniston £125
89. Whoopi Goldberg £35
90. Jessica Lange £175
91. Courtney Cox £85
92. Warren Beatty £100
93. Tim Roth £125
94. Emilio Estevez £45
95. Ian Wright £65
96. Richard Harris £75
97. Liza Minnelli £75
98. Ralph Fiennes £85
99. Alicia Silverstone £125
100. Leonard Cohen £375
101. Elizabeth Taylor £375
102. Robin Williams £50
103. Brian Lara £75
104. Aretha Franklin £125
105. Kylie Minogue £175

(All prices quoted by Fraser's and all autographs are on photos of the people concerned)

10 CELEBRITIES WHO STARTED THE DRAW FOR THE NATIONAL LOTTERY

1. Elkie Brooks
2. Andrew Sachs
3. Stephanie Cole
4. Su Pollard
5. Jill Dando
6. Darren Day
7. Kate O'Mara
8. Andrew O'Connor
9. Frank Thornton
10. Roy Hudd

9 CELEBRITIES WHO WON PIPE SMOKER OF THE YEAR AWARDS

1. Fred Trueman (1974)
2. Magnus Magnusson (1978)
3. Sir Ranulph Fiennes (1994)
4. Sir John Harvey-Jones (1991)
5. Jeremy Brett (1989)
6. David Bryant (1986)
7. Edward Fox (1980)
8. James Galway (1981)
9. Dave Lee Travis (1982)

10 CELEBRITIES WHO WERE CHILD STARS BUT WHO WENT ON TO BECOME EVEN MORE FAMOUS AS ADULTS

1. Phil Collins
2. Anthony Newley
3. Patsy Kensit
4. Dennis Waterman
5. Mickey Dolenz
6. Jodie Foster
7. George Cole
8. Petula Clark
9. Richard O'Sullivan
10. Julie Andrews

10 CELEBRITIES WHO SURVIVED ASSASSINATION ATTEMPTS

1. Charles de Gaulle
2. Adolf Hitler
3. Ronald Reagan
4. Pope John Paul II
5. Queen Victoria
6. Margaret Thatcher
7. Fidel Castro
8. Shah of Iran
9. Yasser Arafat
10. Queen Elizabeth I

10 CELEBRITIES WHO MADE IT TO 100 YEARS OLD

1. George Burns (Comedian)
2. Hal Roach (Film producer)
3. Rose Kennedy (Mother of the Kennedy clan)
4. Irving Berlin (Songwriter)
5. Sir Thomas Sopwith (Aviation pioneer)
6. Manny Shinwell (Politician)
7. Dame Freya Stark (Explorer)
8. Athene Seyler (Actress)
9. Eubie Blake (Pianist)
10. Geoffrey Dearmer (WW1 poet)

10 CELEBRITIES WHO HAD THEATRES NAMED AFTER THEM

1. Bob Hope (Eltham)
2. Sir John Gielgud (London)
3. Dame Peggy Ashcroft (Croydon)
4. Neil Simon (New York)
5. Sir Michael Redgrave (Farnham)
6. Sir Laurence Olivier (London)
7. Kenneth More (Ilford)
8. Dame Sybil Thorndike (Leatherhead)
9. Tony O'Reilly (Pittsburgh)
10. Dame Flora Robson (Newark)

10 CELEBRITIES WHO HAD NOVELS DEDICATED TO THEM

1. Christopher Isherwood (*Myra Breckinridge* by Gore Vidal)
2. Brigid Brophy (*The Good Apprentice* by Iris Murdoch)
3. Robert Bolt (*Second Fiddle* by Mary Wesley)
4. Diana Mosley (*Vile Bodies* by Evelyn Waugh)
5. Philip Larkin (*Lucky Jim* by Kingsley Amis)
6. Kingsley Amis (*XX Poems* by Philip Larkin)
7. Robert Conquest (*Hearing Secret Harmonies* by Anthony Powell)
8. William Makepeace Thackeray (*Jane Eyre* by Charlotte Bronte)
9. Iris Murdoch (*The Sweets of Pimlico* by A. N. Wilson)
10. Ivy Compton-Burnett (*The Spoilt City* by Olivia Manning)

31 CELEBRITIES AWARDED THE FREEDOM OF THE CITY OF . . .

1. Sean Connery (Edinburgh)
2. Brigitte Bardot (Paris)
3. Jimmy Carter (Swansea)
4. Michelle Smith (Dublin)
5. The Duchess of York (York)
6. Nelson Mandela (Glasgow)
7. Jayne Torvill (Nottingham)
8. Christopher Dean (Nottingham)
9. Lord James Callaghan (Sheffield)
10. Lord Robert Runcie (Canterbury)
11. Sir David Attenborough (Leicester)
12. Lord Richard Attenborough (Leicester)
13. Baroness Barbara Castle (Bradford)
14. Jack Charlton (Dublin)
15. Sir Simon Rattle (Birmingham)
16. Norman Wisdom (Tirana)
17. Brian Clough (Nottingham)
18. Kenny Dalglish (Glasgow)
19. Mikhail Gorbachev (Aberdeen)
20. Helen Sharman (Sheffield)
21. Sir Paul McCartney (Liverpool)
22. Prince Philip (London)
23. Lisa Clayton (Birmingham)
24. Bill Clinton (Dublin)
25. John Moores (Liverpool)
26. Baroness Margaret Thatcher (Westminster)
27. John Tusa (London)
28. Sir Rhodes Boyson (London)
29. Pope John Paul II (Dublin)
30. Prince Charles (Swansea)
31. Stephen Roche (Dublin)

35 CELEBRITIES WHO ARE MEMBERS OF THE GROUCHO CLUB

1. Robbie Coltrane
2. Mel Smith
3. Michael Elphick
4. Stephen Fry
5. Gary Lineker
6. Barry Norman
7. Will Carling
8. Harold Pinter
9. Peter Bowles
10. Ken Follett
11. Douglas Adams
12. Larry Adler
13. Bob Mortimer
14. Angus Deayton
15. Wayne Sleep
16. Emma Freud
17. Simon Gray
18. Bel Mooney
19. Griff Rhys-Jones
20. Sir Tim Rice
21. Richard Wilson
22. Timothy West
23. Sir John Harvey-Jones
24. Sir Clement Freud
25. Sam Mendes
26. Desmond Wilcox
27. Michael Nicholson
28. John Sessions
29. Michael Atherton
30. Sue Townsend
31. Patrick Barlow
32. Melvyn Bragg
33. Rabbi Julia Neuberger
34. Raymond Briggs
35. Ben Elton

10 CELEBRITIES WHOSE WIVES WON BEST ACTRESS OSCARS

1. Richard Burton (Elizabeth Taylor)
2. Roald Dahl (Patricia Neal)
3. Kenneth Branagh (Emma Thompson)
4. Paul Newman (Joanne Woodward)
5. Douglas Fairbanks Senior (Mary Pickford)
6. Laurence Olivier (Vivien Leigh)
7. Mel Brooks (Anne Bancroft)
8. Prince Rainier (Grace Kelly)
9. Ronald Reagan (Jane Wyman)
10. Blake Edwards (Julie Andrews)

10 CELEBRITIES WHO ARE FLUENT IN RUSSIAN

1. Eddie George
2. Prince Michael of Kent
3. Alan Bennett
4. Sir John Harvey-Jones
5. A.N. Wilson
6. Michael Frayn
7. Sir Peter Ustinov
8. Madeleine Albright
9. Ivan Lendl
10. Geoffrey Robinson MP

8 CELEBRITIES WHO ARE PROFICIENT MAGICIANS

1. David Hemmings
2. Prince Charles
3. Adam Faith
4. Greville Janner
5. Christo Van Rensburg
6. Muhammad Ali
7. Norman Schwarzkopf
8. Michael Jackson

9 CELEBRITIES WHO CAN COMMUNICATE IN SIGN LANGUAGE

1. Jane Fonda
2. Holly Hunter
3. Desmond Wilcox
4. William Hurt
5. Richard Griffiths
6. Hugh Grant
7. Sinead O'Connor
8. Richard Dreyfuss
9. Louise Fletcher

8 CELEBRITIES WHO ARE VINEYARD OWNERS

1. Sir Peter Ustinov
2. Francis Ford Coppola
3. Gerard Depardieu
4. Antonio Pinto
5. Jean Tigana
6. Chay Blyth
7. Michel Roux
8. Luciano Benneton

9 CELEBRITIES WHO BOUGHT ISLANDS

1. Marlon Brando (Tetiaroa)
2. Richard Branson (Necker)
3. Carla Lane (St Tedwell's East)
4. Charles Haughey (Inis Mhicileain)
5. Lord Peter Palumbo (Ascrib)
6. Bjorn Borg (Kattilo)
7. David & Frederick Barclay (Brecqhou)
8. Malcolm Forbes (Lacaula)
9. Nick Faldo (Bartrath)

12 CELEBRITIES WHO ARE QUALIFIED PILOTS

1. Ted Dexter
2. John Travolta
3. Nicholas Lyndhurst
4. Greg Norman
5. Darius Guppy
6. Stephen Dorrell
7. Prince Charles
8. Niki Lauda
9. Kurt Russell
10. Gary Numan
11. Lord Norman Tebbit
12. Michael Bywater

13 CELEBRITIES WHO WERE EACH LEFT $378.79 IN BOB FOSSE'S WILL TO "GO OUT AND HAVE DINNER ON" HIM

1. Janet Leigh
2. Jessica Lange
3. Buddy Hackett
4. Ben Gazzara
5. Dustin Hoffman
6. Elia Kazan
7. Roy Scheider
8. Ben Vereen
9. Liza Minnelli
10. Julie Hagerty
11. Melanie Griffith
12. E.L. Doctorow
13. Neil Simon

2 CELEBRITIES WHO WERE DEPUTY HEAD BOYS

1. Phil Neville (Elton High)
2. Jack Straw (Brentwood)

2 CELEBRITIES WHO HAD HOTEL SUITES NAMED AFTER THEM

1. Sir Arthur C. Clarke (at the Hotel Club Oceanic, Sri Lanka)
2. James Galway (at the Tara Hotel, London)

14 CELEBRITIES WHO DIED INTESTATE

1. Jayne Mansfield
2. George Gershwin
3. Rita Hayworth
4. Howard Hughes
5. Abraham Lincoln
6. Pablo Picasso
7. Duke Ellington
8. Lenny Bruce
9. Paolo Gucci
10. Pat Phoenix
11. Robert Holmes à Court
12. Phil Lynott
13. J.B. Morton (Beachcomber)
14. Sylvia Plath

34 CELEBRITIES AND THE COUNTRIES WHOSE STAMPS THEY'VE APPEARED ON

1. Ian Botham (St Vincent)
2. Arnold Schwarzenegger (Mali)
3. Clive Lloyd (Guyana)
4. Dolly Parton (Grenada)
5. Viv Richards (Antigua)
6. Frank Sinatra (St Vincent)
7. David Platt (Lesotho)
8. Jimmy Connors (Lesotho)
9. Carl Lewis (Niger)
10. Eddie Murphy (Tanzania)
11. Muhammad Ali (Liberia)
12. Baroness Thatcher (Kenya)
13. Nick Faldo (St Vincent)
13. Stevie Wonder (Tanzania)
14. Gladys Knight (Tanzania)
15. Bruce Springsteen (Grenada)
16. Barbra Streisand (St Vincent)
17. George Michael (St Vincent)
18. Robert De Niro (Gambia)
19. Boris Becker (Central African Republic)
20. (The Artist Formerly Known As) Prince (St Vincent)
21. Tina Turner (Tanzania)
22. Bjorn Borg (Ivory coast)
23. Paul Newman (The Maldives)
24. Elliott Gould (Gambia)
25. Gary Lineker (Gambia)
26. Pelé (Brazil)
27. John McEnroe (Sierra Leone)
28. Martina Navratilova (Ivory Coast)
29. Kirk Douglas (Mali)
30. Michael Jackson (Tanzania)
31. Sir Elton John (Grenada)
32. Mick Jagger (St Vincent)
33. Whitney Houston (Tanzania)
34. Cher (Grenada)

Chapter 8

Politics and Religion

37 CELEBRITIES WHO'VE SUPPORTED THE LABOUR PARTY

1. Anita Roddick
2. Patrick Stewart
3. John Mortimer
4. Stephen Fry
5. Michael Cashman
6. Steve Cram
7. Richard Wilson
8. Alex Ferguson
9. Kathy Lette
10. Sir David Puttnam
11. Michelle Collins
12. Simon Mayo
13. Melvyn Bragg
14. Sinead Cusack
15. Paul McGann
16. Ben Elton
17. Neil Pearson
18. Helen Mirren
19. Pam St Clement
20. Anna Carteret
21. Kevin Whateley
22. Timothy West
23. Lord Richard Attenborough
24. Lenny Henry
25. Hugh Laurie
26. Robbie Coltrane
27. Claire Rayner
28. Anthony Sher
29. Colin Welland
30. Tony Robinson
31. Tom Watt
32. Prunella Scales
33. Ken Follett
34. Jo Brand
35. Paul Weller
36. Brian Clough
37. Billy Bragg

51 CELEBRITIES WHO'VE SUPPORTED THE CONSERVATIVE PARTY

1. Ian Botham
2. William Roache
3. Lord Andrew Lloyd Webber
4. Cilla Black
5. Jimmy Tarbuck
6. Paul Daniels
7. Jim Davidson
8. Jimmy Greaves
9. Sarah Brightman
10. Sharron Davies
11. Mike Gatting
12. Nigel Havers
13. Jenny Seagrove
14. Rob Andrew
15. Joan Armatrading
16. Duncan Goodhew
17. Patrick Moore
18. Bruce Oldfield
19. Bob Monkhouse
20. Ruth Madoc
21. Henry Cooper
22. Ronnie Corbett
23. Anthony Andrews
24. Tony Britton
25. Sir Tim Rice
26. Matthew Pinsent
27. Shirley Bassey
28. Elaine Paige
29. Lynsey de Paul
30. Sir Clive Sinclair
31. Bob Willis
32. Dame Vera Lynn
33. Terry Venables
34. Steve Davis
35. Stan Boardman
36. Bill Beaumont
37. Michael Winner
38. John Barnes
39. Suzanne Dando
40. Sonia
41. Fatima Whitbread
42. Adam Faith
43. Bill Wyman
44. Joan Collins
45. Nigel Mansell
46. Gloria Hunniford
47. Emlyn Hughes
48. Fred Trueman
49. Ken Dodd
50. Stephen Redgrave
51. Bryan Forbes

10 CELEBRITIES WHO ARE SCIENTOLOGISTS

1. Tom Cruise
2. Nicole Kidman
3. John Travolta
4. Priscilla Presley
5. Kirstie Alley
6. Isaac Hayes
7. Ann Archer
8. Kelly Preston
9. Mimi Rogers
10. Sharon Stone

10 CELEBRITIES WHO CONVERTED TO ISLAM

1. Muhammad Ali
2. Darius Guppy
3. Jemima Khan
4. Mike Tyson
5. Malcolm X
6. Gerard Depardieu (although he later converted back to Christianity)
7. Art Blakey
8. Cat Stevens
9. Soraya Khashoggi
10. Chris Eubank

10 CELEBRITIES WHO ARE/WERE CHRISTIAN SCIENTISTS

1. John Simpson (TV news reporter)

2. Joyce Grenfell (Actress, comedienne and broadcaster)

3. Ginger Rogers (Actress and dancer)

4. Jim Henson (Creator of The Muppets)

5. Dame Gwen Ffrangcon-Davies (Actress)

6. William Webster (Former head of the FBI)

7. Ellen Pollock (Actress)

8. H.R. Haldeman (President Nixon's closest aide)

9. Sir Harold Hobson (Drama critic)

10. Dorothy Dickson (Actress)

8 CELEBRITIES WHO WERE THE CHILDREN OF CHRISTIAN SCIENTISTS

1. Sir V.S. Pritchett

2. Elizabeth Taylor

3. Peter Barkworth

4. Dudley Moore

5. Jeffrey Bernard

6. J.P. Getty

7. Lady Menuhin

8. Carol Channing

16 CELEBRITIES WHO WENT ON THE ORIGINAL CND MARCHES

1. Jeremy Beadle

2. Vanessa Redgrave

3. Humphrey Lyttelton

4. Rod Stewart

5. George Melly

6. Doris Lessing

7. Bryan Pringle

8. Arnold Wesker

9. Lindsay Anderson

10. Robert Bolt

11. Peter Vaughan

12. John Braine

13. John Arden

14. Michael Foot

15. Sheila Delaney

16. Anita Roddick

10 CELEBRITIES WHOSE FATHERS WERE MPs

1. Fred Perry
2. Sir James Goldsmith
3. Emma Soames
4. Captain Marryat
5. Bertrand Russell
6. Malcolm Muggeridge
7. Sarah Hogg
8. Lord Montagu of Beaulieu
9. Jeremy Thorpe
10. Susie Orbach

10 CELEBRITIES WHO WERE MEMBERS OF THE COMMUNIST PARTY

1. Pablo Picasso
2. Julie Burchill
3. Sir Stephen Spender
4. Dame Iris Murdoch
5. Roger Woddis
6. A.J.P. Taylor
7. Sir Alfred Sherman
8. Laurie Lee
9. Jessica Mitford
10. Lord Denis Healey

28 CELEBRITIES WHO ARE ROMAN CATHOLICS

1. Bruce Springsteen
2. Delia Smith
3. Billy Connolly
4. Germaine Greer
5. Marina Warner
6. Baroness Sarah Hogg
7. Naim Attallah
8. Jon Bon Jovi
9. Brigadier Andrew Parker Bowles
10. Richard Harris
11. John Gummer
12. Elvis Costello
13. Bob Geldof
14. Cary Elwes
15. John Birt
16. Lady Antonia Fraser
17. Piers Paul Read
18. Roger McGough
19. Conrad Black
20. Madonna
21. Marianne Faithfull
22. Sir Peregrine Worsthorne
23. Carmen Callil
24. David Lodge
25. Frankie Valli
26. Chris de Burgh
27. Sara Wheeler
28. Whoopi Goldberg

10 CELEBRITIES WHO WERE RECTOR OF ST ANDREWS UNIVERSITY

1. John Stuart Mill (1865-68)
2. Sir J.M. Barrie (1919-22)
3. Rudyard Kipling (1922-25)
4. Sir Learie Constantine (1967-70)
5. John Cleese (1970-73)
6. Alan Coren (1973-76)
7. Frank Muir (1976-79)
8. Tim Brooke-Taylor (1979-82)
9. Nicholas Parsons (1988-91)
10. Nicky Campbell (1991-93)

14 CELEBRITIES WHO'VE BEEN LAY PREACHERS

1. Sir David Frost
2. David Blunkett
3. George Foreman
4. Dr Brian Mawhinney
5. Peter Pollock
6. Jimmy Armfield
7. Alan Beith
8. Paul Daniels
9. Dave Merrington
10. Frank Williams
11. Lord Peter Archer
12. Jaci Stephen
13. Sir James Anderton
14. Hartley Booth

10 CELEBRITIES WHO ARE/WERE THE CHILDREN OF LAY PREACHERS

1. Frank Bruno
2. David Bellamy
3. Baroness Thatcher
4. Brian Moore
5. John Poulson
6. Jonah Lomu
7. Alistair Cooke
8. James Baldwin
9. Paula Jones
10. Herol Graham

10 CELEBRITIES WHO ARE/WERE AGNOSTICS

1. Arthur Hailey
2. Brian Sewell
3. A.A. Milne
4. Dennis Potter
5. Michael Palin
6. Ken Livingstone
7. Nicky Campbell
8. Esther Rantzen
9. David Bowie
10. Professor Stephen Hawking

9 CELEBRITIES WHO ARE ATHEISTS

1. Dr David Starkey
2. John Mortimer
3. Paul McKenna
4. Raymond Briggs
5. Dave Allen
6. Bernie Grant
7. Mary Peters
8. Robin Cook
9. Douglas Adams

22 CELEBRITIES WHO ARE PRACTISING BUDDHISTS

1. Uma Thurman
2. Stephanie Beacham
3. Keanu Reeves
4. Cindy Crawford
5. Susan Sarandon
6. Sandie Shaw
7. Woody Harrelson
8. Tina Turner
9. Billy Connolly
10. Courtney Love
11. Harrison Ford
12. Richard Gere
13. Gaynor Faye
14. Julie Peasgood
15. Koo Stark
16. Oliver Stone
17. Pamela Stephenson
18. Claudia Schiffer
19. Lulu
20. Boy George
21. Annie Lennox
22. Louise Jameson

11 CELEBRITIES WHO ARE BORN-AGAIN CHRISTIANS

1. Glenn Hoddle
2. Andre Agassi
3. Marcus Gayle
4. Rosemary Conley
5. Cyrille Regis
6. Jonathan Edwards
7. Tommy Cannon
8. Bobby Ball
9. Donna Summer
10. Pat Boone
11. Samantha Fox

12 CELEBRITIES WHO BELIEVE IN REINCARNATION

1. Jesper Parnevik
2. Glenn Hoddle
3. Eric Cantona
4. Joan Collins
5. Louise Jameson
6. Sheryl Lee
7. k d lang
8. Nesta Wyn Ellis
9. Keanu Reeves
10. Conchita Martinez
11. Tori Amos
12. Shirley Maclaine (well, this list wouldn't have been complete without her)

10 CELEBRITIES WHO ARE/WERE QUAKERS

1. Dame Judi Dench
2. Sheila Hancock
3. Paul Eddington
4. Joel Cadbury
5. Margaret Drabble
6. Richard Nixon
7. James Michener
8. Anna Wing
9. A.S. Byatt
10. Sir Richard Body

Note that Inspector Morse is also a Quaker

Chapter 9

Music

10 CELEBRITIES AND THE SONGS ON WHICH THEY SANG BACKING VOCALS

1. Sir Tim Rice: *Lily The Pink* (The Scaffold)
2. Eric Clapton: *All You Need Is Love* (The Beatles)
3. Donovan: *Yellow Submarine* (The Beatles)
4. Mick Jagger: *You're So Vain* (Carly Simon)
5. Paul Young: *Black Coffee In Bed* (Squeeze)
6. Phil Spector: *My Sweet Lord* (George Harrison)
7. Bruce Springsteen: *Street Hassle* (Lou Reed)
8. Luther Vandross: *Young Americans* (David Bowie)
9. Sir Paul McCartney: *Mellow Yellow* (Donovan)
10. John Lennon: *Fame* (David Bowie)

30 CELEBRITIES ON THE COVER OF SERGEANT PEPPER'S LONELY HEARTS CLUB BAND

1. Tony Curtis
2. Oliver Hardy
3. Stan Laurel
4. George Bernard Shaw
5. Max Miller
6. Bob Dylan
7. Shirley Temple
8. Dion
9. Tyrone Power
10. Lewis Carroll
11. Tommy Hanley
12. Stuart Sutcliffe
13. Fred Astaire
14. Mae West
15. Carl Jung
16. Oscar Wilde
17. Sonny Liston
18. Karl Marx
19. Diana Dors
20. Marlon Brando
21. Marlene Dietrich
22. Lenny Bruce
23. Aldous Huxley
24. Albert Einstein
25. Marilyn Monroe
26. Edgar Allan Poe
27. H.G. Wells
28. Dylan Thomas
29. T.E. Lawrence
30. W.C. Fields

19 CELEBRITIES WHO HAVE BEEN IMMORTALISED IN SONG TITLES

1. Smokey Robinson: *When Smokey Sings* (ABC)

2. Joe Strummer: *Joe Strummer's Wallet* (The Stingrays)

3. Grigori Rasputin: *Rasputin* (Boney M)

4. Buddy Holly: *I Feel Like Buddy* Holly (Alvin Stardust)

5. Otis Redding: *Ode to Otis Redding* (Mark Johnson)

6. Elvis Presley: *Elvis Presley and America* (U2)

7. Dolly Parton: *Dolly Parton's Guitar* (Lee Hazlewood)

8. Jackie Wilson: *Jackie Wilson Said* (Van Morrison)

9. Bo Diddley: *The Story of Bo Diddley* (The Animals)

10. Hank Williams: *The Night Hank Williams Came to Town* (Johnny Cash)

11. Michael Caine: *Michael Caine* (Madness)

12. Dickie Davies: *Dickie Davies Eyes* (Half-Man Half-Biscuit)

13. Benito Mussolini: *Do The Mussolini* (Cabaret Voltaire)

14. Robert De Niro: *Robert De Niro's Waiting* (Bananarama)

15. Bonnie Parker & Clyde Barrow: *Ballad of Bonnie And Clyde* (Georgie Fame)

16. James Callaghan: Jim Callaghan (Mr John Dowie)

17. Sean Penn: *Sean Penn Blues* (Lloyd Cole And The Commotions)

18. Christine Keeler: *Christine Keeler* (The Glaxo Babies)

19. Kaiser Wilhelm II: *I Was Kaiser Bill's Batman* (Whistling Jack Smith)

10 CELEBRITY MARRIED COUPLES WHO HAD HITS

1. Paul and Linda McCartney *Back Seat Of My Car*

2. Ashford and Simpson *Solid*

3. Sonny and Cher *I Got You Babe*

4. Womack and Womack *Teardrops*

5. Rita Coolidge and Kris Kristofferson *A Song I'd Like To Sing*

6. Captain and Tennille *Do That To Me One More Time*

7. Ike and Tina Turner *River Deep Mountain High*

8. John and Yoko/Plastic Ono Band with the Harlem Community Choir Happy *Xmas (War Is Over)*

9. Carly Simon and James Taylor *Mockingbird*

10. Esther and Abi Ofarim *Cinderella Rockefella*

4 CELEBRITIES WHO STARTED THEIR OWN RECORD LABELS

1. Paul Weller: Respond
2. Sir Elton John: Rocket Records
3. Dave Stewart: Anxious Records
4. Madonna: Maverick records

10 CELEBRITIES WHO HAD POSTHUMOUS HITS

*Peak position reached in the charts

1. Bob Marley (Buffalo Soldier) 1983 (4*)
2. Freddie Mercury (Living on My Own) 1993 (1*)
3. Otis Redding (Sittin' On The Dock of The Bay) 1968 (3*)
4. Jim Reeves (Distant Drums) 1966 (1*)
5. Eddie Cochran (Three Steps To Heaven) 1960 (1*)
6. Jackie Wilson (Reet Petite) 1986 (1*)
7. Buddy Holly (It Doesn't Matter Any More) 1959 (1*)
8. John Lennon (Woman) 1981 (1*)
9. Jimi Hendrix (Voodoo Chile) 1970 (1*)
10. Laurel and Hardy (The Trail of The Lonesome Pine) 1975 (2*)

10 CELEBRITIES WHO CHOSE MY WAY ON DESERT ISLANDS DISCS

1. Sir David Frost
2. Geoffrey Boycott
3. Russell Harty
4. David Broome
5. Jimmy Jewel
6. Gareth Edwards
7. Barry John
8. Johnny Speight
9. Alan Minter
10. Stewart Granger

10 SOAP OPERA CELEBRITIES WHO MADE RECORDS

1. Anita Dobson (Angie Watts in *EastEnders*): *Anyone Can Fall In Love*

2. Malandra Burrows (Kathy Merrick in *Emmerdale*): *Just This Side Of Love*

3. Danny McCall (Owen in *Brookside*): *Whose Love Is It Anyway*

4. Nick Berry (Wicksy in *EastEnders*): *Every Loser Wins*

5. Stefan Dennis (Paul Robinson in *Neighbours*): *Don't It Make You Feel Good*

6. Sue Nicholls (Audrey Roberts in *Coronation Street*): *Where Will You Be*

7. Dannii Minogue (Emma in *Home And Away*): *Love And Kisses*

8. Wendy Richard (Pauline Fowler in *EastEnders*): *Come Outside* (with Mike Sarne)

9. *Trevor Harrison (Eddie Grundy in *The Archers*): *Lambs To The Slaughter*

10. Tom Watt (Lofty Holloway in *EastEnders*): *Subterranean Homesick Blues*

11. Will Mellor (Jambo in *Hollyoaks*) *When I Need You*

*Trevor Harrison who plays Eddie Grundy in *The Archers* recorded this as Eddie Grundy.

10 CELEBRITIES AND WHO THEY DUETTED WITH

1. Michael J. Fox (with Joan Jett on *Light of Day* 1986)

2. Victoria Principal (with Andy Gibb on *All I Have To Do Is Dream* 1981)

3. Joan Collins (with Bing Crosby on *Let's Not Be Sensible* 1962)

4. Madeline Kahn (with Frankie Laine on *Blazing Saddles* in 1973)

5. Alain Delon (with Shirley Bassey on the album *Shirley Bassey & Alain Delon* 1984)

6. Catherine Zeta Jones (with David Essex on *True Love Ways* 1994)

7. Rock Hudson (with Rod McKuen on *Love of The Common Celebrities* 1970)

8. Peter Sellers (with Sophia Loren on *Goodness Gracious Me* 1959)

9. Don Johnson (with Barbra Streisand on *Till I Loved You (Love Theme From 'Goya')* 1988)

10. Beavis And Butt-Head (with Cher on *I Got You Babe* 1994)

10 CELEBRITIES WHO HAVE SUNG DUETS WITH ELTON JOHN

1. Kiki Dee: *Don't Go Breaking My Heart* (1976)

2. John Lennon: I *Saw Her Standing There* (1981)

3. Millie Jackson: *Act of War* (1985)

4. Sir Cliff Richard: *Slow Rivers* (1986)

5. Jennifer Rush: *Flames of Paradise* (1987)

6. Aretha Franklin: *Through The Storm* (1989)

7. George Michael: *Don't Let The Sun Go Down On Me* (1991)

8. Eric Clapton: *Runaway Train* (1992)

9. Marcella Detroit: *Ain't Nothing Like The Real Thing* (1994)

10. Luciano Pavarotti: *Live Like Horses* (1996)

27 CELEBRITIES WHO RELEASED SOLO ALBUMS

1. Eddie Murphy (*Love's Alright* 1993)

2. Kurt Russell (*Kurt Russell* 1970)

3. Honor Blackman (*Everything I've Got* 1965)

4. Steve Cauthen (*And Steve Cauthen Sings Too!* 1977)

5. David Hemmings (*David Hemmings Happens* 1967)

6. Jack Palance (*Palance* 1970)

7. Dennis Weaver (*Celebrities Songs* 1974)

8. Goldie Hawn (*Goldie* 1972)

9. Bruce Willis (*Heart of Soul* 1990)

10. Sally Field (*The Star of 'The Flying Nun'* 1967)

11. Clint Eastwood (*Cowboy Favorites* 1959)

12. Leonard Nimoy (*Two Sides of Leonard Nimoy* 1968)

13. John Le Mesurier (*What Is Going To Become of Us All* 1976)

14. Jack Lemmon (*A Twist of Lemmon* 1958)

15. Rock Hudson (*Pillow Talk* 1959)

16. Anthony Quinn (*In My Own Way . . . I Love You* 1969)

17. Bette Davis (*Miss Bette Davis* 1976)

18. George Hamilton (*By George* 1966)

19. Dame Barbara Cartland (*Album of Love Songs* 1978)

20. Chevy Chase (*Chevy Chase* 1980)

21. James Brolin (*James Brolin Sings* 1974)

22. Richard Chamberlain (*Sings* 1964)

23. Albert Finney (*The Albert Finney Album* 1977)

24. Burgess Meredith (*Songs From How The West Was Won* 1963)

25. Sidney Poitier (*Poitier Meets Plato* 1964)

26. Uri Geller (*Uri Geller* 1975)

27. Cybill Shepherd (*Cybill Does It . . . To Cole Porter* 1974)

14 CELEBRITIES WHO APPEAR IN THE BONZO DOG DOO-DAH BAND'S "THE INTRO AND THE OUTRO"

1. John Wayne – Xylophone
2. Robert Morley – Guitar
3. Billy Butlin – Spoons
4. Princess Anne – Sousaphone
5. Liberace – Clarinet
6. Harold Wilson – Violin
7. Eric Clapton – Ukelele ("Hi, Eric")
8. Sir Kenneth Clark – Bass saxophone ("A great honour, sir")
9. Peter Scott – Duck Call
10. Casanova – Horn
11. General de Gaulle – Accordion ("Really wild General. Thank you, sir")
12. Max Jaffa – Bell Ringing and Pealing
13. Val Doonican – Himself
14. J. Arthur Rank – Gong

Not forgetting The Count Basie Orchestra on triangle, Adolf Hitler "looking very relaxed" on vibres, Lord Snooty and his pals tap dancing, Incredible Shrinking Man on euphonium, Roy Rogers on Trigger, Wild Man of Borneo on bongos and Quasimodo on bells – to name but a part of the most sensational line-up in musical history.

23 CELEBRITIES WHO RELEASED SINGLES

1. Peter Fonda (*Catch The Wind* 1968)
2. Linda Evans (*Don't You Need* 1979)
3. Britt Ekland (*Do It To Me* 1979)
4. Sir Anthony Hopkins (*A Distant Star* 1986)
5. Oliver Reed (*Lonely For A Girl* 1965)
6. Rebecca De Mornay (*Oh Jimmy* 1985)
7. Gene Wilder (*Pure Imagination* 1970)
8. Raquel Welch (*This Girl's Back In Town* 1987)
9. Burt Reynolds (*I Like Having You Around* 1974)
10. Robert Mitchum (*Ballad of Thunder Road* 1958)
11. Princess Stephanie of Monaco (*Live Your Life* 1986)
12. Dyan Cannon (Having It All 1980)
13. Billy Crystal (The Christmas Song 1984)
14. Meryl Streep (*Amazing Grace* 1984)
15. Ingrid Bergman (*This Old Man* 1958)
16. Richard Chamberlain (*Love Me Tender* 1962)
17. Patrick Swayze (*Raisin' Heaven And Hell Tonight* 1989)
18. David Copperfield (*Summer Days* 1976)
19. Farrah Fawcett (*You* 1978)
20. Elizabeth Taylor (*Wings In The Sky* 1976)
21. Sissy Spacek (as 'Rainbo') (*John You Went Too Far This Time* 1969)
22. Boris Karloff (*Come, My Laurie, With Me* 1955)
23. Lon Chaney Jnr. (*Monster Holiday* 1964)

10 SONGS IN WHICH THE CELEBRITIES REFER TO THEMSELVES BY NAME

1. *Universal* (The Small Faces – Steve Marriott on vocals 1968)
2. *I Feel For You* (Chaka Khan 1984)
3. *Blue Motel Room* (Joni Mitchell 1976)
4. *My Name Is Prince* (Prince 1992)
5. *Sweet Baby James* (James Taylor 1970)
6. *Strong Persuader* (Robert Cray 1986)
7. *Creeque Alley* (The Mamas And The Papas – Mama Cass on vocals 1967)
8. *The Mind of Love* (k.d. lang 1992)
9. *Float On* (The Floaters – all of them individually 1977)
10. *Wannabe* (The Spice Girls – all of them individually 1996)

22 CELEBRITIES WHO USED TO BE IN POP GROUPS/ROCK BANDS

1. Ruud Gullit used to play bass guitar in a band named Revelation Time
2. Richard Hannon, the racehorse trainer, used to be a drummer with The Troggs
3. Loyd Grossman was the singer and guitarist with a group called Jet Bronx And The Forbidden which got to Number 49 in 1977 with *Ain't Doin' Nothin'*
4. Melvyn Bragg was lead singer of a group named Memphis 5. He was also in a skiffle group playing tea-chest bass.
5. Keith Chegwin was the lead singer in Kenny (which had a Number 3 hit in 1975 with *The Bump)*
6. Nigel Havers was in a pop group with his brother (they used to sing Herman's Hermits type songs)
7. Su Pollard was the singer with the pop group Midnight News
8. Dani Behr started her career as one third of the group Faith, Hope and Charity
9. Martine McCutcheon (Tiffany in *EastEnders*) was the lead singer of a three-girl group named Milan
10. Leslie Ash was a backing singer in the group Smiley & Co
11. Emma Freud was a backing singer for Mike Oldfield
12. Tony Blair was the lead singer in the university band, The Ugly Rumours which also included the broadcaster Mark Ellen
13. Michael Howard played in a skiffle band
14. Michelle Collins started her career as a backing singer with Mari Wilson
15. Nigel Short, the chess champion and world title contender, played in a rock band named The Urge
16. Asil Nadir played in a rock group called The Asils
17. Damon Hill played guitar in a punk band named Sex Hitler And The Hormones (with fellow aspiring racing drivers)
18. Neil Kinnock played guitar in a skiffle group called The Rebels
19. Vince Earl (Ron Dixon in *Brookside*) played the tea-chest bass in a skiffle group called The Teenage Rebels.
20. Chevy Chase played keyboards for Chameleon Church
21. Mike Myers played in a band called Ming Tea
22. Will Mellor was a vocalist in the band Right Now

13 FEMALE CELEBRITIES WHO HAD SONGS WRITTEN FOR THEM

1. Meg Matthews: *Wonderwall* (Oasis)

2. Elizabeth Taylor: *Emotionally Yours* (Bob Dylan)

3. Angie Bowie: *Angie* (The Rolling Stones)

4. Nancy Sinatra: *Nancy With The Laughing Face* (Frank Sinatra)

5. Patti Boyd: *Layla* (Derek And The Dominoes)

6. Christie Brinkley: *Uptown Girl* (Billy Joel)

7. Caroline Kennedy: *Sweet Caroline* (Neil Diamond)

8. Carole King: *Oh Carol* (Neil Sedaka)

9. Frances Tomelty: *Every Breath You Take* (The Police)

10. Patti D'Arbanville: *Lady D'Arbanville* (Cat Stevens)

11. Joni Mitchell: *Our House* (Crosby, Stills and Nash)

12. Jenny Boyd: *Jennifer Juniper* (Donovan)

13. Rosanna Arquette: *Rosanna* (Toto)

2 CELEBRITIES WHO HAD SONGS WRITTEN ABOUT THEM BY STING

1. Rod Stewart (*Peanuts*)

2. Quentin Crisp (*An Englishman In New York*)

2 CELEBRITIES WHO NAMED THEIR CHILDREN AFTER MOTOWN STARS

1. Bryan Ferry (son Otis, after Otis Redding)

2. Paul Young (daughter Levi, after Levi Stubbs)

2 CELEBRITIES WHO AUDITIONED UNSUCCESSFULLY FOR THE MONKEES

1. Charles Manson

2. Stephen Stills

5 CELEBRITIES WHO SANG IN FILMS

1. Sean Connery (*Darby O'Gill And The Little People* 1959)

2. Robert Redford (*Situation Hopeless . . . But Not Serious* 1965)

3. Richard Attenborough (*Doctor Dolittle* 1967)

4. Robert De Niro (*New York, New York* 1977)

5. James Caan (*Harry And Walter Go To New York* 1976)

Chapter 10

Words and Pictures

17 CELEBRITIES WHO'VE MADE GUEST APPEARANCES IN *THE BILL*

1. Roger Lloyd Pack
2. Rik Mayall
3. Paul O'Grady (aka Lily Savage)
4. Kathy Burke
5. Dorothy Tutin
6. Pete Postlethwaite
7. Brian Glover
8. Maurice Denham
9. Ray Winstone
10. Craig Charles
11. Nicholas Ball
12. Leslie Phillips
13. Freddie Jones
14. Letitia Dean
15. Anita Dobson
16. Alfred Burke
17. Colin Baker

11 CELEBRITIES WHO BECAME FAMOUS AS A RESULT OF A SUPPORTING ROLE IN A SIT. COM.

1. Andrew Sachs (*Fawlty Towers*)
2. Tony Robinson (*Blackadder*)
3. Penelope Keith (*The Good Life*)
4. Lesley Joseph (*Birds Of A Feather*)
5. Angela Thorne (*To The Manor Born*)
6. Julia Sawalha (*Absolutely Fabulous*)
7. Clive Dunn (*Dad's Army*)
8. Su Pollard (*Hi De Hi*)
9. Judy Cornwell (*Keeping Up Appearances*)
10. Kathy Staff (*Last Of The Summer Wine*)
11. Buster Merryfield (*Only Fools And Horses*)

70 CELEBRITIES AND THE PRODUCTS THEY'VE ADVERTISED

1. Jonathan Ross (Harp)
2. Maureen Lipman (BT)
3. Lloyd Cole (Amaretto, Italy)
4. Jack Charlton (Shredded Wheat)
5. & 6. Leonard Rossiter and Joan Collins (Cinzano)
7. Sir David Frost (Black Douglas whisky, Australia)
8. Frank Bruno (HP Sauce)
9. Steve Ovett (Mother's Pride)
10. Gary Lineker (Walkers Crisps)
11. John Cleese (Sony)
12. & 13. Sir Edward Heath and Ken Livingstone (British cheese)
14. Sir Peter Ustinov (Gallo Wine, USA)
15. Felicity Kendal (Flora, Australia)
16. Mollie Sugden (Heinz Baked Beans)
17. Severiano Ballesteros (Quorum)
18. Sharron Davies (Shredded Wheat)
19. Paul Gascoigne (Walkers Crisps)
20. Rory McGrath (BT)
21. Quentin Tarantino (Kansai mobile phones)
22. & 23. Damon Hill and Murray Walker (Pizza Hut)
24. Cilla Black (Typhoo)
25. Dennis Waterman (Oxo)
26. Will Carling (Quorn)
27. 28. and 29. Chris Waddle, Stuart Pearce and Gareth Southgate (Pizza Hut)
30. 31. & 32. George Cole, David Bailey & Earl Patrick Lichfield (Olympus Trip)
33. Steve Cram (Start)
34. Jimmy Tarbuck (Sharp Microwaves)
35. Ronnie Barker (Sekonda Watches)
36. Diane Keen (Nescafé)
37. Ronald Reagan (Chesterfield cigarettes)
38. 39. & 40. Terry Venables, Graham Taylor & Bobby Robson (Yellow Pages)
41. Paul Hogan (Fosters)
42. & 43. Leo McKern and Nigel Havers (Lloyds Bank)
44. Nanette Newman (Fairy Liquid)
45. David Platt (TicTac mints)
46. Sebastian Coe (Horlicks)
47. Penelope Keith (Heinz, Australia)
48. Karl Howman (Walls sausages)
49. Ryan Giggs (Quorn)
50. Liz McColgan (Eggs)
51. Pat Cash (Robinsons)
52. Geoffrey Palmer (Lamb)
53. John Barnes (Mars)
54. Geoffrey Boycott (Shredded Wheat)
55. Bob Geldof (Milk)
56. Sir Harry Secombe (Woolworth's)
57. 58. & 59. Henry Cooper, David Hemery and Barry Sheene (Brut)
60. Griff Rhys Jones (Holsten Pils)
61. Bob Hoskins (BT)
62. Gareth Hunt (Nescafé)
63. Steve Davis (Heinz Baked Beans)
64. Lynn Redgrave (Weight Watchers, U.S.)
65. Sally Gunnell (Quorn)
66. Eric Cantona (*The Guardian*)
67. Robbie Coltrane: (Persil)
68. Liza Goddard: (Lenor)
69. Dervla Kirwan (BT)
70. Harold Evans (*The Guardian*)

10 CELEBRITIES WHO HAVE APPEARED IN ADVERTISEMENTS FOR GAP

1. Neneh Cherry
2. Matt Dillon
3. John Barnes
4. Oliver Stone
5. Marianne Faithfull
6. Richard E. Grant
7. Kim Basinger
8. Whoopi Goldberg
9. Spike Lee
10. Joely Richardson

9 CELEBRITIES WHO APPEARED IN *GRANGE HILL*

1. Susan Tully
2. Letitia Dean
3. Sean Maguire
4. Todd Carty
5. Alex Kingston
6. Michelle Gayle
7. Patsy Palmer
8. John Alford
9. Steven Woodcock

22 CELEBRITIES AND THE PRODUCTS THEY'VE ADVERTISED IN JAPAN

1. Arnold Schwarzenegger (Nissin Cup Noodles)
2. Brooke Shields (Aloe Mine)
3. Winona Ryder (Subaru Impreza)
4. Ringo Starr (Ringosutta apple sauce)
5. Brad Pitt (Honda Integra)
6. Dennis Hopper (Tsumura Bathclin)
7. Harrison Ford (Kirin beer)
8. Sylvester Stallone (Itoh sausages)
9. Charlie Sheen (Tokyo Gas)
10. Madonna (Jun liquor)
11. Gene Hackman (Kirin beer)
12. Richard Gere (Japan Airlines)
13. Bruce Willis (NTT mobile phones)
14. Michael Bolton (Georgia Coffee)
15. Jodie Foster (Honda Civic)
16. David Bowie (Sake)
17. Kevin Costner (Kirin beer)
18. Boy George (Shochu)
19. Jeffrey Archer (Suntory)
20. Sting (Kirin beer)
21. Sean Connery (Itoh sausages)
22. Sandy Lyle (Mizuno sportswear)

26 CELEBRITIES WHO'VE 'APPEARED' ON *THE SIMPSONS*

1. Danny De Vito (Herb Powell)
2. Jack Lemmon (Frank Ormand, The Pretzel Man)
3. Donald Sutherland (Hollis Hurlbut)
4. Joe Mantegna (Fat Tony)
5. Willem Dafoe (Commandant)
6. Tracey Ullman (Emily Winthrop)
7. Johnny Cash (Coyote)
8. Kirk Douglas (Chester J. Lampwick)
9. Rodney Dangerfield (Larry Burns)
10. Anne Bancroft (Dr Zweig)
11. Penny Marshall (Ms Botz)
12. Harvey Fierstein (Karl)
13. Glenn Close (Mother Simpson)
14. Gillian Anderson (Scully)
15. David Duchovny (Mulder)
16. Jackie Mason (Rabbi Krustofski)
17. Beverly D'Angelo (Lurleen Lumpkin)
18. Kelsey Grammer (Sideshow Bob)
19. Michelle Pfeiffer (Mindy Simmons)
20. Sam Neill (Molloy)
21. Kathleen Turner (Stacy Lovell)
22. Winona Ryder (Allison Taylor)
23. Meryl Streep (Jessica Lovejoy)
24. Patrick Stewart (Number One)
25. Susan Sarandon (The Ballet Teacher)
26. Mandy Patinkin (Hugh Parkfield)

20 CELEBRITIES WHO STARTED IN SOAP OPERAS

1. Demi Moore (*General Hospital*)
2. Kevin Kline (*Search For Tomorrow*)
3. Alec Baldwin (*The Doctors*)
4. Tommy Lee Jones (*One Life To Live*)
5. Morgan Freeman (*Another World*)
6. Kevin Bacon (*Guiding Light*)
7. Meg Ryan (*As The World Turns*)
8. Ted Danson (*Somerset*)
9. Charles Grodin (*The Young Marrieds*)
10. Hal Holbrook (*The Brighter Day*)
11. Christopher Walken (*Guiding Light*)
12. Marisa Tomei (*As The World Turns*)
13. Sigourney Weaver (*Somerset*)
14. Ray Liotta (*Another World*)
15. Marsha Mason (*Love Of Life*)
16. Tom Berenger (*One Life To Live*)
17. Susan Sarandon (*Search For Tomorrow*)
18. Christian Slater (*Ryan's Hope*)
19. Ellen Burstyn (*The Doctors*)
20. Tom Selleck (*The Young And The Restless*)

10 CELEBRITIES WHO PLAYED COMIC STRIP CHARACTERS

1. Robin Williams (Popeye)
2. Christopher Reeve (Superman)
3. Anouska Hempel (Tiffany Jones)
4. Glynis Barber (Jane)
5. Gil Gerard (Buck Rogers)
6. Michael Keaton (Batman)
7. Jerry Lewis (The Sad Sack)
8. John Goodman (Fred Flintstone)
9. Lynda Carter (Wonder Woman)
10. Warren Beatty (Dick Tracy)

16 CELEBRITIES WHO APPEARED IN *THE AVENGERS*

1. Ron Moody
2. Anthony Valentine
3. Stratford Johns
4. Joss Ackland
5. Peter Cushing
6. John Junkin
7. Julian Glover
8. Arthur Lowe
9. Roy Kinnear
10. Gerald Harper
11. Gordon Jackson
12. Peter Wyngarde
13. Frank Windsor
14. Jon Pertwee
15. Yootha Joyce
16. Penelope Keith

19 CELEBRITIES WHO APPEARED IN THE *BATMAN* TV SERIES

1. Ethel Merman (Lola Lasagne)
2. Tallulah Bankhead (Mrs Max Black)
3. Anne Baxter (Olga, Queen of The Cossacks)
4. Bruce Lee (Kato)
5. Glynis Johns (Lady Penelope Peasoup)
6. Jock Mahoney (Leo, one of Catwoman's accomplices)
7. James Brolin (Ralph Staphylococcus)
8. Michael Rennie (The Sandman)
9. Edward G. Robinson (Cameo role)
10. George Raft (Cameo role)
11. Phyllis Diller (Cameo role)
12. Jerry Lewis (Cameo role)
13. Gypsy Rose Lee (Cameo role)
14. Rob Reiner (Cameo role)
15. Sammy Davis Jnr. (Cameo role)
16. Eartha Kitt (Catwoman)
17. Shelley Winters (Ma Parker)
18. Liberace (unknown)
19. Zsa Zsa Gabor (Minerva)

Celebrities who wanted to appear in cameo roles but couldn't be fitted in: Robert F. Kennedy, Frank Sinatra, Jose Ferrer, Yul Brynner, Elizabeth Taylor and Gregory Peck.

THE FIRST 10
CELEBRITIES ON
*THIS IS YOUR
LIFE* WHEN IT
TRANSFERRED TO
ITV IN 1969

1. Des O'Connor
2. Bobby Charlton
3. Harry Driver
4. Twiggy
5. Honor Blackman
6. The Beverley Sisters
7. John Fairfax
8. Henry Cooper
9. Jackie Stewart
10. Sir Jimmy Savile

65 CELEBRITIES AND THEIR CODENAMES FOR *THIS IS YOUR LIFE*

1. Faith Brown: Hope
2. Bob Holness: Block
3. Pat Jennings: Hands
4. Jeffrey Archer: Dan
5. Joe Johnson: Powder
6. Bobby Davro: Double
7. Rod Hull: Attack
8. Jim Watt: Steam
9. Mickie Most: Disc
10. Richard Vernon: Pools
11. Bob Champion: Wonder
12. Elaine Paige: Book
13. Denis Quilley: Pen
14. David Broome: Sweep
15. Clare Francis: Drake
16. Wayne Sleep: Rest
17. Jimmy Cricket: Stump
18. Sarah Brightman: Shine
19. Freddie Starr: Planet
20. Liza Goddard: Polish
21. Richard Branson: Island
22. Robert Carrier: Pigeon
23. Roy Barraclough: Wedding
24. Alvin Stardust: Twinkle
25. Pam Ferris: Wheel
26. Bernard Cribbins: Cot
27. Bob Monkhouse: Abbot
28. Angela Rippon: Reader
29. Max Boyce: Touch
30. Richard Harris: Tweed
31. Harry Carpenter: Wood
32. Denis Law: Barrister
33. Dame Barbara Cartland: Pink
34. Frazer Hines: Beans
35. Graham Gooch: County
36. Barry Sheene: Gloss
37. Gillian Lynne: Cat
38. Keith Floyd: Soup
39. Sir Donald Sinden: Butler
40. Dudley Moore: Arthur
41. Peter Bowles: Manor
42. Viv Richards: Willow
43. Bill Beaumont: Bees
44. Danny La Rue: Street
45. Thelma Barlow: Till
46. Omar Sharif: Sand
47. Windsor Davies: Whisper
48. Dame Kiri Te Kanawa: Katie
49. Hannah Hauxwell: Dale
50. Gemma Craven: Slipper
51. Nobby Stiles: Gate
52. Alex Higgins: Gale
53. Topol: Slate
54. Jim Bowen: Bull
55. Patrick Macnee: Bowler
56. Derek Fowlds: Beat
57. Lynda Bellingham: Cube
58. Terry Lawless: Order
59. Carl Davis: Theme
60. Mickey Rooney: Andy
61. Julie Goodyear: Bar
62. Zandra Rhodes: Greece
63. Pam Ayres: Verse
64. Juliet Mills: Romeo
65. Dick Francis: Thriller

10 CELEBRITIES WHO APPEARED IN *EMMERDALE*

1. Anna Friel (Poppy Bruce)
2. Diane Keen (Hotel receptionist)
3. Jenny Hanley (Biddy Middleton)
4. Joanne Whalley (Angela Reid)
5. Gorden Kaye (Gerry)
6. Ross Kemp (Graham Lodsworth)
7. Melanie Brown (aka Mel B, as an extra)
8. Gilly Coman (Linda)
9. Pam St Clement (Mrs Eckersley)
10. Tim Healy (Steven)

10 CELEBRITIES WHO APPEARED IN *CORONATION STREET*

1. Ben Kingsley (Ron Jenkins)
2. Max Wall (Harry Payne)
3. Bill Maynard (Mickey Malone)
4. Gilly Coman (Sugar La Marr)
5. Paul Shane (Frank Draper)
6. Kenneth Cope (Jed Stone)
7. Tony Anholt (David Law)
8. Kathy Staff (Vera Hopkins)
9. Leonard Sachs (Sir Julius Berlin)
10. Michael Elphick (Douglas Wormold)

10 CELEBRITIES WHO APPEARED ON *NEW FACES*

1. Jim Davidson
2. Lenny Henry
3. Victoria Wood
4. Marti Caine
5. Michael Barrymore
6. Roger De Courcey
7. Patti Boulaye
8. Les Dennis
9. Malandra Burrows
10. Peter Andre

17 CELEBRITIES WHO HAVE GUESTED IN *FRIENDS*

1. George Clooney
2. Julia Roberts
3. Elliott Gould
4. Noah Wyle
5. Chris Isaak
6. Tom Selleck
7. Morgan Fairchild
8. Brooke Shields
9. Jean-Claude Van Damme
10. Charlie Sheen
11. Charlton Heston
12. The Duchess of York
13. Hugh Laurie
14. Jennifer Saunders
15. June Whitfield
16. Tom Conti
17. Richard Branson

32 CELEBRITIES WHO APPEARED AS GUEST STARS IN *DOCTOR WHO*

1. Jean Marsh (played Joanna in 1965 – Note: she was actually once married to the future Doctor, Jon Pertwee)

2. Julian Glover (played King Richard The Lionheart in 1965)

3. Kenneth Kendall (appeared as himself in 1966)

4. John Cleese (played an art critic in 1979)

5. Eleanor Bron (played an art critic in 1979 and played Kara in 1985)

6. Martin Jarvis (made his TV debut as Captain Hilio in 1965. He went on to play Butler in 1974 and The Governor in 1985)

7. Hywel Bennett (made his TV debut as Rynian in 1965)

8. Hannah Gordon (played Kirsty in 1966-7)

9. Pauline Collins (played Samantha Briggs in 1967 – Note: she was asked if she wanted to become one of the Doctor's companions but declined because she didn't want to become typecast)

10. Nerys Hughes (played Todd in 1982 opposite the veteran British actor Richard *Todd*)

11. Tim Pigott-Smith (played Harker in 1971 and then played Marco in 1976)

12. Carmen Silvera (played Clara in 1966 and Ruth in 1974)

13. Kate O'Mara (played The Rani in 1985 and in 1987)

14. Jason Connery (played Jondar in 1985)

15. Alexei Sayle (played The DJ in 1985)

16. William Gaunt (played Orcini in 1985)

17. Ken Dodd (played Tollmaster in 1987)

18. Richard Briers (played the Chief Caretaker in 1987)

19. Windsor Davies (played Toby in 1967)

20. Peter Sallis (played Penley in 1967)

21. Brian Glover (played Griffiths in 1985)

22. Susan Penhaligon (played Lakis in 1972)

23. Gareth Hunt (played Arak in 1974)

24. Keith Barron (played Captain Striker in 1983)

25. Burt Kwouk (played Lin Futu in 1982)

26. Beryl Reid (played Captain Briggs in 1982)

27. Michael Gough (played Councillor Hedin in 1983)

28. Liza Goddard (played Kari in 1983)

29. Rodney Bewes (played Stein in 1984)

30. Peter Wyngarde (played Timanov in 1984)

31. Faith Brown (played Flast in 1985)

32. Honor Blackman (played Professor Lasky in 1986)

2 CELEBRITIES WHO WERE ASKED BY THE LATE JACKIE ONASSIS (IN HER CAPACITY AS A PUBLISHER) TO WRITE BOOKS BUT REFUSED

1. Camilla Parker Bowles

2. Frank Sinatra

2 CELEBRITIES WHO APPEARED IN *BAYWATCH*

1. Sir Paul McCartney

2. Little Richard

11 CELEBRITIES WHO HAVE BEEN GUEST EDITORS

1. Lord Snowdon: *Country Life*
2. Cherie Blair: *Prima*
3. Mario Testino: *Visionaire*
4. Damien Hirst: *The Big Issue*
5. Joan Collins: *Marie Claire* (U.K.)
6. Eva Herzigova: *Mirror Woman*
7. Jenny Eclair: *Loaded*
8. Isabelle Huppert: *Cahiers Du Cinema*
9. Gwyneth Paltrow: *Marie Claire* (U.S.)
10. & 11. Jennifer Saunders and Joanna Lumley: *Marie Claire* (U.K.)

10 ROCK CELEBRITIES WHO WROTE BOOKS

1. John Lennon: *In His Own Write*
2. Sandie Shaw: *The World At My Feet*
3. Bob Geldof: *Is That It?*
4. Bob Dylan: *Tarantula*
5. Bill Wyman: *Stone Alone*
6. Hank Wangford: *Hank Wangford Volume III, The Middle Years*
7. Charlie Watts: *From One Charlie To Another – A Biography of Charlie Parker*
8. Ronnie Spector: *Be My Baby*
9. George Harrison: *I, Me, Mine*
10. Chuck Berry: Chuck Berry, *The Autobiography*

10 CELEBRITY ACTORS WHO WROTE NOVELS

1. Carrie Fisher (*Postcards From The Edge*)
2. Robert Shaw (*The Sun Doctor*)
3. Anthony Sher (*Middlepost*)
4. Sarah Bernhardt (*In The Clouds*)
5. George Kennedy (*Murder On Location*)
6. Dirk Bogarde (*West of Sunset*)
7. Jean Harlow (*Today Is Tonight*)
8. Joan Collins (*Prime Time*)
9. Leslie Caron (*Vengeance*)
10. Mae West (*The Constant Sinner*)

3 CELEBRITIES WHO WROTE DIET BOOKS

1. Lynn Redgrave (*Diet For Life*)
2. Lord Nigel Lawson (*The Nigel Lawson Diet*)
3. Miriam Stoppard (*Lose Seven Pounds In Seven Days*)

11 CELEBRITY COUPLES WHO HAVE SUFFERED THE CURSE OF HELLO!

1. Jane Seymour and David Flynn
2. Bill Wyman and Mandy Smith
3. The Duke and Duchess of York
4. Tim Vincent and Elise Hyslop
5. Julia Roberts and Kiefer Sutherland
6. Tamara Beckwith and Michael Stone
7. Joanne Ridley and Guy Bellingham
8. David Hemmings and Tessa Dahl
9. Jason Priestley and Christine Elise
10. Amanda de Cadenet and John Taylor
11. Marina Ogilvy and Paul Mowatt

Chapter 11

Films

97 CELEBRITIES WHO WERE NOT ACTORS – AND THE FILMS THEY APPEARED IN

1. Sir Paul McCartney: *Eat The Rich*

2. Jackie Collins: *All At Sea*

3. Jools Holland: *Spiceworld The Movie*

4. Roy Orbison: *The Fastest Gun Alive*

5. Sir Yehudi Menuhin: *The Magic Bow*

6. James Taylor: *Two Lane Blacktop*

7. Craig Stadler: *Tin Cup*

8. Edwina Currie: *News Hounds*

9. Norman Hartnell: *The Beauty Contest*

10. Clarence Darrow: *From Dusk To Dawn*

11. Lech Walesa: *Man of Iron*

12. Ben Bradlee: *Born Yesterday*

13. Bob Geldof: *The Wall*

14. Billy Idol: *Trigger Happy*

15. Tina Turner: *Mad Max Beyond Thunderdome*

16. Victor Lowndes: *Fledglings*

17. Pablo Picasso: *The Testament of Orpheus, Life Begins Tomorrow*

18. Herb Alpert: *The Ten Commandments*

19. Buffalo Bill Cody: *The Indian Wars*

20. Donald Trump: *Another You*

21. Earl Haig: *Remembrance*

22. Sir Len Hutton: *The Final Test*

23. Bianca Jagger: *The Great American Success Company*

24. Koo Stark: *Star Wars*

25. Ty Cobb: *Angels In The Outfield*

26. Shakira Caine: *The Man Who Would Be King*

27. Sir Arthur Conan Doyle: *The $5,000,000 Counterfeiting Plot*

28. Colonel Harland Sanders (of KFC): *The Big Mouth*

29. Michael Johnson: *Space Jam*

30. Earl Spencer: *Another Country*

31. Woodrow Wilson: *The Adventures of A Boy Scout*

32. Gore Vidal: *Bob Roberts*

33. Quentin Crisp: *Orlando*

34. Thomas Keneally: *The Devil's Playground*

35. Barry Sheene: *Space Riders*

36. Allen Ginsberg: *Ciao! Manhattan*

37. The Prince of Wales: *Grimes Goes Green*

38. Patty Hearst: *Cry Baby*

39. Ilie Nastase: *Players*

40. Robbie Robertson: *Carnie*

41. Peter Benchley: *Jaws*

42. Ivana Trump: *Pantau*

43. André Previn: *Pepe*

44. Jimmy Carter: *Special Counsel*

45. Magic Johnson: *Grand Canyon*

46. Robert Graves: *Deadfall*

47. Nicholas Parsons: *Mr Jolly Lives Next Door*

48. Jomo Kenyatta: *Sanders of The River*

49. Adam Ant: *Slam Dance*

50. Truman Capote: *Murder By Death*

51. Dr Ruth Westheimer: *One Woman Or Two*

52. Pelé: *Hotshot*

53. Althea Gibson: *The Horse Soldiers*

54. Ernest Hemingway: *The Old Man And The Sea*

55. Jean-Claude Killy: *Snow Job*

56. Leopold Stokowski: *100 Men and A Girl*

57. Sir Matt Busby: *Cup Fever*

58. Germaine Greer: *Universal Soldier*

59. Ella Fitzgerald *Let No Man Write My Epitaph*

60. Stephen King: *Creepshow*

61. Maria Callas: *Medea*

62. Jene Simmons: *Runaway*

63. Christie Brinkley: *National Lampoon's Vacation*

64. Stirling Moss: *Casino Royale*

65. Paloma Picasso: *Immoral Tales*

66. Johnny Mathis: *Lizzie*

67. Sonny Bono: *Hairspray*

68. Ronnie Biggs: *The Great Rock 'n' Roll Swindle*

69. Tony Bennett: *The Oscar*

70. Christopher Isherwood: *Rich And Famous*

71. Andy Williams: *I'd Rather be Rich*

72. Suzanne Lenglen: *Things Are Looking Up*

73. Dionne Warwick: *Slaves*

74. David Copperfield: *Terror Train*

75. Jerry Hall: *Running Out of Luck*

76. Osvaldo Ardiles: *Escape To Victory*

77. Pat Benatar: *Union City*

78. Leon Trotsky: *My Official Wife*

79. Erich Maria Remarque: *A Time To Love And A Time To Die*

80. Mario Andretti: *Speed Fever*

81. Lenny Bruce: *Dance Hall Racket*

82. Fats Domino: *Every Which Way You Can*

83. Vijay Amritraj: *Octopussy*

84. Joan Rivers: *The Swimmer*

85. Eddie Izzard: *The Avengers*

86. Cecil B. De Mille: *Sunset Boulevard*

87. Faron Young: *Daniel Boone, Trail Blazer*

88. Timothy Leary: *Fatal Skies*

89. Billy Graham: *Two A Penny*

90. Buzz Aldrin: *The Boy In The Plastic Bubble*

91. John Cougar Mellencamp: *Falling From Grace*

92. Johnny Cash: *Door-to-Door Maniac*

93. Cyndi Lauper: *Vibes*

94. Conway Twitty: *College Confidential*

95. Mama Cass: *Pufushf*

96. Chynna Phillips: *The Invisible Kid*

97. Yoko Ono: *Satan's Bed*

12 CELEBRITIES WHO WROTE (OR CO-WROTE) SCREENPLAYS

1. Jack Nicholson *(Head)*
2. Melvyn Bragg *(Isadora)*
3. Martin Amis *(Saturn 3)*
4. Erich Segal *(Yellow Submarine)*
5. John Wells *(Princess Caraboo)*
6. George MacDonald Fraser *(Octopussy)*
7. Roald Dahl *(You Only Live Twice)*
8. Christopher Logue *(Savage Messiah)*
9. Denis Norden *(Buona Sera, Mrs Campbell)*
10. Mike Sarne *(The Lightship)*
11. Paul Theroux *(Saint Jack)*
12. Clare Boothe Luce *(Come To The Stable)*

12 CELEBRITIES WHO SHAVED THEIR HEADS FOR ROLES

1. Tom Bell *(Bent)*
2. Vanessa Redgrave *(Playing For Time)*
3. Demi Moore *(G.I. Jane)*
4. Tom Courtenay *(One Day In The Life of Ivan Denisovich)*
5. Yul Brynner *(The King & I)*
6. Sigourney Weaver *(Alien III)*
7. Anthony Quinn *(The Magus)*
8. Bruce Willis *(Twelve Monkeys)*
9. Sir Anthony Hopkins *(Surviving Picasso)*
10. Ewan McGregor *(Trainspotting)*
11. Tommy Lee Jones *(Cobb)*
12. Timothy Spall *(Still Crazy)*

47 CELEBRITIES WHO HAD HIGH PROFILES IN THEIR VERY FIRST FILMS

1. Ned Beatty: *Deliverance* (1972)
2. Orson Welles: *Citizen Kane* (1941)
3. Rob Lowe: *The Outsiders* (1983)
4. Dan Aykroyd: *1941* (1979)
5. Kathleen Turner: *Body Heat* (1981)
6. Kevin Kline: *Sophie's Choice* (1982)
7. Barbra Streisand: *Funny Girl* (1968)
8. Hywel Bennett: *The Family Way* (1966)
9. Lauren Bacall: *To Have And Have Not* (1943)
10. Eddie Murphy: *48 Hours* (1982)
11. Sean Penn: *Taps* (1981)
12. Kirk Douglas: *The Strange Love of Martha Ivers* (1946)
13. Joanne Woodward: *Count Three And Pray* (1955)
14. Michael Keaton: *Night Shift* (1982)
15. Sir Anthony Hopkins: *The Lion In Winter* (1968)
16. Terence Stamp: *Billy Budd* (1962)
17. William Hurt: *Altered States* (1980)
18. Cybill Shepherd: *The Last Picture Show* (1971)
19. Julie Andrews: *Mary Poppins* (1964)
20. Warren Beatty: *Splendor In The Grass* (1961)
21. Sarah Miles: *Term of Trial* (1962)
22. Marlon Brando: *The Men* (1950)
23. Doris Day: *Romance On The High Seas* (1948)
24. Whoopi Goldberg: *The Color Purple* (1985)
25. Walter Matthau: *The Kentuckian* (1955)
26. Paul Newman: *The Silver Chalice* (1954)
27. Robert Redford: *War Hunt* (1961)
28. Shirley Maclaine: *The Trouble With Harry* (1955)
29. Tatum O'Neal: *Paper Moon* (1973)
30. Sir Dirk Bogarde: *Esther Waters* (1947)
31. Helena Bonham Carter: *Lady Jane* (1984)
32. Dean Stockwell: *The Valley of Decision* (1945)
33. Hayley Mills: *Tiger Bay* (1959)
34. Cliff Robertson: *Picnic* (1955)
35. Lily Tomlin: *Nashville* (1975)
36. Jane Russell: *The Outlaw* (1963)
37. Robin Williams: *Popeye* (1980)
38. Dame Maggie Smith: *Nowhere To Go* (1958)
39. Charlton Heston: *Dark City* (1950)
40. Bruce Willis: *Blind Date* (1987)
41. Michael York: *The Taming of The Shrew* (1967)
42. Liza Minnelli: *Charlie Bubbles* (1968)
43. Dame Diana Rigg: *The Assassination Bureau* (1968)
44. Katharine Hepburn: *A Bill of Divorcement* (1932)
45. Norman Wisdom: *Trouble In Store* (1953)
46. Susannah York: *Tunes of Glory* (1960)
47. Robert Stack: *First Love* (1939)

49 CELEBRITIES WHO HAD LOW PROFILES IN THEIR VERY FIRST FILMS

1. Danny De Vito: *Dreams of Glass* (1968)

2. Sharon Stone: *Stardust Memories* (1980)

3. Rebecca De Mornay: *One From The Heart* (1982)

4. Clint Eastwood: *Revenge of The Creature* (1955)

5. Tom Cruise: *Endless Love* (1981)

6. Goldie Hawn: *The One And Only Genuine Original Family Band* (1968)

7. Richard Dreyfuss: *The Graduate* (1967)

8. Al Pacino: *Me, Natalie* (1969)

9. Tom Selleck: *Myra Breckinridge* (1970)

10. Christopher Reeve: *Gray Lady Down* (1977)

11. Daryl Hannah: *The Fury* (1978)

12. Dustin Hoffman: *The Tiger Makes Out* (1967)

13. Harrison Ford: *Dead Heat On A Merry Go Round* (1966)

14. Willem Dafoe: *Heaven's Gate* (1980)

15. Jane Fonda: *Tall Story* (1960)

16. James Caan: *Irma La Douce* (1963)

17. Nicolas Cage: *Fast Times At Ridgemont High* (1982)

18. Melanie Griffith: *The Harrad Experiment* (1973)

19. Diane Keaton: *Lovers And Other Strangers* (1970)

20. Jeremy Irons: *Nijinsky* (1980)

21. Steve Martin: *Sgt. Pepper's Lonely Hearts Club Band* (1978)

22. Gene Hackman: *Mad Dog Coll* (1961)

23. Drew Barrymore: *Altered States* (1980)

24. Jeff Goldblum: *Death Wish* (1974)

25. Sean Connery: *No Road Back* (1955)

26. Meryl Streep: *Julia* (1977)

27. Martin Short: *Lost And Found* (1979)

28. Holly Hunter: *The Burning* (1981)

29. Keanu Reeves: *Youngblood* (1986)

30. Anjelica Huston: *Sinful Davey* (1968)

31. Julia Roberts: *Blood Red* (1986)

32. Alan Alda: *Gone Are The Days* (1963)

33. Jacqueline Bisset: *The Knack* (1964)

34. Sylvester Stallone: *A Party At Kitty And Stud's* (1970)

35. Tony Curtis: *Criss Cross* (1948)

36. Robert De Niro: *The Wedding Party* (1963)

37. William Devane: *The Pursuit of Happiness* (1971)

38. Farrah Fawcett: *A Man I Like* (1967)

39. Sir Alec Guinness: *Evensong* (1933)

40. John Travolta: *The Devil's Rain* (1975)

41. Susan Hampshire: *Upstairs And Downstairs* (1959)

42. Richard Harris: *Alive And Kicking* (1958)

43. Karl Malden: *They Knew What They Wanted* (1940)

44. Richard Gere: *Report To The Commissioner* (1975)

45. Bette Midler: *Hawaii* (1965)

46. Mickey Rourke: *1941* (1979)

47. Jon Voight: *The Hour of The Gun* (1967)

48. Donald Sutherland: *The World Ten Times Over* (1963)

49. Lynn Redgrave: *Tom Jones* (1963)

10 CELEBRITIES WHO WERE ADULTS WHEN THEY PLAYED CHILDREN

1. Colin Welland (*Blue Remembered Hills*)
2. Richard Attenborough (*The Guinea Pig*)
3. Terry Scott (*Curly Wurly TV commercial*)
4. Ginger Rogers (*The Major And The Minor*)
5. Keith Barron (*Stand Up, Nigel Barton*)
6. Denholm Elliott (*School Play*)
7. Joan Fontaine (*Letter From An Unknown Woman*)
8. Michael Elphick (*Blue Remembered Hills*)
9. Cary Grant (*Monkey Business*)
10. Bette Davis (*Payment On Demand*)

10 CELEBRITIES WHO FAILED SCREEN TESTS

1. Robert De Niro
2. Clark Gable
3. Shirley Temple
4. Cary Grant
5. Jane Russell
6. Maurice Chevalier
7. Brigitte Bardot
8. Laurence Olivier
9. Tallulah Bankhead
10. Fred Astaire ("Can't act, can't sing . . . can dance a little")

10 CELEBRITIES WHO CO-STARRED WITH ELVIS

1. Walter Matthau: *King Creole*
2. Angela Lansbury: *Blue Hawaii*
3. Charles Bronson: *Kid Galahad*
4. Ursula Andress: *Fun In Acapulco*
5. Burgess Meredith: *Stay Away Joe*
6. Ann-Margret: *Viva Las Vegas*
7. Vincent Price: *The Trouble With Girls*
8. Barbara Stanwyck: *Roustabout*
9. Ed Asner: *Change Of Habit*
10. Elsa Lanchester: *Easy Come Easy Go*

10 CELEBRITIES WHO PLAYED AUTHORS

1. Vanessa Redgrave: Agatha Christie in *Agatha*
2. Danny Kaye: Hans Christian Andersen in *Hans Christian Andersen*
3. Ian Holm: Sir J.M. Barrie in *The Lost Boys*
4. Stacy Keach: Ernest Hemingway in *Hemingway*
5. Olivia de Havilland: Charlotte Brontë in *Devotion*
6. Malcolm McDowell: H.G. Wells in *Time After Time*
7. Christopher Plummer: Rudyard Kipling in *The Man Who Would Be King*
8. James Mason: Gustave Flaubert in *Madame Bovary*
9. Paul Muni: Emile Zola in *The Life of Emile Zola*
10. Richard Chamberlain: F. Scott Fitzgerald in *F. Scott Fitzgerald And The Last Of The Belles*

30 CELEBRITIES AND THE FILMS THEY DIRECTED

1. Norman Mailer: *Tough Guys Don't Dance* (1987)
2. Frank Sinatra: *None But The Brave* (1965)
3. Joan Rivers: *Rabbit Test* (1978)
4. Nora Ephron: *Sleepless In Seattle* (1993)
5. Christopher Guest: *Attack of The 50ft Woman* (1993)
6. Clive Barker: *Night Breed* (1990)
7. Anthony Quinn: *The Buccaneer* (1958)
8. Rossano Brazzi: *The Christmas That Almost Wasn't* (1966)
9. James Clavell: *To Sir, With Love* (1967)
10. Arnold Schwarzenegger: *Christmas In Connecticut* (1992)
11. Marlon Brando: *One-Eyed Jacks* (1960)
12. Ruth Prawer Jhabvala: *The Courtesan of Bombay* (1985)
13. James Caan: *Hide In Plain Sight* (1980)
14. Michael Crichton: *Westworld* (1973)
15. Albert Finney: *Charlie Bubbles* (1968)
16. Stephen King: *Maximum Overdrive* (1986)
17. Anthony Perkins: *Psycho III* (1986)
18. Sidney Sheldon: *Dream Wife* (1953)
19. Patrick McGoohan: *Catch My Soul* (1973)
20. Jack Lemmon: *Kotch* (1971)
21. Timothy Leary: *Cheech And Chong's Nice Dream* (1981)
22. Tom Stoppard: *Rosencrantz & Guildenstern Are Dead* (1990)
23. Michael Nesmith: *Doctor Duck's Super Secret All-Purpose Sauce* (1985)
24. Charles Laughton: *The Night of The Hunter* (1955)
25. Salvador Dali: *Un Chien Andalou* (1928)
26. Ringo Starr: *Born To Boogie* (1972)
27. William Peter Blatty: *The Exorcist III* (1990)
28. Howard Hughes: *Hell's Angels* (1930)
29. Larry Hagman: *Son of Blob* (1972)
30. Richard Burton: *Dr Faustus* (1967)

10 CELEBRITIES WHO DIED DURING FILMING

1. Marilyn Monroe *(Something's Got To Give 1962)*
2. James Dean *(Giant 1955)*
3. Jean Harlow *(Saratoga 1937)*
4. John Candy *(Wagons East! 1994)*
5. Bruce Lee *(Game of Death 1973)*
6. Brandon Lee *(The Crow 1993)*
7. Roy Kinnear *(Return of The Musketeers 1989)*
8. River Phoenix *(Dark Blood 1993)*
9. Vic Morrow *(The Twilight Zone 1982)*
10. Natalie Wood *(Brainstorm 1981)*

Chapter 12

Just for Fun!

15 FEMALE CELEBRITIES FROM 5' TO 6' 2"

5' Dawn French

5' 1" Kylie Minogue

5' 2" Holly Hunter

5' 3" Julia Sawalha

5' 4" Madonna

5' 5" Belinda Carlisle

5' 6" Pauline Quirke

5' 7" Laura Bailey

5' 8" Jill Dando

5' 9" Claire Rayner

5' 10" Naomi Campbell

5' 11" Emma Donoghue

6' Eva Herzigova

6' 1" Janet Street-Porter

6' 2" Julie T. Wallace

10 CELEBRITY SNORERS

1. Will Carling
2. George Washington
3. Richard Pitman
4. Beau Brummell
5. Bill Clinton
6. Benito Mussolini
7. King George II
8. Abraham Lincoln
9. Scott Hastings
10. Theodore Roosevelt

3 CELEBRITIES WHO BOUGHT BLACK CABS

1. Stephen Fry
2. Prince Philip
3. Naim Attallah

10 CELEBRITIES AND THEIR E-MAIL ADDRESSES

1. Bob Hoskins:
   75300.1313@compuserve.com
2. John Grisham:
   71035.1742@compuserve.com
3. Bill Gates: billg@microsoft.com
4. Charles Grodin:
   CharlesGrodin@aol.com
5. Tom Clancy: tomclancy@aol.com
6. Billy Idol: idol@well.sf.ca.us
7. James Woods: jameswoods@aol.com
8. Douglas Adams:
   76206.2507@compuserve.com
9. H. Ross Perot:
   71511.460@compuserve.com
10. Ed Asner:
    72726.357@compuserve.com

10 FEMALE CELEBRITIES FROM SHOE SIZE 2 TO 11

1. Dr Ruth Westheimer (2)
2. Clare Grogan (3)
3. Marilyn Monroe (4)
4. Sally Gunnell (5)
5. Amelia Earhart (6)
6. Princess Michael of Kent (7)
7. Gabrielle (8)
8. Corinne Drewery (of Swing Out Sister) (9)
9. Laura Davies (10)
10. Daryl Hannah (11)

12 MALE CELEBRITIES FROM SHOE SIZE 4 TO 15

1. (The Artist Formerly Known As) Prince (4)
2. Juninho (5)
3. Nelson Piquet (6)
4. Eddie Izzard (7)
5. Chris Evans (8)
6. John Motson (9)
7. Hunter (James Crossley) (10)
8. Martin Clunes (11)
9. Nick Faldo (12)
10. Angus Fraser (13)
11. Terry Waite (14)
12. Jonah Lomu (15)

14 CELEBRITIES WHO WEIGH BETWEEN 7 AND 20 STONES

1. Bonnie Langford (7)
2. Twiggy (8)
3. Prince Naseem Hamed (9)
4. The Duchess of York (10)
5. Robbie Williams (11)
6. Harry Enfield (12)
7. Tommy Lee Jones (13)
8. Bill Clinton (14)
9. Liam Botham (15)
10. Peter Schmeichel (16)
11. Roger Cook (17)
12. Jonah Lomu (18)
13. Warrior (Mike Ahearne) (19)
14. John Goodman (20)

12 NUMBERPLATES AND THE CELEBRITIES WHO OWN THEM

1. COM 1C (Jimmy Tarbuck)
2. 1 PRO (Ray Reardon)
3. HRH 1 (The Queen)
4. FAL 1C (John Entwhistle of The Who)
5. 777 SM (Stirling Moss)
6. MOOS KAR (Michael J. Fox)
7. 1 CUE (Jimmy White)
8. X CZECH (Martina Navratilova)
9. K7 (Duke of Kent)
10. RAD 10 (Tommy Steele)
11. OFF 1A (Martin Offiah)
12. 8 DEB (Paul and Debbie Daniels)

12 CELEBRITIES FAMOUS FOR WEARING BOW TIES

1. Frank Muir
2. Frank Sinatra
3. John McCririck
4. Keith Floyd
5. Alfred Kinsey
6. Lord Grey Gowrie
7. Sir Robin Day
8. Timmy Mallett
9. Roger Levitt
10. Lord Woodrow Wyatt
11. Peter Fiddick
12. Neil Hamilton

20 CELEBRITIES WITHOUT A SINGLE OSCAR NOMINATION BETWEEN THEM

1. Al Jolson
2. Tallulah Bankhead
3. Audie Murphy
4. Yvonne De Carlo
5. Errol Flynn
6. Hedy Lamarr
7. Sir Dirk Bogarde
8. Raquel Welch
9. Boris Karloff
10. Veronica Lake
11. Olivia Hussey
12. Glenn Ford
13. Jacqueline Bisset
14. Martin Sheen
15. Dorothy Lamour
16. Peter Cushing
17. Brigitte Bardot
18. Roger Moore
19. Jane Russell
20. Harry Belafonte

34 CELEBRITIES WHO WILL BE 40 IN 1998

1. Paul Weller
2. Miranda Richardson
3. Rik Mayall
4. Michael Jackson
5. Anneka Rice
6. Nick Park
7. Michelle Pfeiffer
8. Sandi Toksvig
9. Peter Scudamore
10. Jennifer Saunders
11. Kate Bush
12. Neville Southall
13. Paul Ackford
14. Belinda Carlisle
15. Sandy Lyle
16. Lenny Henry
17. Caroline Langrishe
18. Bruce Dickinson
19. Simon Mayo
20. Toyah Willcox
21. Daley Thompson
22. Neil Adams
23. Malcolm Marshall
24. Joan Jett
25. Kriss Akabusi
26. Simon Le Bon
27. Gary Numan
28. Jamie Lee Curtis
29. Christopher Dean
30. Ian Woosnam
31. Mick Skinner
32. Marie Osmond
33. Terry Butcher
34. Nik Kershaw

22 MALE CELEBRITIES FROM 5' 1" TO 6' 10"

1. Ronnie Corbett 5' 1"
2. Dudley Moore 5' 2"
3. Mickey Rooney 5' 3"
4. Michael J. Fox 5' 4"
5. Sachin Tendulkar 5' 5"
6. Martin Amis 5' 6"
7. Mick Jagger 5' 7"
8. Phil Collins 5' 8"
9. Vic Reeves 5' 9"
10. Harry Enfield 5' 10"
11. George Michael 5' 11"
12. Terry Wogan 6'
13. Pete Sampras 6' 1"
14. Russ Abbot 6' 2"
15. Michael Barrymore 6' 3"
16. Frank Bruno 6' 4"
17. Mick Fleetwood 6' 5"
18. Dolph Lundgren 6' 6"
19. Terry Waite 6' 7"
20. Wade Dooley 6' 8"
21. Michael Crichton 6' 9"
22. Martin Bayfield 6' 10"

10 CELEBRITY ESSEX BOYS

1. Sir Alf Ramsey (Dagenham)
2. Michael Nicholson (Romford)
3. Mike Smith (Hornchurch)
4. Joseph Lister (Upton)
5. Rik Mayall (Harlow)
6. John Fowles (Leigh-on-Sea)
7. Bobby Moore (Barking)
8. Ian Holm (Ilford)
9. Dudley Moore (Dagenham)
10. Neil Innes (Danbury)

10 CELEBRITY ESSEX GIRLS

1. Charlotte Rampling (Sturmer)
2. Joan Sims (Laindon)
3. Sandie Shaw (Dagenham)
4. Jenny Powell (Ilford)
5. Millicent Martin (Romford)
6. Sarah Miles (Ingatestone)
7. Carol Leader (Colchester)
8. Alison Moyet (Basildon)
9. Lynn Fontanne (Mrs Alfred Lunt, Woodford)
10. Maggie Smith (Ilford)

6 CELEBRITIES WHO ARE *STAR TREK* FANS

1. Sir Cliff Richard
2. Lorraine Kelly
3. Wolf
4. Jim Davidson
5. Adam Woodyatt
6. Gordon Brand Jnr

13 CELEBRITIES WHO WOULD HAVE TURNED 100 IN 1998

1. Rene Clair
2. George Gershwin
3. John Grierson
4. Golda Meir
5. Paul Robeson
6. Bertholt Brecht
7. Enzo Ferrari
8. Lillian Gish
9. Gene Tunney
10. Gertrude Lawrence
11. Amelia Earhart
12. Beatrice Lillie
13. Rene Magritte

6 CELEBRITIES WHO HAD PUBS NAMED AFTER THEM

1. Fred Trueman (Fiery Fred in Yorkshire)
2. Jack Walker (Uncle Jack's in Blackburn)
3. Lord Harold Wilson (Pipe and Gannex in Liverpool)
4. Henry Cooper (Henry Cooper in London)
5. Tom Finney (Tom Finney in Preston)
6. General Sir Jeremy Moore (The General Moore in Plymouth)

Chapter 13

Pastimes

14 CELEBRITIES WHO COLLECT ANTIQUES

1. Gary Barlow
2. John Schlesinger
3. Leslie Caron
4. Tony Allcock
5. Susannah Fellows
6. Joan Collins
7. Antony Worrall-Thompson
8. Erin Pizzey
9. Annabel Croft
10. Graeme Le Saux
11. Elaine Paige
12. Leslie Thomas
13. Judy Parfitt
14. Chris De Burgh

16 CELEBRITIES WHO ARE KEEN PHOTOGRAPHERS

1. Koo Stark
2. Lord Denis Healey
3. Naim Attallah
4. John Suchet
5. David Suchet
6. Steven Berkoff
7. Valerie Singleton
8. Anthony Newley
9. Michael Bond
10. Nigel Dempster
11. Sir Harry Secombe
12. Keith Michell
13. Leo McKern
14. Prince Andrew
15. Bryan Forbes
16. Sir Ranulph Fiennes

8 CELEBRITIES WHO ARE BALLET LOVERS

1. Brian Moore
2. Elizabeth Emanuel
3. Raymond Keene
4. Frank Johnson
5. Monique Javer
6. Celia Brayfield
7. Don Foster MP
8. Jayne Torvill

3 CELEBRITIES WHO OWN HOTELS

1. Jean Shrimpton
2. Anouska Hempel
3. Michael Elphick

14 CELEBRITIES WHO ARE MEMBERS OF PRATT'S (A Gentlemen's Club)

1. Jonathan Aitken
2. Alan Clark
3. J. Paul Getty II
4. Max Hastings
5. Sir Edward Heath
6. Lord Roy Jenkins
7. Lord King of Wartnaby
8. Lord Palumbo
9. Anthony Powell
10. Lord St John of Fawsley
11. Nicholas Soames
12. Sir Denis Thatcher
13. William Waldegrave
14. Sir Peregrine Worsthorne

20 CELEBRITIES WHO SMOKE CIGARS

1. Tommy Lee Jones
2. James Belushi
3. Billy Connolly
4. Kenneth Clarke
5. Sharon Stone
6. Jack Nicholson
7. Demi Moore
8. Michael Grade
9. Jennifer Tilly
10. Ted Danson
11. Linda Evangelista
12. George Cole
13. Famke Janssen
14. Bruce Willis
15. Madonna
16. Danny De Vito
17. Gina Gershon
18. Lord Hanson
19. Arnold Schwarzenegger and, of course,
20. Sir Jimmy Savile

5 CELEBRITIES WHO ARE KEEN SCULPTORS

1. Gina Lollobrigida
2. John de Lorean
3. Gerard Depardieu
4. Tommy Steele
5. Gerald Scarfe

10 CELEBRITIES WHO ARE KEEN TABLE-TENNIS PLAYERS

1. Norman Lamont
2. Chief Rabbi Jonathan Sacks
3. Roger McGough
4. Arthur C. Clarke
5. Paul Gascoigne
6. Anne Hobbs
7. Mavis Nicholson
8. Dr Canaan Banana
9. Julian Bream
10. Kenneth Kaunda

11 CELEBRITIES WHO ARE KEEN BRIDGE PLAYERS

1. Omar Sharif
2. Alan Coren
3. Raymond Illingworth
4. David Nobbs
5. Maeve Binchy
6. Joel Cadbury
7. Nick Ross
8. Gordon Honeycombe
9. James Mates
10. Bruce Critchley
11. Arnold Palmer

10 CELEBRITIES WHO HAVE BEEN FOX HUNTING

1. Jeremy Irons
2. Chay Blyth
3. Jilly Cooper
4. Jane Seymour
5. Mickey Dolenz
6. Davy Jones
7. Richard Todd
8. Dick Francis
9. Willie Carson
10. Jimmy Hill

8 CELEBRITIES WHO ARE KEEN BACKGAMMON PLAYERS

1. Roger Whittaker
2. Sir Clement Freud
3. James Galway
4. Julian Bream
5. Chris Cowdrey
6. Jim Slater
7. Johnnie Walker
8. Robbie Williams

53 CELEBRITIES WHO ARE KEEN GARDENERS

1. Penelope Keith
2. Michael Caine
3. Anna Ford
4. Prunella Scales
5. Tony Britton
6. Bob Carolgees
7. Wendy Richards
8. Kenneth Kendall
9. Mollie Sugden
10. Jimmy Greaves
11. Sian Phillips
12. Charlie Parsons
13. Ken Livingstone MP
14. Roger Lloyd Pack
15. Elizabeth Hurley
16. John Gummer MP
17. Nerys Hughes
18. Michael Brunson
19. Ian Carmichael
20. Jack Cunningham MP
21. Nicola Pagett
22. Virginia McKenna
23. Michael Heseltine MP
24. Gillian Shephard MP
25. John Mortimer
26. Nigel Hawthorne
27. Julian Pettifer
28. Wendy Craig
29. Paddy Ashdown MP
30. Nigel Davenport
31. Edward De Souza
32. Jane Corbin
33. Edward Fox
34. Sir Jeremy Child
35. Joan Ruddock MP
36. Nigel Havers
37. Sam Neill
38. Robert Kilroy-Silk
39. Peter Barkworth
40. Nicholas Parsons
41. Keith Michell
42. John Kettley
43. Freddie Jones
44. Richard Briers
45. Trevor Phillips
46. Hannah Gordon
47. Rita Tushingham
48. Susannah York
49. Susan Hampshire
50. Lynn Redgrave
51. Wendy Richard
52. Jenny Seagrove
53. Sir Roy Strong

26 CELEBRITIES WHO HAVE BEEN THE GUILD OF BRITISH TIE MAKERS' 'TIE WEARERS OF THE YEAR'

1. Sir David Frost
2. Chris Tarrant
3. Harry Carpenter
4. Derek Jameson
5. Frank Bruno
6. Desmond Lynam
7. John Inman
8. John Fashanu
9. Trevor McDonald
10. Nicholas Parsons
11. Alan Whicker
12. Jimmy Tarbuck
13. Jim Davidson
14. John Virgo
15. Julia Somerville
16. Kevin Keegan
17. Paddy Ashdown
18. Su Pollard
19. John Prescott
20. Maureen Lipman
21. Lionel Blair
22. Bob Holness
23. Wendy Richard
24. Michael Fish
25. Alastair Stewart
26. Barry Norman

10 CELEBRITIES WHO HAVE SPONSORED CHILDREN IN THE THIRD WORLD

1. Michael Aspel
2. Marie Helvin
3. Twiggy
4. Jane Lapotaire
5. Matthew Kelly
6. Virginia McKenna
7. Susan Gilmore
8. Lawrie McMenemy
9. Dr. Miriam Stoppard
10. Amanda Redman

THE LUXURIES CHOSEN BY 100 CELEBRITIES ON DESERT ISLAND DISCS

1. Bath salts (Esther Rantzen)
2. A guitar (Harry Carpenter)
3. Model of the Tower of London (Denis Norden)
4. A suicide pill (Stephen Fry)
5. Radio 4 (Neil Kinnock)
6. A fishing rod (Ian Botham)
7. Needles, cotton and material (Mary Archer)
8. Apricot brandy (Sir Alec Guinness)
9. The Mona Lisa (Arthur Scargill)
10. Silk underwear (Helen Mirren)
11. Iron and ironing board (Sue Lawley)
12. Two tape recorders (Rolf Harris)
13. Bag of cricket gear (Sir Tim Rice)
14. A stick of marijuana (Norman Mailer)
15. A large bottle of moisturiser (Joan Collins)
16. A car to clean (Rowan Atkinson)
17. A replica of Broadcasting House (Sir Harry Secombe)
18. A kettle and tea-bags (Tony Benn)
19. Madge Allsop (Dame Edna Everage – the only time a 'person' has been allowed as a luxury on the show)
20. A guitar (Eric Clapton)
21. A picture of Marilyn Monroe (Bob Monkhouse)
22. A high-powered radio (Reverend Ian Paisley)
23. Electrical device to heat shaving foam (Billy Connolly)
24. Big bag of plaster to make heads of friends (Virginia Ironside)
25. A manicure set and nail varnish (Cilla Black)
26. Cold cream (Twiggy)
27. A Barclaycard (Spike Milligan)
28. A radio (Boy George)
29. Beer and cigarette machine (Harry Enfield)
30. A bathtub and soap (Lord Hailsham)
31. Linen sheets (David Bellamy)
32. The laws of the land (so he could break them) (Benjamin Zephaniah)
33. A comfortable bed with pillows and sheets (Anita Roddick)
34. An unlisted radio telephone (Salman Rushdie)
35. Graphic novels (Lenny Henry)
36. A sand wedge and a crate of golf balls (Eric Sykes)
37. A telescope (Bob Hoskins)
38. An Edwardian bath (Chris Patten)
39. Pens and paper (Sian Phillips)
40. A guitar (Joan Armatrading)
41. Endless supply of A4 paper and 4B pencils (Sir Terence Conran)
42. A hot bath with extra tap for cold champagne (Jane Asher)
43. Laptop computers (Paddy Ashdown)
44. A steamer for cooking (Anton Mosimann)
45. A guitar (Charles Dance)
46. Watercolour paints, brushes and paper (Dame Vera Lynn)
47. A set of cricket equipment (David Essex)
48. Suntan lotion (Sir Edward Heath)

49. Golf clubs and balls (Bruce Forsyth)

50. Cleansing milk (Dame Thora Hird)

51. A snooker table (Sir Rocco Forte)

52. A fish smoker (Enoch Powell)

53. Paper and pencils (Pauline Collins)

54. Notebooks and pens (Richard Branson)

55. The front seat of a Porsche (Iain Banks)

56. A distillery (Sir Dirk Bogarde)

57. Tennis wall, balls and racket (Baroness Tessa Blackstone)

58. A fishing rod (Loyd Grossman)

59. A sack of seed potatoes (Ned Sherrin)

60. A home gym (Peter Blake)

61. A case of Bordeaux wine (Lord Roy Jenkins)

62. An aircraft carrier (Katharine Hamnett)

63. A piano (Anthony Minghella)

64. A circular knitting needle with a point at each end (Richard Rodney Bennett)

65. Space invaders (Clive James)

66. A fountain pen (Jonathon Porritt)

67. A mink-lined hammock (Janet Suzman)

68. A word processor (Rose Tremain)

69. A pair of binoculars (Penelope Lively)

70. A grand piano (Jools Holland)

71. Tenor saxophone (Warren Mitchell)

72. A solar-powered lamp (The Duchess of Kent)

73. A metal detector (Leslie Grantham)

74. Vodka (Terry Wogan)

75. An oriental rug (Jenny Agutter)

76. Make-up (Dame Barbara Cartland)

77. A sports car (Tommy Steele)

78. Tennis practice equipment (Charlton Heston)

79. A piano (Jack Lemmon)

80. Garlic (Derek Nimmo)

81. Cooking knives (Dame Kiri Te Kanawa)

82. Havana cigars (George Cole)

83. Hot spices (Germaine Greer)

84. Poppy seeds (Wayne Sleep)

85. Video recorder and cassettes of his own performances (Placido Domingo)

86. A case half-filled with Black Label and half-filled with Dom Perignon (Saeed Jaffrey)

87. Potato crisps (Sir David Frost)

88. A multi-language dictionary (Vivienne Westwood)

89. Toothbrushes (Wendy Craig)

90. Perfume (Felicity Kendal)

91. A bicycle (Luciano Pavarotti)

92. An oyster knife (Lionel Blair)

93. A car to listen to music in (Sir Michael Gambon)

94. Lavatory and lavatory paper (Mike Leigh)

95. Video recorder with cassettes of his family (Roger Moore)

96. A cricket bat and bowling machine (David Hare)

97. A pipe (Magnus Magnusson)

98. A river painting by Turner (Gerald Scarfe)

99. Amazonian rain-maker (Maria Aitken)

100. Feather-filled pillow (Michael Palin)

THE BOOKS CHOSEN BY 49 CELEBRITIES ON *DESERT ISLAND DISCS*

1. *One Hundred Years of Solitude* by Gabriel Garcia Marquez (Mike Leigh)
2. *Four Books of Architecture* by Palladio (Jools Holland)
3. *Fun In A Chinese Laundry* by Josef Von Sternberg (Maria Aitken)
4. *A Brief History Of Time* by Stephen Hawking (Rose Tremain)
5. *Treasure Island* by Robert Louis Stevenson (Loyd Grossman)
6. *Scene And Hird* by Dame Thora Hird (Dame Thora Hird)
7. *Power Of Positive Thinking* by Norman Vincent-Rees (Virginia Ironside)
8. *Huckleberry Finn* by Mark Twain (Arthur Scargill)
9. *Middlemarch* by George Eliot (Baroness Blackstone)
10. *The Works of Homer* (Lord Hailsham)
11. *Remembrance of Things Past* by Marcel Proust (Tony Blair)
12. *No Bed For Bacon* by Caryl Brahms (Ned Sherrin)
13. *History of The World* by H.G. Wells (Sir Terence Conran)
14. *The Collected Works of P.G. Wodehouse* (Terry Wogan)
15. *The Rattle Bag* by Seamus Heaney and Ted Hughes (Chris Patten)
16. *The Poems of John Donne* (Paddy Ashdown)
17. *The Picture of Dorian Gray* by Oscar Wilde (Anita Dobson)
18. *Robinson Crusoe* by Daniel Defoe (Leslie Grantham)
19. *The Odyssey* by Homer (Lord Robert Runcie)
20. *Ulysses* by James Joyce (Seamus Heaney)
21. *Don Juan* by Lord Byron (Michael Foot)
22. *Remembrance of Things Past* by Marcel Proust (Mary Archer)
23. *The Old Testament* in Hebrew and *The New Testament* in Greek (Enoch Powell)
24. *Smell of Sunday Dinner* by Sid Chaplin (Alan Plater)
25. *Ripley's Fascinating Facts* (Eric Sykes)
26. *A Dream In The Luxembourg* by Richard Aldington (Charles Dance)
27. *Reader's Digest Now Do-It-Yourself Manual* (Duchess of Kent)
28. *Why Didn't They Ask Evans?* by Agatha Christie (Joan Armatrading)
29. *Essays On Equality* by R.H. Tawney (Neil Kinnock)
30. *The Oxford English Dictionary* (Germaine Greer)
31. *I Ching* (Katharine Hamnett)
32. *Bleak House* by Charles Dickens (Harry Enfield)
33. *Who Was Who* (Lord Roy Jenkins)
34. *At Play In The Fields of Our Lord* by Peter Matheson (Jack Lemmon)
35. *Tess of The D'Urbervilles* by Thomas Hardy (Twiggy)
36. *The Oxford Book of English Verse* (Sir Trevor Huddleston)
37. *Uncle Fred In Springtime* by P.G. Wodehouse (Rowan Atkinson)
38. *The Oxford Book of Twentieth Century Verse* (Lord Douglas Hurd)
39. *Akenfield* by Ronald Blythe (Sir Dirk Bogarde)
40. *The Jeeves Omnibus* by P.G. Wodehouse (Stephen Fry)
41. *Les Miserables* by Victor Hugo (Mark McCormack)
42. *The biggest volume of pure maths* (Rabbi Lionel Blue)
43. *Catch 22* by Joseph Heller (Lenny Henry)
44. *The Dictionary of National Biography* (Lucinda Lambton)
45. *Das Kapital* by Karl Marx (Tony Benn MP)
46. *The Divine Comedy* by Dante (Sir Rocco Forte)
47. *Larousse Gastronomique* (David Hare)
48. *Remembrance of Things Past* by Marcel Proust (Sir Stephen Spender)
49. *Moby Dick* by Herman Melville (Penelope Lively)

11 CELEBRITIES WHO SOLD THEIR POSSESSIONS AT AUCTION

1. Sir Elton John (Outfits and possessions in 1996)
2. Janet Street-Porter (Dresses in 1997)
3. Barbra Streisand (20th Century furniture in 1993)
4. Britt Ekland (Contents of Chelsea home and various possessions in 1996)
5. Michael Caine (Paintings and furniture from Hollywood home in 1996)
6. Frank Sinatra (Car, golf cart and various possessions in 1995)
7. Eric Clapton (Paintings in 1997)
8. Andrew Lloyd Webber (Wine in 1997)
9. Joan Sutherland (Opera clothes and costumes in 1996)
10. The Princess of Wales (Dresses in 1997)
11. Paul Gambaccini (Record collection in 1997) 6

25 CELEBRITIES WHO ARE OPERA LOVERS

1. Derek Jameson
2. Elvis Costello
3. Bella Emberg
4. Clive James
5. Anita Dobson
6. Omar Sharif
7. David 'Kid' Jensen
8. Lulu
9. Eric Clapton
10. John Major
11. John Gosden
12. Bob Willis
13. Lord Robert Runcie
14. Brian Barron
15. Alan Freeman
16. Brian Hayes
17. John Mortimer
18. Sir Hardy Amies
19. Ruth Rendell
20. Naim Attallah
21. Christopher Lee
22. Phillip Hodson
23. Lindka Cierach
24. Clare Francis
25. Margaret Hodge MP

10 CELEBRITIES WHO ARE MEMBERS OF THE DENNIS THE MENACE FAN CLUB

1. Joan Armatrading
2. Lenny Henry
3. Paul Gascoigne
4. Timmy Mallett
5. Suzanne Dando
6. Ian Woosnam
7. Mark Hamill
8. Mike Read
9. Auberon Waugh
10. David Jenkins (the former Bishop of Durham who was enrolled by one of his ministers)

17 CELEBRITIES WHO ARE KEEN CHESS PLAYERS

1. Stephen Fry
2. Jonathan Edwards
3. Loyd Grossman
4. Art Buchwald
5. Garry Bushell
6. Roger Lloyd Pack
7. Greta Scacchi
8. James Galway
9. Patrick Moore
10. Johnny Ball
11. Martin Amis
12. Ellery Hanley
13. Michael Foot
14. Joe Bugner
15. Emma Nicholson
16. Michael Jayston
17. Brian Walden

10 CELEBRITIES WHO ARE CLASSIC CAR AFICIONADOS

1. Robbie Coltrane
2. Lord David Steel
3. Mary Ann Sieghart
4. Stephen Fry
5. Alan Clark MP
6. June Brown
7. Chris Barrie
8. Michael Barrymore
9. Joan Armatrading
10. Peter Waterman

10 CELEBRITIES WHO DO NEEDLEPOINT

1. Elizabeth Hurley
2. Dillie Keane
3. Katie Boyle
4. Nanette Newman
5. Dame Joan Sutherland
6. Elizabeth Jane Howard
7. Wendy Richards
8. Sian Phillips
9. Lea Salonga
10. Judy Parfitt

10 CELEBRITIES WHO BECAME PATRONS OF PIPEDOWN (the campaign against piped music)

1. Spike Milligan
2. George Melly
3. Stephen Fry
4. Joanna Lumley
5. Tony Parsons
6. Julian Lloyd Webber
7. Sir Yehudi Menuhin
8. A.N. Wilson
9. Claire Tomalin
10. Sir Kingsley Amis

10 CELEBRITIES WHO KEEP KOI CARP

1. Pete Waterman
2. Jim Davidson
3. John Major
4. Aaron Spelling
5. Kenneth Branagh
6. Felix Dennis
7. Alexandra Bastedo
8. Peter Sissons
9. Francis Rossi
10. Brian Blessed

23 CELEBRITIES WHO ARE KEEN PAINTERS

1. Rabbi Lionel Blue
2. Dame Vera Lynn
3. Paul Johnson
4. James Herbert
5. Dr Desmond Morris
6. Joss Ackland
7. David Hemmings
8. Ray Bradbury
9. Acker Bilk
10. George Melly
11. Beryl Bainbridge
12. Prince Charles
13. David Bowie
14. Sheila Kitzinger
15. Max Bygraves
16. Eric Cantona
17. David Bailey
18. Robbie Coltrane
19. Jan Leeming
20. Will Carling
21. Cherie Lunghi
22. Timmy Mallett
23. Tommy Steele

12 CELEBRITIES WHOSE HOBBIES INCLUDE WINE

1. Sir David Frost
2. Peter Alliss
3. Sir Peter O'Sullevan
4. Spike Milligan
5. Carol Barnes
6. Paddy Ashdown
7. Michael Bond
8. Leslie Grantham
9. Justin de Blank
10. Michael Ignatieff
11. Colonel John Blashford-Snell
12. Michael Bogdanov

12 CELEBRITIES WHOSE HOBBIES INCLUDE SLEEPING

1. Terry Jones
2. Jeremy Paxman
3. Phil Tufnell
4. Beryl Bainbridge
5. Jane Corbin
6. Roy Hudd
7. Lee Sharpe
8. Lord St John of Fawsley
9. Joyce Hopkirk
10. Jonathan Miller
11. Wolf Mankowitz
12. Brian Sedgemore MP

8 CELEBRITIES WHO BELIEVE IN ASTROLOGY

1. Nick Faldo
2. Sylvester Stallone
3. Bryan Ferry
4. Gloria Estefan
5. The Duchess of York
6. Pete Waterman
7. Nancy Reagan
8. Boy George

2 CELEBRITIES WHO SMOKE ROLL-UPS

1. Kate Winslet
2. Arthur Smith

69 CELEBRITIES AND THEIR PETS

CELEBRITY	ANIMAL	NAME
1. The Queen	Dogs (Corgis)	Fable, Myth, Shadow, Jolly and Chipper But not Fergie.
2. Barry Gibb	Dog	Duane
3. Carrie Fisher	Dog (Rottweiler)	Sweetie
4. Courtney Love	Dog	Bob Dylan
5. Bill Treacher	Dog	Toto
6. Paul Newman	Dog (Collie)	Smokey
7. Zsa Zsa Gabor	Dog (Yorkshire Terrier)	Susie
8. Susan Dey	Dog	Molly
9. Ringo Starr	Dogs	Ying and Yang
10. Ian Botham	Dog (Boxer)	Tigger
11. Brad Pitt	Dog	Saudi
12. Keith Chegwin	Dog	Muffin
13. Axl Rose	Dog	Sumner (Sting's surname at birth).
14. Susan Penhaligon	Dog	Bronwyn
15. Julia Roberts	Dog	Gatsby
16. Tim Brooke-Taylor	Cat	Muriel (the name of his wife in *Me & My Girl*)
17. Sheena Easton	Dog	Poker
18. Rodney Bewes	Cat	Beryl
19. Anna Carteret	Cat	Michael Jackson (it is not known whether Michael Jackson has a moggy named Anna Carteret)
20. Cyndi Lauper	Cat	Weasel
21. George Hamilton	Dog (Yorkshire Terrier)	Mitzi
22. Su Pollard	Cat	Dulcie
23. Mike Smith	Carp	Kevin
24. Linda Evans	Cat	Sassy
25. Sandy Gall	Dog (Labrador)	Solomon
26. Isabella Rossellini	Dog (Dachshund)	Ferdinando
27. Jimmy Hill	Dog (Labrador)	George
28. Tony Britton	Cat	Tiger
29. Henry Kissinger	Dog (Retriever)	Tyler
30. Michael Aspel	Dog	Cressie
31. Victoria Principal	Dog	Gorby
32. Russell Grant	Dog (Labrador)	Amber
33. Jaclyn Smith	Dog (Poodle)	Vivien Leigh
34. Sir Alec Guinness	Parrot	Percy

CELEBRITY	ANIMAL	NAME
35. William Shatner	Dog (Doberman Pinscher)	Kirk
36. Richard Briers	Cat	Tigger
37. Sylvester Stallone	Dog (Boxer)	Gangster
38. Fiona Armstrong	Cat	Max
39. Janet Jackson	Dog	Snow White
40. Dudley Moore	Dog	Chelsea
41. Princess Beatrice	Dog (Terrier)	Wat
42. Roy Barraclough	Dog (West Highland Terrier)	Whisky
43. Faith Brown	Dog	Use
44. Maggie Philbin	Cat	Pooh
45. James Garner	Dog	Nikki
46. Chris Patten	Dogs	Whisky and Soda
47. Malandra Burrows	Dog	Bonkers
48. Morgan Fairchild	Cat	Stinky
49. Gina Bellman	Cat	Bobo
50. Val Singleton	Cat	Pansy
51. Cheryl Baker	Dog	Malcolm
52. Patrick Swayze	Dog	Derek
53. Arnold Schwarzenegger	Dog (Labrador)	Conan
54. Darren Gough	Dog (Jack Russell)	Jack
55. Charles Bronson	Dog	Cassie
56. Uma Thurman	Dog (Chow Chow)	Muffy
57. Jonathan Pryce	Dog	Boots
58. Dustin Hoffman	Dog	Maggie
59. Bill Clinton	Cat	Socks
60. The Duke of Kent	Dog	Muff
61. Michael Foot	Dog (Terrier)	Dizzy (the nickname of former PM, Benjamin Disraeli).
62. Michael J. Fox	Dog (Pit Bull Terrier)	Burnaby
63. Gyles Brandreth	Cat	GB
64. Quincy Jones	Cat	Lucy
65. Rob Lowe	Dog	Spot
66. Bob Hope	Dog (Basset Hound)	Recession
67. Prunella Scales	Cats	Lily and Baylis (named after the great theatre manager, Lillian Baylis)
68. Steve Martin	Cat	Dr Carlton B. Forbes
69. Anne Bancroft	Dog (Staffordshire Bull Terrier)	Pongo

Chapter 14

Past Times

9 CELEBRITIES WHO USED TO BE WAITERS/WAITRESSES

1. Richard Gere (and he once served Robert De Niro)
2. Annie Lennox
3. Rickie Lee Jones
4. Jacqueline Bisset
5. Dame Diana Rigg
6. Ellen Barkin
7. Paula Abdul
8. Alec Baldwin
9. Antonio Banderas

2 CELEBRITIES WHO USED TO LIVE IN THEIR CARS

1. Brad Pitt
2. Chris Tarrant

10 DEAD CELEBRITIES WHO OWNED ROLLS-ROYCES

1. Vladimir Lenin
2. Grigori Rasputin
3. T.E. Lawrence
4. Rudyard Kipling
5. Idi Amin
6. John Lennon
7. Benito Mussolini
8. Mae West
9. George Bernard Shaw
10. Elvis Presley

8 CELEBRITIES WHO USED TO BE POLICEMEN

1. Christopher Dean
2. Lord Jeffrey Archer
3. Dave Dee
4. Ray Reardon
5. Paul Ackford
6. Geoff Capes
7. John Arlott
8. Josef Locke

14 CELEBRITIES WHOSE FATHERS WERE KILLED IN WAR

1. Bill Cash MP (WW2)
2. Norman Stone (WW2)
3. Dame Barbara Cartland (WW1)
4. Leslie Thomas (WW2)
5. Nick Raynsford MP (WW2)
6. Sir Ludovic Kennedy (WW2)
7. Alfred Shaughnessy (WW1)
8. David Niven (WW1)
9. Norma Major (WW2)
10. Henry Cecil (WW2)
11. Lord Killanin (WW1)
12. Tim Rathbone (WW2)
13. Lord Longford (WW1)
14. Sir Ranulph Fiennes (WW2)

10 CELEBRITIES WHO USED TO WORK IN CINEMAS/THEATRES AS USHERS OR USHERETTES

1. Sylvester Stallone
2. Barbra Streisand
3. Marianne Jean-Baptiste
4. Charlene Tilton
5. George Michael
6. Elizabeth Garvie
7. George Segal
8. Nadia Sawalha
9. Jayne Irving
10. Kirk Douglas

7 CELEBRITIES WHO DIED ON THEIR BIRTHDAYS

1. William Shakespeare (23rd April, 1564-1616)
2. Joe Mercer (9th August, 1914-1990)
3. Raphael (6th April, 1483-1520 and for good measure both days fell on Good Friday)
4. Ingrid Bergman (29th August, 1915-82)
5. Frans Francken (6th May, 1581-1642)
6. Keith Boyce (11th October, 1943-96)
7. Lord Victor Matthews (5th December, 1919-1995)

10 CELEBRITIES WHO USED TO HAVE BEARDS

1. Ian Botham
2. Prince Philip
3. Jimmy Hill
4. Billy Connolly
5. John McEnroe
6. Sir Paul McCartney
7. Liam Gallagher
8. Ringo Starr
9. John Gummer
10. Sir Peter Ustinov

80 CELEBRITIES WHO WERE SCOUTS OR GUIDES

1. Janet Street-Porter
2. Rolf Harris
3. Marjorie "Mo" Mowlam MP
4. President Bill Clinton
5. David Bellamy
6. Angela Rippon
7. Bobby Robson
8. Mark Spitz
9. Anita Roddick
10. Russell Grant
11. Peter Barkworth
12. Simon Mayo
13. Georgie Fame
14. Helen Sharman
15. Derek Nimmo
16. Richard Gere
17. Trevor Brooking
18. Björk
19. Chris Smith MP
20. Tom O'Connor
21. Sir Derek Jacobi
22. Mike Harding
23. Frank Bough
24. Lord David Owen
25. Lady Annabel Goldsmith
26. Neil Armstrong
27. Michelle Gayle
28. Richard Meade
29. President Jacques Chirac
30. Linda Robson
31. Neil Kinnock
32. Sir David Attenborough
33. Sally Magnusson
34. Leslie Thomas
35. Michael Elphick
36. Clare Short MP
37. Robin Knox-Johnston
38. Penny Junor
39. Emma Forbes
40. Gerry Marsden
41. Lord Brian Rix
42. Emma Thompson
43. Michael Parkinson
44. Austin Mitchell MP
45. Anne Gregg
46. Lord Jeffrey Archer
47. Diana Quick
48. Jason Donovan
49. Roger Rees
50. Baroness Thatcher
51. Denis Norden
52. Diana Moran
53. Brian Clough
54. Nigel Clough
55. Ann Widdecombe MP
56. Paul Shane
57. Stirling Moss
58. Belinda Lang
59. Princess Margaret
60. Tony Benn
61. Teresa Gorman MP
62. Lord Geoffrey Howe
63. Lewis Collins
64. Sally Oppenheimer
65. Norman Wisdom
66. Danny La Rue
67. Alice Beer
68. James Stewart
69. Lord Richard Attenborough
70. Richard Baker
71. Glenda Jackson MP
72. Richard Branson
73. The Princess Royal
74. Adrian Moorhouse
75. John Craven
76. Pauline Quirke
77. Peter Lilley
78. Susan Tully
79. Edward Woodward
80. Keith Richards

2 CELEBRITIES WHO WERE MODELS FOR TEEN PHOTO-ROMANCE STORIES

1. Hugh Grant
2. George Michael

10 CELEBRITIES WHO USED TO OWN HARLEY-DAVIDSONS

1. Steve McQueen
2. Jim Bowen
3. Errol Flynn
4. Elvis Presley
5. Malcolm Forbes
6. T.E. Lawrence
7. Bill Haley
8. George Sanders
9. Clark Gable
10. Howard Hughes

13 CELEBRITIES WHO STARTED OUT AS BUTLIN'S REDCOATS

1. Ted Rogers
2. Des O'Connor
3. Roy Hudd
4. Michael Barrymore
5. Russell Grant
6. Darren Day
7. Jimmy Tarbuck
8. Ken Dodd
9. William G. Stewart
10. Dave Allen
11. Sir Cliff Richard
12. Johnny Ball
13. Shane Ritchie

5 CELEBRITIES WHO DIED IN THE BATHROOM

1. Judy Garland
2. Elvis Presley
3. King George II
4. Lenny Bruce
5. Jim Morrison

11 CELEBRITIES WHO WORKED AS SINGING TELEGRAMS

1. Julian Clary
2. Sinead O'Connor
3. Carol Smillie
4. Chris Evans
5. Mandy Smith
6. Virginia Madsen
7. Michaela Strachan
8. Helen Lederer
9. Emma Freud
10. Rosalind Sutherland
11. Keith Duffy

10 CELEBRITIES WHO LITERALLY DIED ON STAGE

1. Tommy Cooper
2. Sid James
3. Leonard Rossiter
4. Marie Lloyd
5. Simon Barere (Pianist)
6. Lee Harvey (Stone The Crows musician – electrocuted by touching a live microphone with wet feet in 1972)
7. Richard Versalle (Opera singer – after singing the line "Too bad you can only live so long" in 1996)
8. Linda Wright (Nightclub singer)
9. Leonard Warren (Opera singer)
10. Sylvia Syms (Singer)

2 CELEBRITIES WHO DIED IN AN APARTMENT OWNED BY HARRY NILSSON

1. Mama Cass Elliott
2. Keith Moon

11 CELEBRITIES WHO HAVE OWNED PORSCHES

1. Prince Naseem Hamed
2. Sir Elton John
3. Rick Parfitt
4. Daley Thompson
5. Chris Evans
6. Julian Dicks
7. Angus Deayton
8. Jurgen Klinsmann
9. King Hussein
10. David Bailey
11. Rupert Allason

8 CELEBRITIES WHO SHOPLIFTED

1. Nick Ross
2. Farrah Fawcett
3. Liam Gallagher
4. Noel Gallagher
5. Tracy Shaw
6. Quentin Tarantino
7. Roseanne
8. Julie Burchill

19 CELEBRITIES AND WHAT THEY ORIGINALLY INTENDED TO BE

1. Whitney Houston: Vet
2. Alec Baldwin: Lawyer
3. Nick Berry: Professional footballer
4. Mike Read: Singer
5. Rowan Atkinson: Electrical engineer
6. Georgie Fame: Professional Rugby League player
7. Gareth Hale: Vet
8. William Baldwin: Professional baseball player
9. Soraya Khashoggi: Professional Photographer
10. Bob Dole: Doctor
11. Britt Ekland: Vet
12. Paul Theroux: Doctor
13. Eddie Izzard: Accountant
14. Zeinab Bedawi: Doctor
15. Kate O'Mara: Concert pianist
16. Michael Palin: Explorer
17. Jeremy Irons: Vet
18. Gary Numan: Airline pilot
19. Anneka Rice: Actress

15 CELEBRITIES WHO WERE PALLBEARERS FOR OTHER CELEBRITIES

1. Donald Dewar: John Smith
2. Ben Crenshaw: Harvey Penick
3. Jack Lemmon: Rosalind Russell
4. Andrew Farriss: Michael Hutchence
5. John McEnroe: Vitas Gerulaitis
6. Phil Everly: Buddy Holly
7. Emerson Fittipaldi: Ayrton Senna
8. James Stewart: Clark Gable
9. Hubert de Givenchy: Audrey Hepburn
10. Ian Botham: Colin Milburn
11. Tom Mix: Wyatt Earp
12. Joe Louis: Sonny Liston
13. King Edward VII: William Gladstone
14. Tiny Rowland: Sir Hugh Fraser
15. Kenny Rogers: Vincente Minnelli

86 CELEBRITIES AND WHAT THEY DID BEFORE BECOMING FAMOUS

1. Dawn French: Teacher

2. Peter Gabriel: Milliner

3. Janice Long: Air stewardess on Laker Airways

4. Freddie Starr: Bricklayer

5. Jim Davidson: Fork-lift truck driver

6. Elvis Costello: Computer programmer

7. Anthony Andrews: Farm labourer

8. Bob Geldof: Meat-packer

9. Alexei Sayle: Illustrator

10. Shane MacGowan: Worked in a record shop

11. Christie Brinkley: Painter

12. Pierce Brosnan: Mini-cab driver

13. Charlie Watts: Designer in advertising

14. Edward Woodward: Trainee sanitary engineer

15. Gabriel Byrne: Plumber

16. Michael Keaton: Cab driver

17. Rolf Harris: Postman

18. Steve Wright: Insurance broker

19. Ken Dodd: Coal Delivery Assistant

20. Ken Kercheval: Sold plots of land in a cemetery

21. Paul Newman: Encyclopaedia salesman

22. Gareth Hale: P.E. Teacher

23. Tom Jones: Glove cutter

24. Ben Kingsley: Penicillin tester

25. Madonna: Worked in Burger King

26. Mike Yarwood: Commercial traveller

27. Robert Redford: Pavement artist

28. Tina Turner: Maid

29. Joe Cocker: Plumber

30. Giorgio Armani: Window dresser

31. Edna O'Brien: Trainee pharmacist

32. Anita Roddick: Teacher

33. Madonna: Lifeguard

34. Sir Elton John: Messenger boy

35. Rutger Hauer: Electrician

36. Roy Barraclough: Draughtsman

37. Paul Young: Apprentice toolmaker at Vauxhall

38. Johnny Briggs: Was in the chorus of an Italian opera company.

39. Gary Kemp: Prices clerk for the Financial Times

40. Willem Dafoe: Magazine binder at Penthouse

41. Gloria Estefan: Spanish and French interpreter for the customs at an American airport

42. Bill Withers: Manufactured aeroplane loo seats

43. Tom Hanks: Bellhop

44. James Caan: Rodeo rider

45. Jon Bon Jovi: Served in Burger King

46. Lynne Perrie : Cabaret singer – performing on the same bill as The Rolling Stones and The Beatles

47. Bob Newhart: Accountant

48. Kylie Minogue: Video shop worker

49. Anthea Turner: Worked for the AA's information and breakdown service

50. Jimmy Somerville: Baker

51. Kathy Bates: Cashier in the gift shop in New York's Museum of Modern Art

52. Danny De Vito: Janitor

53. Steve Wright: British Telecom engineer

54. Mickey Rourke: Sold pretzels

55. Anthony Quinn: Shoe shine boy

56. Simon Le Bon: Lumberjack
57. Mick Jagger: Hospital porter
58. Walter Matthau: Filing clerk
59. Charles Dance: Window-dresser at Burton's
60. Roger Daltrey: Sheet metal worker
61. Helen Lederer: Social Worker
62. Cher: Receptionist in a department store
63. Bob Monkhouse: Animator
64. Adam Faith: Messenger boy
65. Desmond Dekker: Welder
66. Anthony Quinn: Fruit picker
67. Ringo Starr: Barman
68. Leo Sayer: Illustrator
69. Ozzy Osbourne: Slaughterhouse labourer
70. Michael Aspel: Bedding salesman
71. Annie Lennox: Fish filleter
72. Bob Hoskins: Nightclub bouncer
73. Jon Bon Jovi: Floor sweeper
74. Rod Stewart: Grave digger
75. Kim Wilde: Hospital cleaner
76. Vic Reeves: Pig Farmer
77. Warren Beatty: Cocktail bar pianist
78. Bernard Manning: Cigarette Factory worker
79. Reg Presley: Bricklayer
80. Joan Armatrading: Accounts assistant
81. Anita Dobson: Insurance clerk
82. Beck: Refrigerator mover and YMCA I.D. photographer
83. Cuba Gooding Jr.: Construction worker
84. Rene Russo: Eye Glass factory worker
85. Kate Winslet: Worked in a delicatessen
86. Jeremy Beadle: Mini Cab Driver

40 DEAD CELEBRITIES AND THE PRICE OF THEIR AUTOGRAPHS

1. Cary Grant: £2,500
2. John Lennon: £1,400
3. Vivien Leigh: £750
4. Sir Alfred Hitchcock: £775
5. Sir Laurence Olivier: £575
6. Grace Kelly: £850
7. Bob Marley: £750
8. Ingrid Bergman: £425
9. Judy Garland: £1,500
10. Jim Morrison: £4,950
11. Cesar Romero: £25
12. Fred Astaire: £325
13. James Cagney: £325
14. Celia Johnson: £150
15. Lionel Barrymore: £375
16. Stewart Granger: £85
17. Peter Cushing: £250
18. Marlene Dietrich: £175
19. John Candy: £150
20. Vincent Price: £150
21. Wilfred Brambell: £225
22. Gene Kelly: £375
23. Chuck Connors: £175
24. Rock Hudson: £275
25. Jon Pertwee: £50
26. Brandon Lee: £750
27. Bette Davis: £225
28. Hattie Jacques: £125
29. Joseph Cotten: £75
30. Dorothy Lamour: £275
31. Dean Martin: £200
32. Ray Milland: £125
33. Audie Murphy: £750
34. River Phoenix: £300
35. Sir Ralph Richardson: £275
36. Peter Sellers: £150
37. Phil Silvers: £375
38. Bobby Moore: £125
39. Elvis Presley: £1,500
40. Donald Pleasence: £95

81 CELEBRITIES WHO DIED FROM THE AGES OF 21 TO 101

1. Sid Vicious
2. Buddy Holly
3. River Phoenix
4. James Dean
5. Brian Jones
6. Otis Redding
7. Jimi Hendrix
8. Ruth Ellis
9. Marc Bolan
10. Emily Brontë
11. Keith Moon
12. Bruce Lee
13. Carole Lombard
14. Yuri Gagarin
15. Jayne Mansfield
16. Marilyn Monroe
17. Vincent Van Gogh
18. Charlotte Bronte
19. Dr Martin Luther King
20. John Lennon
21. Jane Austen
22. Elvis Presley
23. Natalie Wood
24. Tony Hancock
25. James Hunt
26. Graham Hill
27. Judy Garland
28. David Janssen
29. Marty Feldman
30. Steve McQueen
31. Bobby Moore
32. Roy Orbison
33. Russell Harty
34. Peter Sellers
35. Julius Caesar
36. Ludwig Van Beethoven
37. Humphrey Bogart
38. Eric Morecambe
39. Rock Hudson
40. Anthony Perkins
41. Ernest Hemingway
42. Kenneth Williams
43. Audrey Hepburn
44. Sammy Davis Jnr.
45. Walt Disney
46. Joe Louis
47. Benny Hill
48. Paul Eddington
49. Richard Burton
50. Telly Savalas
51. Louis Armstrong
52. John Wayne
53. Bing Crosby
54. Stan Laurel
55. Duke Ellington
56. Beryl Reid
57. Jules Verne
58. John Ford
59. Ella Fitzgerald
60. Burt Lancaster
61. Bette Davis
62. Sir Laurence Olivier
63. Gene Kelly
64. Greta Garbo
65. Dame Agatha Christie
66. James Cagney
67. Malcolm Muggeridge
68. Sir Charlie Chaplin
69. Compton Mackenzie
70. Marlene Dietrich
71. Pablo Picasso
72. Greer Garson
73. Sir P.G. Wodehouse
74. George Bernard Shaw
75. Leopold Stokowski
76. Pablo Casals
77. Bertrand Russell
78. Dame Eva Turner
79. Lillian Gish
80. George Burns
81. Irving Berlin

34 CELEBRITIES WHO SERVED IN THE RAF

1. Bill Wyman
2. Des O'Connor
3. Ted Rogers
4. Arthur C. Clarke
5. Peter Alliss
6. Alan Bates
7. Arthur Hailey
8. Max Bygraves
9. Brian Moore
10. David Hamilton
11. Pete Murray
12. Eric Sykes
13. Lord Norman Tebbit
14. Lord Richard Attenborough
15. Sandy Gall
16. Frank Muir
17. Joe Ashton
18. Sir Alec Bedser
19. Ron Moody
20. Alan Sillitoe
21. Fred Emery
22. Cliff Michelmore
23. Johnny Ball
24. Bill Treacher
25. George Cole
26. Bob Holness
27. Rodney Bewes
28. Michael Nicholson
29. Barry Took
30. Richard Briers
31. Dickie Davies
32. Roy Hudd
33. Arnold Wesker
34. Bob Monkhouse

18 CELEBRITIES WHO WERE BEAUTY QUEENS

1. Shakira Caine (Miss Guyana)
2. Marla Maples (Miss Georgia Peach)
3. Leila Williams (Miss Great Britain)
4. Vicki Oyston (Miss Fleetwood)
5. Veronica Lake (Miss Florida)
6. Desiree Washington (Miss Rhode Island)
7. Kim Novak (Miss Deepfreeze)
8. Carolyn Seaward (Miss UK)
9. Anita Ekberg (Miss Sweden)
10. Pamella Bordes (Miss India)
11. Imelda Marcos (Miss Manila)
12. Jayne Mansfield (Miss Flash)
13. Lynda Carter (Miss America)
14. Meg Gallagher (Miss Holiday Guernsey)
15. Dorothy Lamour (Miss New Orleans)
16. Carol Smillie (Miss Parallel Bars)
17. Sylvie Kristel (Miss TV Europe)
18. Kim Basinger (Miss Junior Athens)

16 CELEBRITIES WHO'VE WORKED AS MODELS

1. Brooke Shields
2. Quentin Crisp
3. Jacqueline Bisset
4. Sylvia Kristel
5. Norman Scott
6. Gerald Ford
7. Ali MacGraw
8. Charlotte Rampling
9. George Lazenby
10. Ellen Burstyn
11. Richard Jobson
12. Jonah Barrington
13. Burt Reynolds
14. Jessica Lange
15. Dyan Cannon
16. Rene Russo

16 CELEBRITIES WHO WERE IN THE MERCHANT NAVY

1. Bob Mills
2. John Prescott
3. Bill Treacher
4. Dickie Davies
5. Peter Stringfellow
6. Gareth Hunt
7. Christopher Ellison
8. Rutger Hauer
9. Bob Hoskins
10. Daniel Farson
11. Jack Kerouac
12. Bernie Winters
13. Alan Weeks
14. Vivian Stanshall
15. Allen Ginsberg
16. Roger Scott

7 CELEBRITY BOYS WHO WERE DRESSED AS GIRLS FOR THE FIRST FEW YEARS OF THEIR LIVES

1. Oscar Wilde
2. Peter O'Toole
3. Ernest Hemingway
4. Thomas Wolfe
5. General Douglas MacArthur
6. Bill Tilden
7. Rainer Maria Rilke

14 CELEBRITIES WHO'VE TAKEN HEROIN

1. Shaun Ryder
2. Keith Richards
3. Eric Clapton
4. Marianne Faithfull
5. Will Self
6. Tatum O'Neal
7. Paula Yates
8. Courtney Love
9. Boy George
10. Pete Townshend
11. Patti D'Arbanville
12. Magenta De Vine
13. Fawn Hall
14. Robert Downey Jnr.

33 CELEBRITIES WHO HAD A COCAINE HABIT

1. Sir Elton John
2. Liam Gallagher
3. Noel Gallagher
4. David Bowie
5. Shadow (Jefferson King)
6. Paula Hamilton
7. Stephen Fry
8. Robin Williams
9. Mick Fleetwood
10. Sting
11. Jimmy Mulville
12. Drew Barrymore
13. Kim Basinger
14. Julian Lennon
15. Kirstie Alley
16. Belinda Carlisle
17. Patsy Palmer
18. Daniella Westbrook
19. Sid Owen
20. Jean-Claude Van Damme
21. Simon Gregson
22. Paul Merson
23. James Caan
24. Rick Parfitt
25. Sugar Ray Leonard
26. Bobby Brown
27. Diego Maradona
28. Michael Douglas
29. Dennis Hopper
30. Melanie Griffith
31. Dennis Quaid
32. Chevy Chase
33. Oliver McCall

12 CELEBRITIES WHO STARTED OUT AS SECRETARIES

1. Cilla Black
2. Anneka Rice
3. Caroline Aherne
4. Verity Lambert
5. Sophie Mirman
6. Jan Leeming
7. Su Pollard
8. The Duchess of York
9. Debbie Arnold
10. Mystic Meg
11. Ulrika Jonsson
12. Belinda Carlisle

10 CELEBRITIES WHO WASHED DISHES FOR A LIVING

1. Ronald Reagan
2. Jacques Chirac
3. Burt Reynolds
4. Roseanne
5. Beechy Colclough
6. Little Richard
7. Eddie 'The Eagle' Edwards
8. Roger Moore
9. Steve Collins (the boxer)
10. Chrissie Hynde

12 CELEBRITIES WHO APPEARED IN ADVERTISEMENTS WHEN THEY WERE KIDS

1. Patsy Kensit (Birds Eye Frozen Peas)
2. Simon Le Bon (Persil)
3. Michael Portillo (Ribena)
4. Jodie Foster (Coppertone)
5. Martyn Lewis (Cow & Gate Baby Food)
6. B.B. King (Pepticon Health Tonic)
7. Keith Chegwin (Marathon)
8. Emma Bunton - Baby Spice (Milky Bar)
9. Jonathan Ross (Rice Krispies)
10. Leslie Ash (Fairy Liquid)
11. Kate Winslet (Sugar Puffs)
12. Drew Barrymore (Gainsburgers)
13. Leonardo DiCaprio (Matchbox Cars)

2 CELEBRITIES WHO SMASHED UP THEIR OWN HOMES BECAUSE IT MADE THEM "FEEL GOOD"

1. Axl Rose

2. Sharon Stone

2 CELEBRITIES WHO WORKED AS LION-CAGE CLEANERS

1. Clive James

2. Sylvester Stallone

9 CELEBRITIES WHO WERE ARRESTED

1. Hugh Grant (for performing a 'lewd act' with Divine Brown in 1995 – he was fined and given two years' probation)

2. Brigitte Bardot (for castrating a donkey which was trying to mount her donkey – later she was not only discharged but was also awarded costs against the plaintiff)

3. Johnny Depp (for trashing a hotel suite in 1994 – he agreed to pay for the damage)

4. Billy Preston (Drink-driving and cocaine possession – given a suspended jail sentence and probation in 1992)

5. Johnny Cash (Many times in the early 1960s for being drunk and disorderly)

6. Jodie Foster (for possession of cocaine – given a year's probation in 1983)

7. Brian de Palma (for stealing a motorcycle and for resisting arrest – he was given a suspended sentence in 1963)

8. Carlos Santana (for marijuana possession – community service in 1991)

9. Paul Reubens (aka Pee-Wee Herman) (for 'indecent exposure' in a cinema – i.e. performing the five-finger shuffle during a porn film - he was fined and ordered to do community service)

27 CELEBRITIES WHO'VE BEEN INSIDE

1. James Brown (Carrying a gun and assault in 1988 – served two years; he had also served three years for theft when he was a teenager)

2. Ozzy Osbourne (Burglary – two months in 1966)

3. Don King (Manslaughter in 1966 – three years and 11 months)

4. Zsa Zsa Gabor (Slapping a cop – three days in 1989)

5. Kelsey Grammer (Drugs – two weeks in jail for not doing community service imposed for his offence in 1988)

6. George Best (Drunk driving – twelve weeks in 1984)

7. Sean Penn (Assault and violation of a probation order for an earlier assault – 32 days in 1987)

8. Chuck Berry (Violating the Mann Act – by taking a girl across State borders for 'immoral purposes' – two years in 1962; for income tax evasion – four months in 1979)

9. Ryan O'Neal (Brawling – served 51 days in 1960)

10. Lester Piggott (Income tax evasion – sentenced to three years but only served a year in 1987)

11. Stephen Fry (Stealing credit cards - spent three months in a young offender's institution in 1975)

12. Sir Paul McCartney (Drugs – 9 days in Japan in 1980)

13. Evel Knievel (Assault in 1977 – six months)

14. Christian Slater (Attacking policemen under the influence of cocaine – three months in 1997. In January 1998, Salter was sentenced again for three months for assaulting his girlfriend and a police officer and for being under the influence of cocaine).

15. Robert Downey Jnr (Drugs – sentenced to six months in 1997. In January 1998 [the day before Christian Slater was arrested]. Downey Junior was jailed again for six months for violating probation and slipping back into drug use.

16. Oliver Stone (Drugs – two weeks in 1969 whilst waiting to be tried for possession of marijuana)

16. Taki (Drugs – served three months in 1984-85)

18. Nick Nolte (Reckless driving – 30 nights in jail whilst at college – though he was released during the days to practise his football. More amazingly, he was given a 45-year suspended sentence for faking I.D. papers for underage drinkers in the 1960s)

19. Stacy Keach (Drugs – sentenced to six months in 1984)

20. Gregg Allman (Drink driving – served three days in 1986)

21. Jimmy Nail (GBH – six months in 1977)

22. Sophia Loren (Income tax evasion – 17 days in 1982)

23. Hugh Cornwell (Drugs – five weeks in 1980)

24. Wilson Pickett (Drink driving and causing injury – served a year in 1992)

25. Mark Morrison (Threatening a policeman – served three months in 1997)

26. David Crosby (Drugs and possession of an illegal weapon – sentenced to five years in 1983 but served about a year and a half)

27. Johnny Vaughan (Drugs - four years in 1988)

10 CELEBRITIES WHO WORKED IN THE CIRCUS

1. Harry Houdini (Escapologist)
2. Burt Lancaster (Acrobat)
3. Bob Hoskins (Fire-eater)
4. Rupert Graves (Clown)
5. Jack Higgins (Odd jobs)
6. Tom Major (Father of John; Trapeze artist)
7. W.C. Fields (Elephant attendant)
8. Jeremy Beadle (Ringmaster)
9. Cantinflas (Prizefighter)
10. Graham Cripsey (Snooker player; Rode the wall of death)

2 CELEBRITIES WHO HAD TWIN BROTHERS WHO DIED AT BIRTH

1. Elvis Presley
2. David Jason

10 CELEBRITIES WHO TRAINED AS ENGINEERS

1. John Birt
2. Rowan Atkinson
3. Yasser Arafat
4. Carol Vorderman
5. Clifford Longley
6. Kate Bellingham
7. Nicholas Parsons
8. Eric Porter
9. Naim Attallah
10. The Bachelors

37 CELEBRITIES BORN ON THE SAME DAY AS ANOTHER CELEBRITY DIED

1. Stephen Fry and Ronald Knox: 24.8.1957

2. Donnie Wahlberg and Mies van der Rohe: 17.8.1969

3. Davy Crockett and Frederick the Great: 17.8.1786

4. Richard Stilgoe and Sergei Rachmaninov 28.3.1943

5. Billie Jean King and Lorenz Hart: 22.11.1943

6. Laura Dern and Billy Rose: 10.2.1966

7. Donald Trump and John Logie Baird: 14.6.1946

8. Bryan Ferry and Béla Bartók: 26.9.1945

9. Georges Seurat and John Brown: 2.12.1859

10. Charles Wheeler and Sarah Bernhardt: 26.3.1923

11. Kevin Costner and George Morrow: 18.1.1955

12. Vic Reeves and Cecil B. De Mille: 21.1.1959

13. Rutger Hauer and Edvard Munch: 23.1.1944

14. Phil Collins and C.B. Cochran: 31.1.1951

15. Peter Willey and Leadbelly: 6.12.1949

16. Colin Jackson and Robert Oppenheimer: 18.2.1967

17. Lesley Collier and Angela Brazil: 13.3.1947

18. Janet Jackson and Randolph Turpin: 16.5.1966

19. Debra Winger and James Agee: 16.5.1955

20. Candice Bergen and Booth Tarkington: 19.5.1946

21. Jason Donovan and Helen Keller: 1.6.1968

22. Mark Goodier and Carl Jung: 6.6.1961

23. Donald Trelford and Ramsay MacDonald: 9.11.1937

24. Mike Tyson and Margery Allingham: 30.6.1966

25. Peter De Savary and Lucien Pissarro: 11.7.1944

26. Reece Dinsdale and Preston Sturges: 6.8.1959

27. Jim Dale and Will Rogers: 15.8.1935

28. Graham Chapman and Lord Baden-Powell: 8.1.1941

29. Bernard Levin and Viscount Haldane: 19.8.1928

30. Alan Mullery and P.C. Wren: 23.11.1941

31. Geoffrey Dickens and Frank Harris: 26.8.1931

32. Julio Iglesias and Elinor Glyn: 23.9.1943

33. Chris Cowdrey and Jack Buchanan: 20.10.1957

34. Daniel Ortega and Jerome Kern: 11.11.1945

35. Jack Simmons and Virginia Woolf: 28.3.1941

36. Keith Vaz MP and Tommy Dorsey: 26.11.1956

37. Yoko Ono and Gentleman Jim Corbett: 18.2.1933

11 CELEBRITIES WHO STARTED OUT WITH ANNA SCHER

1. Kathy Burke
2. Pauline Quirke
3. Linda Robson
4. Patsy Palmer
5. Susan Tully
6. Phil Daniels
7. Gillian Taylforth
8. Jesse Birdsall
9. Dexter Fletcher
10. Gary Kemp
11. Martin Kemp

12 CELEBRITIES WHO WERE LIBRARIANS

1. Mao Tse-Tung
2. Sir Ludovic Kennedy
3. Casanova
4. Laurie Taylor
5. Anthea Turner
6. Philip Larkin
7. August Strindberg
8. John Braine
9. David Hockney
10. J. Edgar Hoover
11. Pope Pius XI
12. Jane Gardam

10 CELEBRITIES WHO'VE LIVED ON A HOUSEBOAT

1. Frederick Forsyth
2. Nigel Planer
3. Imogen Stubbs
4. Lemmy
5. Richard Branson
6. Lord David Owen
7. Elizabeth Emanuel
8. David Suchet
9. Dr Conor Cruise O'Brien
10. Lawrence Dallaglio

11 CELEBRITIES WHO SANG IN STAGE MUSICALS

1. Bob Hoskins (*Guys And Dolls* 1982)
2. Ian Carmichael (*I Do! I Do!* 1968)
3. Kevin Kline (*Pirates of Penzance* 1981)
4. Diane Keaton (*Hair* 1967)
5. Alan Alda (*The Apple Tree* 1966)
6. Glenn Close (*Sunset Boulevard* 1995)
7. Anthony Perkins (*Greenwillow* 1960)
8. Jeremy Irons (*Godspell* 1972)
9. Anthony Quinn (*Zorba* 1983)
10. Sir John Mills (*Goodbye Mr Chips* 1982)
11. Tom Courtenay (*Andy Capp* 1982)

10 CELEBRITIES AND THEIR CELEBRITY BIOGRAPHERS IN THE DICTIONARY OF *NATIONAL BIOGRAPHY*

1. Dame Edith Evans (Bryan Forbes)
2. Sir Noel Coward (Michael Denison)
3. John Le Mesurier (Derek Nimmo)
4. Billy Fury (David Jacobs)
5. Dame Margaret Rutherford (Sir John Gielgud)
6. Sir Francis Chichester (Sir Edward Heath)
7. George Formby (Frank Muir)
8. W. Somerset Maugham (Frederic Raphael)
9. Kenneth Horne (Barry Took)
10. Anthony Crosland (Lord (Roy) Jenkins)

108 PAIRS OF CELEBRITIES WHO DIED ON PRECISELY THE SAME DAY OF THE SAME MONTH OF THE SAME YEAR

Not including pairs of people who died *together* – e.g. Adolf Hitler and Eva Braun, Buddy Holly & The Big Bopper or Bonnie Parker & Clyde Barrow)

1. Maria Callas (opera singer) and Marc Bolan (rock star) (16.9.1977)

2. Fred Perry (tennis player) and Donald Pleasence (actor) (2.2.95)

3. Ben Travers (playwright) and Alexei Kosygin (former Soviet premier) (18.12.80)

4. Alfred Marks (actor) and Margot Hemingway (model and actress) (1.7.96)

5. G.K. Chesterton (writer) and Maxim Gorky (writer) (14.6.36)

6. Ronnie Kray (gangster) and Arthur English (comic actor) (17.3.95)

7. Carl Bechstein (maker of the famous Bechstein pianos) and Gottlieb Daimler (motor car manufacturer) (6.3.1900)

8. Woody Guthrie (folk singer) and Sir Malcolm Sargent (orchestral conductor) (3.10.67)

9. Tommy Trinder (comedian) and Mel Blanc (the voice of cartoon characters such as Bugs Bunny) (10.7.89)

10. Mel Appleby (of Mel and Kim) and Bhagwan Shree Rajneesh (guru) (19.1.90)

11. Rudolf Nureyev (ballet dancer) and Dizzy Gillespie (jazz musician) (6.1.93)

12. Lord Silkin of Dulwich (politician) and Zia ul-Haq (President of Pakistan) (17.8.88)

13. Sam Spiegel (film producer) and Ricky Nelson (pop star) (31.12.85)

14. Sir P.G. Wodehouse (writer) and Sir Julian Huxley (scientist) (14.2.75)

15. Freddie Mercury (rock star) and Klaus Kinski (actor) (24.11.91)

16. Louis Braille (the deviser of the system of reading for the blind) and Fanny Wright (social reformer) (6.1.1852)

17. Muddy Waters (Blues musician) and George Balanchine (choreographer) (30.4.83)

18. George Adamson (*Born Free* conservationist) and Diana Vreeland (fashion guru) (21.8.89)

19. Gilbert Harding (broadcaster) and Clark Gable (film star) (16.11.60)

20. Charles Stewart Parnell (Irish leader) and William Henry Smith (the founder of W.H. Smith) (6.10.1891)

21. Mama Cass Elliot (singer) and Erich Kastner (writer of *Emil And The Detectives*) (29.7.74)

22. Marvin Gaye (rock star) and Rene Cutforth (broadcaster) (1.4.84)

23. Serge Gainsbourg (French singer and composer) and Edwin Land (inventor of the Polaroid camera) (3.3.91)

24. Bernie Winters (comedian) and Jerzy Kosinski (writer) (4.5.91)

25. Alberto Giacometti (painter) and Lal Shastri (Indian Prime Minister) (11.1.66)

26. Jim Laker (England cricketer) and Otto Preminger (film producer) (23.4.1986)

27. Ovid (Roman poet) and Livy (Roman historian) (AD 2.1.17)

28. Jaco Pastorius (Jazz and Rock musician) and Dan Rowan (co-presenter of *Rowan and Martin's Laugh-In*) (22.9.87)

29. Colin Milburn (England cricketer) and Greville Wynne (British businessman and alleged spy) (28.2.90)

30. Orson Welles (film director and actor) and Yul Brynner (actor) (10.10.85)

31. Cecil Day-Lewis (poet) and Dame Margaret Rutherford (actress) (22.5.72)

32. Billy Rose (Broadway producer) and Sophie Tucker (singer) (10.2.66)

33. Orville Wright (aviation pioneer) and Mahatma Gandhi (Indian leader) (30.1.1948)

34. Steve Marriott (rock star) and Don Siegel (film director) (20.4.91)

35. Carl Foreman (film producer) and George Gallup (pollster) (26.6.84)

36. Josef Stalin (Soviet dictator) and Sergei Prokofiev (composer who was persecuted by Stalin) (5.3.1953)

37. Ted Heath (bandleader) and Joseph Kennedy (former American ambassador to Britain and head of the Kennedy clan) (18.1169)

38. Princess Beatrice (Queen Victoria's youngest child) and William Temple (Archbishop of Canterbury) (26.10.44)

39. David Niven (actor and author) and Raymond Massey (actor) (29.7.1983)

40. Peter Tosh (musician) and Al Read (comedian) (11.9.87)

41. Sir Anthony Eden, the Earl of Avon (former British Prime Minister) and Peter Finch (actor) (14.1.1977)

42. Issac Bashevis Singer (Nobel Prize-winning writer) and Freddie Brown (England cricketer) (24.7.91)

43. Thelonius Monk (musician) and Lee Strasberg (actor and drama teacher) (17.2.82)

44. Robert Maxwell (businessman) and Fred MacMurray (actor) (5.11.91)

45. Greta Garbo (actress) and Lord Jock Bruce-Gardyne (politician and writer) (15.4.90)

46. Lord Bernard Miles (actor and producer) and Dame Peggy Ashcroft (actress) (14.6.91)

47. John Ruskin (social reformer, artist and writer) and Richard Doddridge Blackmore (writer – of Lorna Doone) (20.1.1900)

48. Randolph Scott (actor) and Joan Greenwood (actress) (2.3.87)

49. John Adams (second U.S. President) and Thomas Jefferson (third U.S. President) (4.7.1826 – U.S. Independence Day)

50. Jean Cocteau (playwright and film director) and Edith Piaf (singer) (11.10.63)

51. Ward Bond (actor) and Mack Sennett (Hollywood producer of silent comedies – The Keystone Kops etc.) (5.11.60)

52. Michael Curtiz (film director) and Stu Sutcliffe (former member of The Beatles) (10.4.62)

53. King Ibn Saud (of Saudi Arabia) and Dylan Thomas (poet) (9.11.1953)

54. Charles Kingsley (author of The Water Babies) and Gustave Doré (painter) (23.1.1883)

55. Geoff Love (bandleader) and James Franciscus (actor) (8.7.91)

56. Dr Hendrik Verwoerd (Prime Minister of South Africa) and Margaret Sanger (American birth control pioneer) (6.9.66)

57. Max Wall (actor and comedian) and Major Pat Reid (Colditz escaper and author) (22.5.90)

58. General Augusto Sandino (Nicaraguan rebel leader after whom the Sandinistas were named) and Sir Edward Elgar (classical composer) (23.2.34)

59. Sammy Davis Jnr. (entertainer) and Jim Henson (the man behind the Muppet Show) (16.5.90)

60. Che Guevara (revolutionary) and André Maurois (French author) (9.10.67)

61. William Powell (film star) and Tito Gobbi (opera singer) (5.3.84)

62. John Snagge (sports commentator) and Ed Muskie (former US Senator and Presidential contender) (26.3.96)

63. Marshal Henri Pétain (French soldier and leader of the wartime Vichy regime) and Robert Flaherty (film-maker and explorer) (23.7.51)

64. Franz Liszt (classical composer) and Frank Holl (painter) (31.7.1888)

65. Erle Stanley Gardner (writer and creator of Perry Mason) and Admiral Richard Byrd (American aviator and explorer) (11.3.57)

66. Dame Christabel Pankhurst (Suffragette) and Georges Roualt (painter) (13.2.58)

67. Ruby Keeler (actress) and Joyce Carey (actress) (28.2.93)

68. Lord Michael Havers (Lord Chancellor of Britain) and Konstantin Sergeyev (ballet dancer and choreographer) (20.4.92)

69. Joyce Grenfell (actress and writer) and Zeppo Marx (member of the Marx Brothers) (30.11.79)

70. Robert Chesebrough (American industrialist who invented Vaseline) and King Feisal (of Iraq) (8.9.33)

71. Dickie Henderson (entertainer) and Axel Springer (German publisher) (22.9.85)

72. Arthur Marshall (writer and broadcaster) and Sir Thomas Sopwith (aviation pioneer) (27.1.89)

73. Teddy Tinling (tennis dress designer) and Rocky Graziano (boxer) (23.5.90)

74. Mary Martin (actress and singer) and Sir David Stirling (founder of the SAS) (4.11.90)

75. Francis Bacon (painter) and Olivier Messiaen (composer) (28.4.92)

76. Graham Chapman (member of the Monty Pythons) and Norman Yardley (England cricketer) (4.10.89)

77. River Phoenix (actor) and Federico Fellini (film director) (31.10.93)

78. Ray Lindwall (Australian cricketer) and Andreas Papandreou (Greek Prime Minister) (23.6.96)

79. Gene Roddenberry (creator of *Star Trek*) and Bill Graham (rock concert impresario) (25.10.91)

80. Mary Astor (actress) and Emlyn Williams (actor and playwright) (25.9.87)

81. Bobby Locke (four-time Open-winning golfer) and Ken Colyer (Jazz musician) (11.3.88)

82. Earl Spencer (Princess Diana's father) and Paul Henreid (actor) (29.3.92)

83. Bob Todd (Benny Hill's comic sidekick) and Jim Garrison (the New Orleans DA who 'uncovered' the conspiracy behind President Kennedy's assassination and was portrayed by Kevin Costner in *JFK*) (21.10.92)

84. Wilkie Collins (novelist) and Eliza Cook (poet) (23.9.1889)

85. Sugar Ray Robinson (boxer) and Abbie Hoffman (American activist and writer) (12.4.89)

86. Arthur Ashe (tennis player) and Lord Sidney Bernstein (businessman and TV mogul) (5.2.93)

87. Bob Crosby (American dance bandleader) and C. Northcote Parkinson (political scientist the inventor of the 'law' – that work expands to fill the time available for its completion – which bears his name) (9.3.93)

88. Mike Hailwood (motor racing driver) and Field Marshal Sir Claude John Auchinleck (soldier) (23.3.81)

89. Basil Rathbone (actor) and Albert Luthuli (President of the African National Congress) (21.7.67)

90. Steve Biko (anti-apartheid activist) and Robert Lowell (American poet) (12.9.77)

91. Simon Cadell (actor) and Lord Douglas Jay (politician) (6.3.96)

92. John F. Kennedy (U.S. President) and Aldous Huxley (writer) (22.11.63)

93. Alan Jay Lerner (lyricist) and Jorge Luis Borges (writer) (14.6.86)

94. Earl Stanley Baldwin (former British Prime Minister) and Will Fyffe (comedian) (14.12.47)

95. Zoltan Kodály (Hungarian composer) and Nelson Eddy (singer and film star) (6.3.67)

96. Alfred, Duke of Edinburgh (son of Queen Victoria) and King Umberto I (of Italy) (30.7.1900)

97. Bill Naughton (writer and creator of *Alfie*) and William Rees-Davies (MP) (8.1.92)

98. Ayatollah Khomeini (Iranian leader) and Cecil Collins (painter) (4.6.89)

99. James Hunt (motor racing driver) and John Connally (Former Texas Governor and U.S. Presidential candidate who was riding in the same car as President Kennedy when he was shot) (15.6.93)

100. Dame Gracie Fields (singer) and Jimmy McCullough (guitarist with Wings) (27.9.79)

101. Wallis Simpson (Duchess of Windsor) and Bill Edrich (England cricketer) (24.4.86)

102. Stella Adler (drama teacher) and Albert King (Blues singer) (21.12.92)

103. Kwame Nkrumah (President of Ghana) and Phil King (musician with Blue Oyster Cult) (27.4.72)

104. Les Dawson (comedian) and Arleen Auger (Opera singer) (10.6.93)

105. Lord Nicholas Ridley (politician) and Art Hodes (Jazz musician) (4.3.93)

106. Frank Capra (film director) and Peggy Ramsey (theatrical agent – played by Vanessa Redgrave in *Prick Up Your Ears*) (4.9.91)

107. H.R. Haldeman (President Nixon's Chief of Staff and Watergate co-conspirator) and Jill Tweedie (writer and journalist) (12.11.93)

108. Sonny Bono (Musician) and David Bairstow (5.1.98)

Index

Armatrading, Joan, 61, 72, 122, 163, 165, 167, 179
Armfield, Jimmy, 35, 125
Armstrong, Fiona, 171
Armstrong, Neil, 174
Armstrong, Louis, 180
Armstrong, Pamela, 72
Arnold, Debbie, 184
Arnold, Matthew, 9
Arnold, Tom, 45
Arquette, Rosanna, 72, 135
Arthur, Bea, 48
Ash, Leslie, 13, 134, 184
Ashcroft, Peggy, 116, 192
Ashdown, Paddy, 8, 107, 161, 162, 163, 165, 169
Ashe, Arthur, 193
Asher, Jane, 42, 54, 92, 163
Ashford, Nick, 129
Ashley, Jack, 33, 64, 79
Ashton, Joe, 181
Asimov, Isaac, 28
Asner, Ed, 22, 150, 153
Aspel, Michael, 36, 57, 76, 109, 113, 162, 170, 179
Asquith, Herbert, 11
Astaire, Fred, 128, 150, 179
Astley, Rick, 37
Astor, Mary, 193
Astor, Nancy, 11
Atherton, Michael, 35, 57, 90, 95, 117
Atkins, Eileen, 84
Atkinson, Rowan, 33, 37, 55, 58, 61, 163, 165, 177, 187
Attallah, Naim, 124, 152, 158, 166, 187
Attenborough, David, 13, 34, 36, 58, 107, 113, 117, 174
Attenborough, Richard, 33, 38, 81, 117, 121, 135, 150, 174, 181
Auchinleck, Claude John, 194
Auden, W.H., 24
Auermann, Nadja, 44
Auger, Arleen, 194
Austen, Jane, 29, 82, 180

Ayckbourn, Alan, 35
Aykroyd, Dan, 148
Ayres, Lew, 41
Ayres, Pam, 54, 76, 141
Azinger, Paul, 80
Aznavour, Charles, 52

Bacall, Lauren, 26, 114, 148
Bacchus, Faoud, 61
Bacharach, Burt, 12, 20
Bachelors, The, 187
Bacon, Francis, 193
Bacon, Kevin, 139
Baddiel, David, 30, 32, 59, 73, 84, 97
Baden-Powell, Lord, 108, 188
Bader, Douglas, 28
Baez, Joan, 13, 45, 85
Baggio, Roberto, 13
Bailey, David, 21, 37, 59, 65, 137, 168
Bailey, Laura, 152
Bailey, Pearl, 12
Bainbridge, Beryl, 23, 60, 168, 169
Baird, John Logie, 108, 188
Bairstow, David, 194
Baker, Cheryl, 27, 43, 52, 97, 171
Baker, Colin, 136
Baker, Danny, 97
Baker, Janet, 15, 34, 113
Baker, Joe Don, 63
Baker, Josephine, 12
Baker, Kenneth, 36
Baker, Richard, 34, 35, 105, 106, 174
Baker, Tom, 66
Bakewell, Joan, 39
Balanchine, George, 191
Balding, Ian, 91, 92, 95
Baldwin, Alec, 49, 114, 139, 177
Baldwin, James, 7, 125
Baldwin, Peter, 79
Baldwin, Stanley, 194
Baldwin, William, 87, 177
Ball, Alan, 13
Ball, Zoë, 24, 40, 44, 71, 84, 97

Ball, Bobby, 127
Ball, Johnny, 24, 34, 167, 175, 181
Ball, Michael, 48
Ball, Nicholas, 136
Ballesteros, Manuel, 27
Ballesteros, Severiano, 27, 57, 137
Balsam, Martin, 105
Banana, Canaan, 160
Bancroft, Anne, 52, 118, 139, 171
Bandaranaike, Solomon, 61
Banderas, Antonio, 172
Bankhead, Tallulah, 140, 150, 155
Banks, Iain, 164
Banks, Lynne Reid, 38
Banks, Morwenna, 32
Banks, Tony, 72, 98
Bannister, Roger, 34
Barber, Glynis, 140
Barclay, David, 119
Barclay, Frederick, 119
Bardot, Brigitte, 53, 66, 114, 117, 150, 155, 185
Barere, Simon, 176
Barker, Clive, 151
Barker, Pat, 7
Barker, Ronnie, 46, 79, 137
Barker, Sue, 40, 81
Barkin, Ellen, 114, 172
Barkworth, Peter, 123, 161, 174
Barlow, Gary, 59, 106, 158
Barlow, Patrick, 117
Barlow, Thelma, 141
Barnardo, Dr, 23
Barnes, Brian, 66
Barnes, Carol, 15, 43, 57, 90, 92, 169
Barnes, John, 43, 122, 137, 138
Barnes, Stewart, 96
Barraclough, Roy, 141, 171, 178
Barrie, Chris, 167
Barrie, J.M., 28, 125, 150
Barrington, Jonah, 182
Barron, Brian, 166
Barron, Keith, 143, 150
Barrow, Clyde, 129

Barrowman, John, 69

Barry, Michael, 76

Barrymore, Drew, 45, 58, 66, 80, 149, 183, 184

Barrymore, Lionel, 179

Barrymore, Michael, 47, 52, 55, 59, 67, 98, 142, 156, 167, 175

Bartók, Béla, 188

Basinger, Kim, 57, 71, 72, 138, 181, 183

Bassey, Shirley, 37, 86, 122, 131

Bastedo, Alexandra, 78, 168

Bates, Alan, 13, 27, 93, 181

Bates, Jeremy, 82

Bates, Kathy, 51, 178

Bates, Ken, 65

Batiste, Spencer, 31

Batty, David, 27

Baudouin, King of Belgium, 107

Baugh, Laura, 77

Baxter, Anne, 140

Baxter, Raymond, 104

Bayfield, Martin, 156

Beacham, Stephanie, 40, 83, 126

Beadle, Jeremy, 37, 56, 123, 187

Bean, Sean, 34, 45, 97

Beardsley, Peter, 84

Beatrice, Princess, 171, 192

Beatty, Ned, 148

Beatty, Warren, 50, 54, 88, 95, 114, 140, 148, 179

Beaulieu, Lord Montagu of, 124

Beaumont, Bill, 122, 141

Beavis, 131

Bechstein, Carl, 191

Beck, Jeff, 72

Beck, 179

Becker, Boris, 120

Beckett, Samuel, 84

Beckett, Wendy, 24

Beckwith, Tamara, 144

Bedawi, Zeinab, 177

Bedelia, Bonnie, 25

Bedser, Alec, 181

Beer, Alice, 174

Beethoven, Ludwig Van, 181

Begley, Ed, 55

Behr, Dani, 57, 134

Beith, Alan, 125

Belafonte, Harry, 155

Bell, Andy, 96

Bell, Derek, 96

Bell, Martin, 30, 36

Bell, Mary Hayley, 54

Bell, Tom, 50, 147

Bellamy, David, 12, 13, 110, 113, 125, 163, 174

Bellingham, Guy, 144

Bellingham, Kate, 187

Bellingham, Lynda, 141

Bellman, Gina, 171

Belushi, James, 159

Benatar, Pat, 53, 146

Benchley, Peter, 145

Bening, Annette, 114

Benn, Nigel, 27, 79, 85, 98

Benn, Tony, 65, 72, 99, 163, 165, 174

Benneton, Luciano, 119

Bennett, Alan, 22, 36, 118

Bennett, Hywel, 29, 143, 148

Bennett, Jill, 9

Bennett, Richard Rodney, 164

Bennett, Tony, 104, 146

Bentine, Michael, 101

Bentley, Derek, 70

Berenger, Tom, 139

Beresford, Bruce, 92

Bergen, Candice, 72, 188

Bergkamp, Dennis, 60, 85

Bergman, Ingrid, 54, 133, 173, 179

Berkoff, Steven, 158

Berlin, Irving, 116, 180

Bermant, Chaim, 28

Bernard, Jeffrey, 35, 123

Bernhard, Sandra, 24

Bernhardt, Sarah, 144, 188

Bernsen, Corbin, 27

Bernstein, Sidney, 193

Berry, Chuck, 106, 144, 186

Berry, Nick, 98, 131, 177

Best, George, 16, 56, 186

Beverley Sisters, The, 109, 141

Bewes, Rodney, 73, 143, 170, 181

Bhutto, Benahzir, 25, 72, 78, 84

Biddlecombe, Terry, 66

Biggins, Christopher, 47

Biggs, Ronnie, 56, 76, 146

Biko, Steve, 194

Bilk, Acker, 56, 168

Binchy, Maeve, 82, 160

Bird, John, 32

Birdsall, Jesse, 189

Birkin, Jane, 16

Birt, John, 124, 187

Bisset, Jacqueline, 15, 24, 109, 149, 155, 172, 182

Björk, 45, 63, 114, 174

Black, Cilla, 8, 42, 47, 53, 56, 69, 74, 109, 122, 137, 163, 184

Black, Conrad, 124

Black, Don, 91

Black, Karen, 16

Black, Roger, 24, 41, 44, 76

Blackburn, Tony, 13, 24, 36, 70

Blackman, Honor, 12, 67, 73, 86, 114, 132, 141, 143

Blackmore, Richard Doddridge, 192

Blackstone, Baroness, 165

Blackstone, Tessa, 164

Blair, Cherie Booth, 40, 144

Blair, Isla, 80, 81

Blair, Lionel, 162, 164

Blair, Tony, 19, 34, 107, 134, 165

Blake, Eubie, 116

Blake, Peter, 164

Blakey, Art, 122

Blanc, Mel, 191

Blanc, Raymond, 80, 82

Blanchflower, Danny, 67

Blank, Justin de, 169

Blashford-Snell, John, 169

Blatt, Melanie, 45

Blatty, William Peter, 151

Bleasdale, Alan, 19, 70, 79

Bleeth, Yasmin, 71

Blessed, Brian, 48, 67, 168

Blethyn, Brenda, 10

Blom-Cooper, Louis, 27

Bloom, Claire, 26

Blue, Lionel, 165, 168

Blundell, Mark, 90

Blunkett, David, 125

Blyth, Chay, 92, 93, 119, 160

Boardman, Andrea, 24

Boardman, Stan, 24, 122

Boateng, Paul, 14, 33, 55

Body, Richard, 127

Bogarde, Dirk, 38, 82, 99, 144, 148, 155, 164, 165

Bogart, Humphrey, 24, 180

Bogdanov, Michael, 31, 169

Boht, Jean, 43, 48

Bolan, Marc, 180, 191

Bolt, Robert, 116, 123

Bolton, Michael, 58, 72, 138

Bon Jovi, John, 22

Bonallack, Michael, 9

Bond, Alan, 13

Bond, Michael, 20, 158, 169

Bond, Ward, 192

Bonham Carter, Helena, 11, 14, 36, 46

Bonington, Chris, 92

Bono, 53, 63

Bono, Edward de, 38

Bono, Sonny, 129, 146, 194

Boo, Betty, 110

Boone, Pat, 127

Boorman, John, 13

Booth, Anthony, 66

Booth, Hartley, 125

Booth, Pat, 12

Boothroyd, Betty, 20, 33, 34

Bordes, Pamela, 72, 181

Borg, Bjon, 43, 50, 69, 119, 120

Borge, Victor, 53

Borges, Jorge Luis, 194

Born, Max, 18

Borotra, Jean, 104

Botham, Ian, 16, 96, 120, 122, 163, 170, 173, 177

Botham, Liam, 154

Bottomley, Virginia, 13, 34, 57, 61

Bough, Frank, 91, 174

Boulaye, Patti, 142

Boulter, John, 112

Boulting, Roy, 27

Bouquet, Carole, 40

Bowen, Jim, 46, 56, 141, 175

Bowie, Angie, 66, 135

Bowie, David, 38, 42, 51, 53, 56, 84, 85, 114, 126, 128, 138, 168, 183

Bowles, Peter, 21, 42, 117, 141

Boyce, Keith, 173

Boyce, Max, 141

Boycott, Geoffrey, 15, 54, 74, 96, 130, 137

Boycott, Rosie, 93

Boyd, Jenny, 135

Boyd, Patti, 135

Boyd, William, 33

Boyle, Katie, 168

Boyson, Rhodes, 46, 117

Bracken, Kyran, 80

Bradbury, Ray, 168

Bradford, Barbara Taylor, 19, 63

Bradlee, Ben, 145

Bradley, Bill, 38

Bradley, Graham, 91

Bradley, Paul, 24

Brady, Karren, 40

Bragg, Billy, 121

Bragg, Melvyn, 19, 21, 56, 97, 117, 121, 134, 147

Braille, Louis, 191

Braine, John, 123, 189

Brake, Patricia, 16

Brambell, Wilfred, 179

Branagh, Kenneth, 59, 118

Brand Jnr, Gordon, 55, 157

Brand, Jo, 97, 121

Brandauer, Klaus Maria, 63

Brando, Marlon, 12, 13, 50, 61, 106, 111, 119, 128, 148, 151

Brandon, Michael, 92, 93

Brandreth, Gyles, 35, 171

Branson, Richard, 35, 92, 98, 119, 141, 142, 164, 174, 190

Brayfield, Celia, 35, 159

Brazil, Angela, 188

Brazzi, Rossano, 103, 151

Bream, Juilan, 160, 161

Brearley, Mike, 35

Brecht, Bertholt, 157

Brendel, Alfred, 111

Brett, Jeremy, 67, 71, 115

Bricusse, Leslie, 32

Briers, Lucy, 24

Briers, Richard, 24, 85, 143, 161, 171, 181

Briggs, Johnny, 97, 178

Briggs, Raymond, 35, 117, 126

Brightman, Sarah, 35, 122, 141

Brinkley, Christie, 72, 112, 135, 146, 178

Brittain, Vera, 23

Britton, Fern, 27

Brittan, Leon, 27, 89

Brittan, Samuel, 27, 35

Britton, Tony, 28, 122, 161, 170

Broad, Chris, 83

Broadhurst, Paul, 27

Brocklehurst, Henry, 28

Broderick, Matthew, 43

Brolin, James, 132, 140

Bron, Eleanor, 32, 36, 113, 143

Bronson, Charles, 12, 53, 150, 171

Brontë, Charlotte, 116, 150, 180

Brontë, Emily, 180

Brooke-Taylor, Tim, 32, 57, 92, 97, 125, 170

Brooke, Rupert, 49

Brookes, Bruno, 13

Brooking, Trevor, 90, 174

Brookner, Anita, 20

Brooks, Elkie, 53, 72, 115

Brooks, Mel, 52, 118

Brooks, Ray, 7

Broome, David, 130, 141
Brophy, Brigid, 72, 116
Brosnan, Pierce, 57, 107, 114, 178
Broudie, Ian, 70
Brown, Bobby, 77, 183
Brown, Gordon, 90
Brown, Faith, 14, 72, 141, 143, 171
Brown, Freddie, 192
Brown, Gordon, 29, 30, 49, 62
Brown, James, 186
Brown, Janet, 46
Brown, Jim, 88
Brown, Joe, 93
Brown, John, 188
Brown, June, 8, 167
Brown, Melanie "Scary Spice", 50, 59, 142
Brown, Roy, 57, 98
Bruce-Gardyne, Jock, 192
Bruce, Steve, 9
Bruce, Rory Knight, 40
Bruce, Lenny, 120, 128, 146, 175
Brummell, Beau, 152
Brundle, Martin, 90
Bruni, Carla, 41
Bruno, Frank, 40, 125, 137, 156, 162
Brunson, Michael, 161
Bryan, Dora, 12, 67, 101
Bryant, David, 115
Brynner, Yul, 140, 147, 192
Buchanan, Jack, 188
Buchwald, Art, 167
Buckman, Rob, 32
Budd, Zola, 14
Buerk, Michael, 27, 36, 74
Bugner, Joe, 167
Bujold, Genevieve, 16, 40
Bullimore, Tony, 44, 86
Bullock, Sandra, 39, 110, 114
Bunton, Emma "Baby Spice", 22, 59, 184
Burchill, Julie, 20, 124, 176
Burgh, Chris de, 35, 46, 53, 124
Burke, Kathy, 21, 40, 136, 189

Burnel, Jean Jacques, 89
Burnet, Alastair, 15, 36, 97
Burns, George, 12, 116, 180
Burns, Gordon, 95
Burrows, Malandra, 58, 131, 142, 171
Burstyn, Ellen, 139, 182
Burton, Amanda, 78
Burton, Richard, 106, 118, 151, 180
Busby, Matt, 112, 146
Bush, George, 105, 107, 111
Bush, Kate, 15, 24, 57, 155
Bushell, Gary, 167
Bussell, Darcey, 107
Butcher, Terry, 155
Butler-Sloss, Elizabeth, 25
Butler, Robin, 40
Butlin, Billy, 133
Butt-Head, 131
Byatt, A.S., 54, 127
Bygraves, Max, 168, 181
Byrd, Richard, 193
Byrne, Gabriel, 114, 178
Byron, Lord, 65, 70
Bywater, Michael, 41, 119

Caan, James, 26, 135, 149, 151, 178, 183
Caballe, Montserrat, 66, 81
Cadbury, Adrian, 91
Cadbury, Joel, 28, 90, 127, 160
Cadell, Simon, 194
Cadenet, Amanda de, 95, 144
Caesar, Julius, 12, 70, 76, 180
Cage, Nicolas, 53, 149
Cagney, James, 12, 179, 180
Caine, Marti, 142
Caine, Michael, 13, 36, 42, 48, 52, 56, 58, 60, 77, 109, 129, 161, 166
Caine, Shakira, 145, 181
Callaghan, James, 62, 117, 129
Callard, Beverley, 73, 94
Callas, Maria, 146, 191
Callil, Carmen, 124
Callow, Simon, 20

Campbell-Savours, Dale, 31
Campbell, Alastair, 65, 67
Campbell, Glen, 13, 17, 18, 45
Campbell, Naomi, 7, 107, 152
Campbell, Nicky, 35, 59, 125, 126
Campbell, Robin, 16
Campbell, Sol, 65
Candy, John, 151, 179
Cannon, Dyan, 26, 133, 182
Cannon, Tommy, 15, 98, 127
Cantinflas, 187
Cantona, Eric, 44, 46, 73, 107, 114, 127, 137, 168
Capes, Geoff, 172
Capote, Truman, 146
Capra, Frank, 194
Capriati, Jennifer, 74
Caprice, 39, 47, 63
Capshaw, Kate, 12
Captain Sensible, 53
Capucine, 63
Cardinale, Claudia, 10
Carey, George, 37, 107
Carey, Joyce, 193
Cargill, Patrick, 102
Carling, Will, 58, 107, 117, 137, 152, 168
Carlisle, Belinda, 15, 58, 72, 152, 155, 183, 184
Carlos, Juan, King of Spain, 83
Carluccio, Antonio, 76
Carlyle, Robert, 22
Carmichael, Ian, 89, 103, 161, 190
Carolgees, Bob, 13, 161
Caron, Leslie, 41, 67, 144, 158
Carpenter, Harry, 141, 162, 163
Carpenter, Sue, 36, 93
Carrey, Jim, 85, 114
Carrier, Robert, 141
Carrington, Lord, 101, 108
Carroll, Dina, 85
Carroll, Lewis, 10, 128
Carrott, Jasper, 24, 96, 97, 109
Carson, Willie, 109, 160
Carter, Helena Bonham, 148

Carter, Jimmy, 78, 117, 145

Carter, Lynda, 140, 181

Carteret, Anna, 121, 170

Cartland, Barbara, 11, 55, 77, 132, 141, 164, 173

Caruso, Enrico, 67

Casals, Pablo, 180

Casanova, 133, 189

Cash, Bill, 173

Cash, Johnny, 77, 139, 146, 185

Cash, Pat, 27, 137

Cashman, Michael, 121

Cass, Mama, 134, 146

Cassidy, David, 23

Casson, Hugh, 113

Castle, Barbara, 34, 99, 117

Castro, Fidel, 7, 62, 115

Catt, Mike, 90

Cauthen, Steve, 132

Cecil, Henry, 173

Cervantes, Miguel de, 44

Chalker, Lynda, 39

Chalmers, Craig, 91

Chalmers, Judith, 35

Chamberlain, Mark, 16

Chamberlain, Richard, 132, 133, 150

Champion, Bob, 80, 141

Chandler, Jeff, 104

Chandler, Raymond, 36

Chanel, Coco, 7

Chaney Jnr, Lon, 55, 133

Channing, Carol, 123

Channing, Stockard, 16

Chaplin, Charlie, 44, 110, 180

Chaplin, Geraldine, 15

Chapman, Graham, 12, 32, 188, 193

Charisse, Cyd, 26

Charlene, 63

Charles, Craig, 136

Charles, Prince, 33, 40, 44, 61, 92, 93, 110, 117, 118, 119, 145, 168

Charlton, Suzanne, 24, 75

Charlton, Bobby, 24, 25, 27, 43, 112, 141

Charlton, Jack, 27, 34, 117, 137

Charteris, Leslie, 64

Chase, Chevy, 52, 54, 77, 87, 132, 134, 183

Checker, Chubby, 36

Chegwin, Keith, 22, 33, 54, 66, 93, 134, 170, 184

Cher, 45, 47, 48, 51, 63, 71, 84, 85, 94, 95, 120, 129, 131, 179

Cherry, Neneh, 138

Chesebrough, Robert, 193

Cheshire, Leonard, 75

Chesterton, G.K., 191

Chevalier, Maurice, 150

Chichester, Francis, 190

Child, Jeremy, 161

Chirac, Jacques, 16, 19, 107, 174, 184

Chisolme, Melanie "Sporty Spice", 45, 97

Christie, Agatha, 150, 180

Christie, Julie, 48, 72, 114

Christie, Linford, 77, 107

Christian, Fletcher, 11

Christian, Terry, 57, 98

Churchill, Caryl, 113

Churchill, Winston, 70

Cierach, Lindka, 166

Clair, Rene, 157

Clancy, Tom, 153

Clapton, Eric, 7, 18, 44, 52, 57, 66, 109, 128, 132, 133, 163, 166, 183

Clark, Alan, 159, 167

Clark, Kenneth, 133

Clark, Petula, 115

Clarke, Arthur C., 30, 160, 181

Clarke, John Cooper, 63

Clarke, Kenneth, 36, 98, 107, 159

Clarke, Margi, 72

Clarke, Vince, 15, 96

Clarkson, Jeremy, 36

Clary, Julian, 29, 35, 43, 61, 176

Claudius, Emperor, 65

Clavell, James, 151

Clayton, Lisa, 117

Cleese, John, 21, 32, 34, 36, 53, 55, 83, 125, 137, 143

Clerk, F.W.de, 107

Clifford, Max, 70, 80

Clinton, Bill, 33, 38, 73, 83, 90, 107, 111, 117, 152, 154, 171, 174

Clinton, Chelsea, 60, 80

Clinton, Hillary, 24, 58, 74

Clooney, George, 114, 142

Close, Glenn, 24, 51, 61, 114, 139, 190

Clough, Brian, 117, 121, 174

Clough, Nigel, 174

Clunes, Martin, 59, 153

Cobb, Ty, 145

Coburn, James, 69

Cochran, C.B., 188

Cochran, Eddie, 130

Cocker, Jarvis, 97

Cocker, Joe, 16, 178

Cocteau, Jean, 192

Cody, Buffalo Bill, 145

Coe, Sebastian, 56, 97, 137

Cohen, George, 80

Cohen, Leonard, 114

Colclough, Beechy, 184

Cochran, C.B., 188

Cole, George, 21, 22, 103, 114, 115, 137, 159, 164, 181

Cole, John, 98

Cole, Lloyd, 137

Cole, Stephanie, 71, 84, 115

Coleman, David, 27, 81, 88

Coleridge, Nicholas, 76

Collier, Lesley, 188

Collins, Cecil, 194

Collins, Jackie, 69, 145

Collins, Joan, 26, 49, 55, 84, 94, 106, 122, 127, 131, 137, 144, 158, 163

Collins, Lewis, 174

Collins, Michelle, 121, 134

Collins, Pauline, 15, 17, 143, 164

Collins, Phil, 43, 49, 115, 156, 188

Collins, Steve, 184

Collins, Wilkie, 193

Collymore, Stan, 44

Coltrane, Robbie, 57, 92, 117, 121, 137, 167, 168
Colyer, Ken, 193
Coman, Gilly, 142
Como, Perry, 18
Compton-Burnett, Ivy, 116
Condon, Paul, 30, 93
Conley, Brian, 45, 58
Conley, Rosemary, 78, 94, 127
Connally, John, 194
Connery, Jason, 24, 143
Connery, Sean, 22, 24, 45, 57, 84, 96, 97, 117, 135, 138, 149
Connick, Harry, 55
Connolly, Billy, 17, 50, 72, 98, 124, 126, 159, 163, 173
Connors, Jimmy, 43, 120
Connors, Chuck, 179
Conrad, Joseph, 76
Conran, Shirley, 35
Conran, Terence, 15, 55, 163, 165
Constantine, Learie, 125
Conti, Tom, 8, 142
Conway, Tom, 54
Coogan, Steve, 112
Cook, Eliza, 193
Cook, Peter, 32
Cook, Robin, 19, 58, 126
Cook, Roger, 73, 80, 154
Cook, Sue, 48
Cooke, Alistair, 62, 125
Cookson, Catherine, 7, 18, 67
Cool, Phil, 72
Coolidge, Rita, 129
Coombs, Pat, 80
Cooper, Alice, 29, 53, 106
Cooper, Henry, 43, 96, 122, 137, 141, 157
Cooper, Jilly, 69, 160
Cooper, Tommy, 176
Cope, Kenneth, 142
Copeland, Stewart, 21, 35
Copperfield, David, 20, 53, 107, 133, 146
Coppola, Francis, 13, 54, 119

Copsey, Tony, 45
Coral, Joem 74
Corbett, Gentleman Jim, 188
Corbett, Ronnie, 96, 122, 156
Corbin, Jane, 161, 169
Coren, Alan, 15, 93, 125, 160
Cornwell, Charlotte, 67, 72
Cornwell, Hugh, 186
Cornwell, Judy, 136
Cosby, Bill, 87
Costello, Elvis, 15, 52, 58, 98, 106, 124, 166, 178
Costner, Kevin, 114, 138, 188, 193
Cotten, Joseph, 179
Cottle, Gerry, 93
Cotton, Bill, 55
Cotton, Fran, 76
Coulthard, David, 80
Courcey, Roger de, 98
Court, Robert Holmes à, 120
Courtenay, Tom, 147, 190
Covington, Julie, 32
Coward, Noel, 28, 190
Cowdrey, Chris, 27, 28, 161, 188
Cowdrey, Colin, 9, 35, 44
Cox, Courtney, 114
Cox, Mark, 16, 36
Crabbe, Buster, 94
Craddock, Johnny, 64
Craig, Wendy, 8, 161, 164
Cram, Steve, 74, 81, 90, 91, 98, 121, 137
Craven, Gemma, 14, 20, 141
Craven, John, 36, 48, 174
Crawford, Cindy, 58, 60, 69, 94, 114, 126
Crawford, Joan, 12
Crawford, Michael, 43, 52, 81, 109
Crawley, John, 35
Cray, Robert, 134
Crenshaw, Ben, 177
Cribbins, Bernard, 141
Crichton, Michael, 151, 156
Cricket, Jimmy, 97, 141
Cripsey, Graham, 187

Crisp, Quentin, 135, 145, 182
Critchley, Bruce, 160
Critchley, Julian, 31, 74
Crockett, Davy, 188
Croft, David, 101
Croft, Annabel, 41, 92, 95, 158
Crosbie, Annette, 20
Crosby, Bing, 131, 180
Crosby, Bob, 193
Crosby, David, 186
Crosland, Anthony, 190
Crow, Sheryl, 61
Crowe, Sarah, 72
Crowther, Leslie, 36
Cruise, Tom, 39, 43, 58, 88, 95, 110, 114, 122, 149
Cruyff, Jordi, 62
Cryer, Barry, 36
Crystal, Billy, 39, 61, 88, 133
Cuellar, Perez de, 111
Cukor, George, 28
Culkin, Macaulay, 7, 25, 61
Culp, Robert, 15
Cumani, Luca, 41
Cunningham, Jack, 161
Currie, Edwina, 21, 35, 44, 47, 73, 145
Curtis, Jamie Lee, 16, 114, 155
Curtis, Tony, 17, 53, 77, 101, 128, 149
Curtiz, Michael, 192
Cusack, Niamh, 80
Cusack, Sinead, 121
Cushing, Peter, 140, 155, 179
Cutforth, Rene, 191

D'Abo, Jennifer, 37
D'Abo, Mike, 13
D'Angelo, Beverly, 139
D'Arbanville, Patti, 135, 183
D'Errico, Donna, 40, 86
D'Oliviera, Basil, 15
Dafoe, Willem, 24, 114, 139, 149, 178
Dahl, Roald, 118, 147

Dahl, Sophie, 23, 74

Dahl, Tessa, 23, 66, 144

Daimler, Gottlieb, 191

Dalai Lama, The, 85, 107

Dale, Jim, 188

Dalglish, Kenny, 96, 117

Dali, Salvador, 151

Dallaglio, Lawrence, 55, 190

Daltrey, Roger, 13, 98, 106, 109, 179

Daly, John, 66, 77, 84, 85, 114

Daly, Tyne, 51

Dana, 53, 63

Dance, Charles, 15, 108, 163, 165, 179

Dando, Jill, 69, 74, 80, 115, 152

Dando, Suzanne, 15, 87, 122, 167

Dangerfield, Rodney, 139

Daniels, Debbie, 154

Daniels, Paul, 8, 22, 90, 125, 154

Daniels, Phil, 189

Dankworth, Johnny, 72

Danson, Ted, 12, 49, 72, 114, 139, 159

Darrow, Clarence, 145

Davenport, Nigel, 62, 161

Davidson, Jaye, 50

Davidson, Jim, 66, 122, 142, 157, 162, 168, 178

Davies, Barry, 93

Davies, Denzil, 30

Davies, Dickie, 27, 74, 79, 82, 93, 113, 129, 181, 182

Davies, Gary, 36

Davies, Jonathan, 96

Davies, Kimberley, 71

Davies, Laura, 153

Davies, Mervyn, 28

Davies, Rudi, 23

Davies, Sharron, 45, 137

Davies, Windsor, 16, 97, 141, 143

Davis, Bette, 12, 62, 132, 150, 179, 180

Davis, Carl, 141

Davis, Lucy, 24

Davis, Geena, 51

Davis Jnr., Sammy, 12, 55, 100, 140, 180, 192

Davis, Steve, 98, 108, 122, 137

Davro, Bobby, 52, 98, 141

Dawn, Elizabeth, 48, 97

Dawson, Les, 194

Day-Lewis, Cecil, 192

Day-Lewis, Daniel, 17, 26, 67, 114

Day, Darren, 80, 115, 175

Day, Doris, 13, 52, 56, 114, 148

Day, Robin, 46, 154

De Blank, Justin, 41

De Burgh, Chris, 96, 158

De Carlo, Yvonne, 155

De Courcey, Roger, 142

De Haan, Ben, 16

De Mille, Cecil B., 146, 188

De Mornay, Rebecca, 114, 133, 149

De Niro, Robert, 19, 27, 43, 57, 61, 87, 109, 114, 120, 129, 135, 149, 150

De Paul, Lynsey, 38, 59

De Savary, Peter, 37, 93, 112, 188

De Souza, Edward, 161

De Vine, Magenta, 183

De Vito, Danny, 59, 61, 72, 139, 149, 159, 178

Dean, Christopher, 95, 107, 117, 155, 172

Dean, James, 151, 180

Dean, Letitia, 35, 81, 136

Dearmer, Geoffrey, 116

Deayton, Angus, 62, 92, 106, 117, 176

Decker, Carol, 72, 106

Dee, Dave, 172

Dee, Kiki, 53, 132

Deighton, Len, 21, 38

Dekker, Desmond, 179

Delaney, Frank, 66

Delaney, Sheila, 123

Delfont, Bernard, 54, 102

Delon, Alain, 131

Dempster, Nigel, 95, 158

Dench, Judi, 23, 24, 36, 127

Denham, Maurice, 136

Denison, Michael, 89, 190

Dennis, Felix, 168

Dennis, Hugh, 40

Dennis, Les, 36, 52, 90, 97, 142

Dennis, Stefan, 131

Denver, John, 12

Depardieu, Gerard, 45, 58, 107, 119, 122, 160

Depp, Johnny, 45, 61, 84, 114, 185

Derek, Bo, 53

Dern, Ann-Margret, 36

Dern, Bruce, 14, 36

Dern, Laura, 110, 188

Dervish, Roger, 65

Des'ree, 63

Detroit, Marcella, 110, 132

Dettori, Frankie, 98

Devane, William, 149

Dewar, Donald, 177

Dexter, Ted, 36, 119

Dey, Susan, 170

Diamond, Anne, 22, 81

Diamond, Neil, 15, 35, 41

Diana, Princess of Wales, 166

Diaz, Cameron, 114

Dibley, Janet, 40

DiCaprio, Leonardo, 72, 114, 184

Dickens, Geoffrey, 188

Dickinson, Bruce, 35, 155

Dicks, Julian, 45, 176

Dickson, Dorothy, 123

Diddley, Bo, 129

Dietrich, Marlene, 64, 106, 128, 179, 180

Digance, Richard, 98

Diller, Phyllis, 140

Dillon, Matt, 114, 138

Dimbleby, David, 35

Dimbleby, Jonathan, 15, 33, 88, 92, 109

Dinsdale, Reece, 98, 188

Dion, Celine, 57, 114

Dion, 63, 128

Disney, Walt, 12, 106, 180

Everage, Dame Edna, 46, 163
Everett, Rupert, 22, 35
Everly, Phil, 177

Fabian, 63
Fabio, 63
Fahd, King of Saudi Arabia, 82
Fairbairn, Nicholas, 41
Fairbanks, Douglas, 55, 118
Fairbrass, Richard, 85, 106
Fairchild, Morgan, 142, 171
Fairfax, John, 141
Faith, Adam, 52, 86, 95, 118, 122, 179
Faithfull, Marianne, 40, 45, 61, 66, 124, 138, 183
Falco, 63
Faldo, Nick, 19, 91, 107, 119, 120, 153, 169
Fame, Georgie, 52, 174, 177
Fantoni, Barry, 72
Farr, Jamie, 109
Farriss, Andrew, 177
Farrow, Mia, 23, 28, 40, 84
Farson, Daniel, 11, 182
Fashanu, John, 21, 27, 89, 162
Fashanu, Justin, 27
Faulds-Wood, Lynn, 22, 80
Fawcett, Farrah, 48, 133, 149, 176
Fawsley, Lord St John of, 159, 169
Faye, Gaynor, 126
Feisal, Kin, 193
Feldman, Marty, 180
Fellini, Federico, 193
Fellows, Susannah, 158
Feltz, Vanessa, 17, 21, 30, 78, 84
Ferdinand, Les, 59
Ferguson, Alex, 9, 28, 34, 91, 121
Ferguson, Ronald, 46
Fernandel, 63
Ferrari, Enzo, 157
Ferrer, Jose, 140
Ferris, Pam, 78, 141
Ferry, Bryan, 21, 80, 106, 135, 169, 188
Ffrangcon-Davies, Gwen, 123

Fiddick, Peter, 154
Field, Sally, 23, 132
Field, Shirley Ann, 15, 23
Fields, W.C., 128, 187
Fields, Gracie, 194
Fiennes, Ralph, 114
Fiennes, Ranulph, 81, 110, 115, 158
Fierstein, Harvey, 139
Finch, Peter, 192
Finnegan, Judy, 8
Finney, Albert, 13, 132, 151
Finney, Tom, 157
Finnigan, Judy, 80
Fish, 63
Fish, Michael, 36, 75, 162
Fisher, Eddie, 106
Fisher, Mark, 15
Fisher, Carrie, 23, 69, 114, 144, 170
Fisher, Eddie, 36
Fisher, Gregor, 23
Fittipaldi, Emerson, 177
Fitzgerald, Ella, 7, 12, 111, 146, 180
Fitzgerald, F. Scott, 108, 150
Fitzgerald, Ella, 180
Flack, Roberta, 56
Flaubert, Gustave, 150
Fleetwood, Mick, 35, 156, 183
Fleming, Ian, 11, 101
Fleming, Matthew, 11
Fletcher, Dexter, 189
Fletcher, Keith, 16
Fletcher, Louise, 118
Flint, Keith, 50
Flint, Rachael Heyhoe, 63, 90, 98
Floyd, Keith, 107, 141, 154
Flynn, David, 144
Flynn, Errol, 11, 17, 61, 155, 175
Flynn, Jerome, 72
Follett, Ken, 117, 121
Fonda, Bridget, 25, 80
Fonda, Henry, 12
Fonda, Jane, 25, 48, 94, 114, 118, 149
Fonda, Peter, 133

Fontaine, Joan, 54, 150
Fontanne, Lynn, 156
Fonteyn, Margot, 33
Foot, Michael, 34, 97, 103, 108, 123, 165, 167, 171
Forbes, Bryan, 122, 158, 190
Forbes, Emma, 23, 57, 174
Forbes, Malcolm, 119, 175
Ford, Anna, 54, 109, 161
Ford, Gerald, 78, 182
Ford, Glenn, 11, 155
Ford, Harrison, 16, 61, 107, 110, 114, 126, 138, 149
Ford, John, 180
Foreman, Carl, 192
Foreman, George, 16, 125
Forman, Milos, 26
Formby, George, 190
Forsyth, Bruce, 22, 49, 64, 96, 98, 112, 164
Forsyth, Frederick, 19, 22, 35, 190
Forte, Rocco, 164, 165
Fossey, Dian, 81
Foster, Brendan, 13
Foster, Don, 159
Foster, Jodie, 51, 53, 114, 115, 138, 184, 185
Fowlds, Derek, 141
Fowles, John, 40, 156
Fowler, Norman, 62
Fowler, Robbie, 59
Fox, Edward, 35, 115, 161
Fox, Michael J., 131, 154, 156, 171
Fox, Samantha, 40, 127
Francis, Clare, 13, 41, 141, 166
Francis, Connie, 12
Francis, Dick, 88, 103, 141, 160
Francis, Gerry, 81
Francisco, Peter, 25
Francisco, Silvino, 25
Franciscus, James, 192
Francken, Frans, 173
Franklin, Aretha, 28, 71, 114, 132
Franklyn, William, 89
Fraser, Angus, 36, 153

Fraser, Lady Antonia, 124

Fraser, Flora, 85

Fraser, George MacDonald, 63, 91, 105, 147

Frayn, Michael, 32, 118

Frederick the Great, 188

Freeman, Alan, 73, 166

Freeman, Morgan, 114, 139

French, Dawn, 68, 152, 178

Freud, Clement, 89, 117, 161

Freud, Emma, 117, 134, 176

Freud, Sigmund, 65

Fricker, Brenda, 64, 66

Friel, Anna, 142

Frischmann, Justine, 41

Frost, David, 13, 29, 32, 86, 89, 125, 130, 137, 162, 164, 169

Frostrup, Mariella, 85

Fry, Stephen, 32, 35, 48, 68, 98, 117, 121, 152, 163, 165, 167, 168, 183, 186, 188

Fullerton, Fiona, 36, 67

Furstenburg, Princess Ira von, 69

Fury, Billy, 190

Fyffe, Will, 194

Gable, Clark, 150, 175, 191

Gabor, Zsa Zsa, 140, 170, 186

Gabriel, Peter, 14, 72, 95, 178

Gabrielle, 84, 153

Gaffiney, Dean, 27

Gagarin, Yuri, 180

Gaines, Rosie, 59

Gainsbourg, Serge, 191

Gall, Sandy, 34, 90, 170, 181

Gallagher, Liam, 45, 46, 71, 83, 98, 114, 173, 176, 183

Gallagher, Meg, 181

Gallagher, Noel, 46, 98, 114, 176, 183

Gallup, George, 192

Galton, Ray, 75

Galway, James, 27, 115, 161, 167

Gambaccini, Paul, 166

Gambon, Michael, 164

Gandhi, Indira, 36

Gandhi, Mahatma, 65, 192

Garbo, Greta, 180, 192

Garcia, Andy, 114

Gardam, Jane, 189

Garden, Graeme, 32, 36

Gardner, Andrew, 36

Gardner, Ava, 9, 44

Gardner, Erie Stanley, 193

Garel-Jones, Tristan, 36, 61

Garfunkel, Art, 41, 61

Garland, Judy, 11, 23, 54, 65, 175, 179, 180

Garner, James, 53, 109, 171

Garrison, Jim, 193

Garsons, Greer, 180

Garvie, Elizabeth, 173

Gascoigne, Bamber, 32, 36

Gascoigne, Jill, 85

Gascoigne, Paul, 35, 57, 107, 137, 160, 167

Gates, Bill, 153

Gatting, Mike, 14, 90, 122

Gaulle, Charles de, 115, 133

Gaultier, Jean-Paul, 19, 107

Gaunt, William, 143

Gaye, Marvin, 68, 191

Gayle, Marcus, 127

Gayle, Michelle, 174

Gazzara, Ben, 16, 119

Geldof, Bob, 22, 43, 60, 124, 137, 144, 145, 178

Geller, Uri, 16, 19, 97, 105, 132

George, Boy, 22, 51, 72, 106, 126, 138, 163, 169, 183

George II, King, 152, 175

George III, King, 65

George VI, King, 65, 70

George, Eddie, 118

Gerard, Gil, 140

Gere, Richard, 61, 72, 87, 114, 126, 138, 149, 172, 174

Gershon, Gina, 159

Gershwin, George, 65, 120, 157

Getty, Aileen, 12

Getty II, J. Paul, 159

Getty, J.P. 123

Giacometti, Alberto, 191

Gibb, Andy, 131

Gibb, Barry, 170

Gibb, Maurice, 66

Gibb, Robin, 46

Gibson, Althea, 146

Gibson, Dale, 75

Gibson, Mel, 55, 57, 66, 81, 107, 110

Gielgud, John, 11, 34, 113, 116, 190

Giggs, Ryan, 7, 137

Giles, Carl, 102

Gill, A.A., 64

Gillespie, Dizzy, 191

Gilliat, Sidney, 75

Gillingham, Nick, 90

Gilmore, Susan, 162

Gilmour, David, 35

Gina G, 69

Gingrich, Newt, 44

Ginsberg, Allen, 145, 182

Giordano, Richard, 111

Gish, Lillian, 157, 180

Givenchy, Hubert de, 177

Givens, Robin 12

Glaser, Paul Michael, 63

Glenamara, Lord, 33

Gless, Sharon, 66, 112

Glitter, Gary, 21, 42, 49, 58, 66

Glover, Brian, 88, 136, 143

Glover, Julian, 36, 140, 143

Glyn, Elino, 188

Gobbi, Tito, 193

Goddard, Liza, 78, 80, 93, 137, 141, 143

Godley, Kevin, 72

Goebbels, Josef, 65

Goldberg, Whoopi, 45, 52, 114, 124, 138, 148

Goldblum, Jeff, 149

Goldsmith, Annabel, 174

Goldsmith, Harvey, 22, 43

Goldsmith, James, 70, 84, 124

Gooch, Graham, 27, 98, 141

Goodall, Howard, 72

Goodhew, Duncan, 14, 36, 122

Goodier, Mark, 16, 188

Gooding Jnr, Cuba, 55, 179

Goodman, Gaynor, 58

Goodman, John, 140, 154

Goodwin, Trudie, 83

Goodyear, Julie, 141

Goosen, Retief, 79, 80

Gorbachev, Mikhail, 16, 97, 107, 117

Gordimer, Nadine, 26

Gordon, Hannah, 109, 143, 161

Gorky, Maxim, 191

Gorman, Teresa, 174

Gosden, John, 91, 166

Gossett Jnr., Louis, 12, 55

Gough, Darren, 56, 171

Gough, Michael, 143

Gough, Sandra, 71

Gould, Brian, 38

Gould, Elliott, 106, 120, 142

Gouldman, Graham, 12

Gower, David, 19, 36, 90, 92

Gowrie, Grey, 154

Grade, Lew, 25, 54

Grade, Michael, 13, 25, 92, 159

Graf, Steffi, 25, 75

Graham, Herol, 125

Graham, Bill, 193

Graham, Billy, 146

Grammer, Kelsey, 61, 77, 139, 186

Grandmaster Flash, 52

Granger, Stewart, 65, 75, 130, 179

Grant, Bernie, 126

Grant, Cary, 150, 179

Grant, Hugh, 55, 97, 107, 114, 118, 175, 185

Grant, Richard E., 65, 73, 96, 138

Grant, Russell, 79, 80, 97, 170, 174, 175

Grant, Ulysses S. President General, 11

Grantham, Leslie, 98, 164, 165, 169

Graveney, David, 25

Graveney, Tom, 25

Graves, Robert, 146

Graves, Rupert, 187

Gray, Andy, 16

Gray, Dulcie, 84

Gray, Simon, 117

Graziano, Rocky, 193

Greaves, Jimmy, 43, 66, 90, 122, 161

Green, Al, 16

Green, Hughie, 20, 65, 100

Green, Lucinda, 36

Green, Peter, 26, 50

Green, Robson, 55, 97

Greene, Graham, 36, 110

Greene, Laura, 75

Greene, Lorne, 105

Greene, Sarah, 112

Greenwood, Debbie, 36

Greenwood, Joan, 192

Greer, Germaine, 32, 124, 146, 164, 165

Gregg, Anne, 174

Gregson, Simon, 29, 183

Grenfell, Joyce, 11, 123, 193

Grierson, John, 157

Griffith, Melanie, 23, 45, 47, 48, 92, 119, 149, 183

Griffiths, Richard, 118

Grisham, John, 153

Grobbelaar, Bruce, 90, 95

Grodin, Charles, 139, 153

Grogan, Clare, 153

Grossman, Loyd, 43, 59, 96, 134, 164, 165, 167

Gucci, Paolo, 120

Guest, Christopher, 151

Guevara, Che, 193

Guinness, Alec, 102, 149, 163, 170

Gullit, Ruud, 7, 43, 134

Gummer, John, 36, 124, 161, 173

Gunnell, Sally, 137, 153

Guppy, Darius, 30, 64, 119, 122

Guscott, Jeremy, 90, 96

Guthrie, Arlo, 26

Guthrie, Woody, 191

Gryn, Hugo, 104

Hackett, Buddy, 119

Hackman, Gene, 38, 55, 61, 138, 149

Hadlee, Richard, 67

Hagerty, Julie, 119

Hagman, Larry, 78, 151

Hague, William, 42, 59, 107

Haig, Earl, 145

Hailey, Arthur, 126, 181

Hailsham, Lord, 101, 163, 165

Hailwood, Mike, 194

Haitink, Bernard, 111

Hakkinen, Mika, 81

Haldane, Viscount, 188

Haldeman, H.R., 123, 194

Hale, Gareth, 61, 80, 177, 178

Hale, Ross, 50

Haley, Bill, 175

Hall, Eric, 85

Hall, Fawn, 183

Hall, Jerry, 22, 114, 146

Hall, Peter, 19, 22, 35, 40, 67, 72

Halliwell, Geri "Ginger Spice", 42, 57, 111

Halpern, Ralph, 36

Hamed, Prince Naseem, 154, 176

Hamill, Mark, 167

Hamilton, David, 181

Hamilton, George, 77, 132, 170

Hamilton, Neil, 154

Hamilton, Paula, 66, 71, 94, 183

Hammer, 53, 63

Hamnett, Katherine, 35, 164, 165

Hampshire, Susan, 13, 66, 93, 149, 161

Hampton, Christopher, 35

Hancock, Nick, 73, 98

Hancock, Sheila, 13, 127

Hancock, Tony, 180

Hanks, Tom, 114, 178

Hanley, Ellery, 167

Hanley, Jenny, 142

Hanley, Tommy, 128

Hann, Judith, 80
Hannah, Daryl, 72, 95, 149, 153
Hannon, Richard, 134
Hansen, Alex, 96
Hanson, Lord, 12, 159
Harding, Gilbert, 191
Harding, Matthew, 76
Harding, Mike, 174
Harding, Warren G., 11
Hardy, Oliver, 62, 128, 130
Hare, David, 35, 164, 165
Harewood, Earl of, 100
Harker, Susannah, 23
Harley, Steve, 74, 94
Harlin, Renny, 96
Harlow, Jean, 144, 151
Harman, Harriet, 33, 35
Harper, Gerald, 140
Harper, Valerie, 12
Harrelson, Woody, 25, 55, 61, 72, 126
Harris, Anita, 73, 78
Harris, Frank, 188
Harris, Philip, 37
Harris, Richard, 75, 87, 114, 124, 141, 149
Harris, Robert, 91
Harris, Rolf, 64, 69, 163, 174, 178
Harris, Rosemary, 23
Harrison, George, 21, 64, 128, 144
Harrison, Rex, 36
Harrison, Trevor, 131
Harrow, Lisa, 76
Harry, Debbie, 49, 51, 96
Hart, Lorenz, 188
Hartnell, Norman, 145
Harty, Russell, 130, 180
Harvey, Brian, 45
Harvey, Steve, 176
Harvey-Jones, John, 34, 82, 92, 110, 115, 117, 118
Harwood, Ronald, 89
Hasselhoff, David, 69
Hastings, Gavin, 35, 90
Hastings, Max, 159

Hastings, Scott, 152
Hatcher, Teri, 19, 114
Hateley, Mark, 15
Hatfield, Bobby, 16
Hattersley, Roy, 98, 108
Hauer, Rutger, 178, 182, 188
Haughey, Charles, 15, 81, 92, 119
Hauxwell, Hannah, 141
Havel, Vaclav, 65
Havers, Nigel, 25, 35, 97, 122, 134, 137, 161, 193
Havilland, Olivia de, 54, 150
Hawke, Bob, 38, 75, 91, 108
Hawkes, Chesney, 98
Hawking, Stephen, 24, 107, 126
Hawn, Goldie, 43, 61, 132, 149
Hawthorne, Nigel, 24, 54, 72, 114, 161
Hayes, Brian, 166
Hayes, Isaac, 122
Hayworth, Rita, 120
Healey, Denis, 30, 34, 35, 46, 99, 124, 158
Healy, Tim, 37, 142
Heaney, Seamus, 165
Hearn, Barry, 91
Hearst, Patty, 145
Heath, Edward, 19, 34, 56, 103, 137, 159, 163, 190
Heath, Ted, 192
Hedren, Tippi, 23
Heinz, 63
Helfgott, David, 67
Heller, Joseph, 80
Helvin, Marie, 74, 162
Hemery, David, 137
Hemingway, Ernest, 18, 146, 150, 180, 183
Hemingway, Margot, 191
Hemingway, Mariel, 18, 60, 114
Hemmings, David, 118, 132, 144, 168
Hempel, Anouska, 140, 159
Henderson, Dickie, 193
Hendrix, Jimi, 111, 130, 180

Hendry, Stephen, 90, 97
Henie, Sonja, 94
Henman, Tim, 57
Henreid, Paul, 193
Henri, Adrian, 16
Henry IV, King, 11
Henry, Lenny, 15, 65, 106, 121, 142, 155, 163, 165, 167
Henshall, Ruthie, 92, 93
Henson, Jim, 123, 192
Henson, Nicky, 13
Hepburn, Dee, 15
Hepburn, Audrey, 103, 180
Hepburn, Katharine, 24, 84, 148
Herbert, James, 168
Herriot, James, 67, 102
Herzigova, Eva, 144, 152
Herzog, Chaim, 111
Heseltine Michael, 19, 34, 81, 108, 161
Heskey, Emile, 55
Heston, Charlton, 49, 82, 111, 114, 142, 148, 164
Hetward, Nick, 16
Higgins, Alex, 96, 141
Higgins, Jack, 34, 187
Hill, Benny, 108, 180
Hill, Bernard, 92, 95
Hill, Damon, 24, 55, 90, 134, 137
Hill, Graham, 24, 180
Hill, Jimmy, 93, 160, 170, 173
Hill, Richard, 40
Hill, Susan, 20, 73
Hill, Vince, 67
Hillary, Edmund, 101
Hines, Frazer, 93, 141
Hingis, Martina, 20, 60
Hird, Thora, 39, 54, 60, 164, 165
Hirst, Damien, 144
Hislop, Ian, 35, 40
Hitchcock, Alfred, 179
Hitler, Adolf, 115
Hobbs, Anne, 160
Hobbs, Lyndall, 12
Hobson, Harold, 74, 123

Hobswam, Eric, 113

Hockney, David, 36, 83, 113, 189

Hoddle, Glenn, 56, 59, 60, 90, 127

Hodes, Art, 194

Hodge, Margaret, 166

Hodge, Patricia, 35

Hodson, Philip, 166

Hoffman, Dustin, 49, 60, 61, 72, 95, 119, 149, 171

Hoffman, Abbie, 193

Hogan, Paul, 137

Hogg, Sarah, 39, 124

Holbrook, Hal, 139

Holden, William, 11

Holdsworth, Dean, 45

Holiday, Billie, 7

Holland, Jools, 25, 36, 145, 164, 165

Hollioake, Ben, 55

Hollis, Roger, 75

Holly, Buddy, 129, 130, 180

Holm, Ian, 150, 156

Holmes, Eamonn, 69, 96, 98

Holmes, Kelly, 80, 86

Holness, Bob, 141, 162, 181

Holroyd, Michael, 34

Holyfield, Evander, 80

Hom, Ken, 20

Home, Lord, 102

Honeycombe, Gordon, 61, 160

Hooker, John Lee, 63

Hoover, J. Edgar, 111, 189

Hope, Bob, 12, 111, 116, 171

Hopkin, Mary, 43

Hopkins, Anthony, 9, 20, 66, 69, 107, 133, 147, 148

Hopkirk, Joyce, 169

Hopper, Dennis, 138, 183

Hordern, Michael, 102

Horne, Kenneth, 190

Hoskins, Bob, 19, 38, 44, 59, 67, 137, 153, 163, 179, 182, 190

Houdini, Harry, 28, 187

Houston, Donald, 94

Houston, Whitney, 28, 60, 72, 85, 110, 120, 177

Howard, Alan, 25

Howard, Elizabeth Jane, 168

Howard, Leslie, 25

Howard, Michael, 15, 134

Howe, Geoffrey, 62, 108, 174

Howerd, Frankie, 67, 70

Howman, Karl, 137

Hucknall, Mick, 19, 33, 42, 45, 46, 97, 106

Hudd, Roy, 38, 115, 169, 175, 181

Huddleston, Trevor, 34, 165

Hudson, Rock, 131, 132, 179, 180

Hughes, Emlyn, 122

Hughes, Howard, 9, 65, 84, 120, 151, 175

Hughes, Nerys, 143, 161

Hughes, Sean, 72, 98

Hughes, Ted, 15

Hull, Rod, 97, 141

Hume, Cardinal, 54, 98

Humperdinck, Engelbert, 53, 75

Humphries, Barry, 13, 66, 68

Humphrys, John, 62

Hunnicutt, Gayle, 20

Hunniford, Gloria, 16, 22, 23, 47, 58, 60, 73, 78, 94, 109, 122

Hunt, Gareth, 137, 143, 182

Hunt, James, 180, 194

Hunter (James Crossley), 153

Hunter, David, 75

Hunter, Holly, 118, 149, 152

Hunter, Ian, 38

Hunter, Rachel, 80

Huppert, Isabelle, 144

Hurd, Douglas, 30, 40, 56, 165

Hurley, Elizabeth, 114, 161, 168

Hurst, Geoff, 56

Hurst, Lee, 73, 98

Hurt, John, 29, 89

Hurt, William, 77, 118, 148

Hussain, Nasser, 90

Hussein, King of Jordan, 80, 176

Hussein, Saddam, 7, 107

Hussey, Olivia, 71, 155

Huston, Angelica, 149

Hutton, Lauren, 55

Hutton, Len, 145

Huxley, Aldous, 128, 194

Hyman, Dorothy, 95

Huxley, Julian, 191

Hynde, Chrissie, 45, 59, 72, 184

Hyslop, Elise, 144

Ian, Janis, 53

Idle, Eric, 13, 32

Idol, Billy, 16, 52, 70, 72, 106, 145, 153

Iglesias, Julio, 15, 87, 188

Ignatieff, Michael, 169

Illingworth, Raymond, 160

Ince, Paul, 55

Ingrams, Richard, 109

Inman, John, 162

Innes, Neil, 156

Ireland, Jill, 12

Irons, Jeremy, 21, 35, 92, 93, 149, 160, 177, 190

Ironside, Virginia, 163, 165

Irvine, Eddie, 90

Irvine, Lucy, 36

Irving, Jane, 173

Isaak, Chris, 142

Isherwood, Christopher, 41, 116, 146

Islam, Yusuf (see also Cat Stevens), 8

Ives, Burl, 12

Izzard, Eddie, 146, 153, 177

Jacklin, Tony, 15

Jackson, Colin, 13, 188

Jackson, Glenda, 13, 22, 84, 174

Jackson, Gordon, 140

Jackson, Janet, 93, 95, 171, 188

Jackson, Jermaine, 27

Jackson, Joe, 72

Jackson, Kate, 12

Jackson, LaToya, 72

Jackson, Michael, 15, 27, 50, 57, 64, 72, 82, 118, 120, 155, 170

Jackson, Millie, 132

Jacobi, Derek, 68, 69, 174
Jacobs, David, 190
Jacobson, Howard, 91
Jacques, Hattie, 179
Jaffa, Max, 133
Jaffrey, Saeed, 164
Jagger, Bianca, 145
Jagger, Mick, 22, 33, 109, 111, 120, 128, 156, 179
Jak, 86
James, Naomi, 13
James, Clive, 19, 32, 106, 164, 166, 185
James, Naomi, 90
James, P.D., 19
James, Sid, 176
James, Wendy, 72
Jameson, Derek, 109, 162, 166
Jameson, Louise, 13, 72, 126, 127
Jamie, Marquis of Blandford, 16
Janner, Greville, 118
Janssen, David, 180
Janssen, Famke, 159
Janus, Samantha, 7, 67
Jarvis, Martin, 143
Jason, David, 96, 187
Javer, Monique, 159
Jay, Douglas, 194
Jay, Peter, 30, 40, 92
Jayston, Michael, 89, 167
Jean-Baptiste, Marianne, 173
Jefferson, Thomas, 192
Jeffrey, John, 93
Jenkins, David, 16, 167
Jenkins, Roy, 20, 33, 103, 159, 164, 165, 190
Jenner, Bruce, 94
Jennings, Pat, 34, 141
Jensen, David, 11, 47, 70, 166
Jet, (Diane Youdale), 94
Jethro, 63
Jett, Joan, 131, 155
Jewel, Jimmy, 130
Jhabvala, Ruth Prawer, 151
Jobson, Richard, 182

Joel, Billy, 26, 66
Joffe, Roland, 36
John Paul II, Pope, 50, 78, 81, 87, 115, 117
John, Barry, 25, 130
John, Sir Elton, 19, 51, 53, 66, 76, 96, 97, 106, 111, 120, 130, 166, 176, 178, 183
Johns, Glynis, 140
Johns, Stratford, 140
Johnson, Ben (athlete), 77
Johnson, Ben (playwright), 70
Johnson, Boris, 40
Johnson, Celia, 179
Johnson, Don, 48, 53, 77, 96, 131
Johnson, Frank, 22, 159
Johnson, Joe, 8, 141
Johnson, Magic, 12, 145
Johnson, Michael, 10, 145
Johnson, Paul, 168
Johnson, Samuel, 76
Johnston, Brian, 101
Jolson, Al, 155
Jones, Aled, 20
Jones, Ann, 95, 113
Jones, Brian, 49, 180
Jones, Catherine Zeta, 63, 80, 98, 131
Jones, Davy, 88, 160
Jones, Freddie, 136, 161
Jones, Griff Rhys, 32, 63, 65, 117, 137
Jones, Jack, 113
Jones, James Earl, 70
Jones, Howard, 72
Jones, Kenny, 93
Jones, Paul, 52
Jones, Paula, 125
Jones, Quincy, 13, 171
Jones, Ricky Lee, 172
Jones, Terry, 35, 169
Jones, Tom, 47, 52, 178
Jones, Tommy Lee, 15, 49, 87, 139, 147, 154, 159
Jones, Vinnie, 45, 90

Jonsson, Ulrika, 19, 45, 59, 184
Jordan, Bill, 13
Joseph, Lesley, 59, 85, 136
Jovi, Jon Bon, 124, 178, 179
Jowell, Tessa, 24
Joyce, James, 108
Joyce, Yootha, 140
Judd, Lesley, 16
Judge Jules, 25
Juliana, Queen, 28
Jung, Carl, 128, 188
Juninho, 153
Junkin, John, 140
Junor, Penny, 36, 72, 174

Kahn, Madeline, 131
Kanawa, Kiri Te, 34, 90, 141, 164
Karloff, Boris, 133, 155
Kasparov, Gary, 26
Kastner, Eric, 191
Kaufman, Gerald, 36
Kaunda, Kenneth, 72, 160
Kavanagh, P.J., 109
Kaye, Danny, 150
Kaye, Gorden, 69, 142
Kazan, Elia, 119
Keach, Stacy, 14, 36, 150, 186
Keane, Dillie, 40, 168
Keating, Caron, 23, 66, 78
Keating, Paul, 107
Keaton, Diane, 12, 43, 52, 106, 149, 190
Keaton, Michael, 53, 114, 140, 148, 178
Kee, Robert, 104
Keegan, Kevin, 37, 162
Keeler, Christine, 129
Keeler, Ruby, 193
Keen, Diane, 137, 142
Keene, Raymond, 159
Keitel, Harvey, 70
Keith, Penelope, 19, 54, 136, 137, 140, 161
Keller, Helen, 188
Kelly, Gene, 179, 180

Kelly, Grace, 118, 179
Kelly, Henry, 13, 81, 98
Kelly, Lorraine, 157
Kelly, Matthew, 47, 162
Kelsey, Ian, 73
Kemp, Martin, 72
Kemp, Gary, 15, 72, 178, 189
Kemp, Martin, 189
Kemp, Ross, 43, 142
Kempinski, Tom, 71
Kendal, Felicity, 58, 60, 137, 164
Kendall, Howard, 16
Kendall, Kenneth, 143, 161
Keneally, Thomas, 145
Kennedy, Caroline, 135
Kennedy, George, 144
Kennedy, Gordon, 35
Kennedy, Helena, 33
Kennedy, John, 55
Kennedy, John F., 33, 82, 140, 193, 194
Kennedy, John Jnr, 45
Kennedy, Joseph, 192
Kennedy, Ludovic, 34, 101, 173, 189
Kennedy, Nigel, 34, 97, 107
Kennedy, Robert F., 140
Kennedy, Rose, 116
Kennedy, Sarah, 40
Kensit, Patsy, 13, 40, 45, 58, 92, 93, 114, 115, 184
Kent, Duchess of, 13, 54, 67, 164, 165
Kent, Duke of, 154, 171
Kent, Prince Michael of, 33, 118
Kent, Princess Michael of, 153
Kenyatta, Jomo, 146
Kercheval, Ken, 66, 178
Kern, Jerome, 23, 188
Kerouac, Jack, 182
Kerr, Jim, 16, 97
Kershaw, Andy, 16, 35
Kershaw, Nik, 72, 155
Kettley, John, 161
Khan, Chaka, 134
Khan, Jahangir, 82

Khan, Jemima, 122
Khan, Majid, 15
Khashoggi, Adnan, 24
Khashoggi, Soraya, 8, 122, 177
Khomeini, Ayatollah, 194
Kidman, Nicole, 95, 114, 122
Killanin, Lord, 31, 32, 173
Killen, Mary, 24
Killy, Jean-Claude, 146
Kilmer, Val, 61, 114
Kilroy-Silk, Robert, 161
King, Albert, 194
King, B.B., 15, 184
King, Billie Jean, 188
King, Carole, 17, 135
King, Claire, 83
King, Don, 186
King, Jonathan, 35, 76
King, Larry, 26
King, Lord, 159
King, Martin Luther, 55, 180
King, Phil, 194
King, Stephen, 44, 79, 146, 151
Kingsley, Ben, 9, 24, 36, 142, 178
Kingsley, Charles, 192
Kingston, Alex, 42
Kinnear, Roy, 140, 151
Kinnock, Glenys, 15, 33
Kinnock, Neil 34, 42, 107, 134, 163, 165, 174
Kinsey, Alfred, 154
Kinski, Klaus, 191
Kinski, Nastassja, 108
Kipling, Rudyard, 125, 150, 172
Kirkbride, Anne, 80
Kirwan, Dervla, 137
Kissinger, Henry, 111, 170
Kitchen, Michael, 92, 93
Kitt, Eartha, 21, 140
Kitzinger, Sheila, 168
Klein, Calvin, 26, 53, 56, 109
Kline, Kevin, 26, 139, 190
Klinsmann, Jurgen, 107, 176
Kluge, Patricia, 12

Knievel, Evel, 186
Knight, Andrew, 75
Knight, Gladys, 14, 72, 120
Knopfler, Mark, 22, 34, 55
Knox-Johnston, Robin, 174
Knox, Barbara, 42
Knox, Ronald, 188
Kodály, Zoltan, 194
Kops, Bernard, 109
Korbut, Olga, 14, 107
Korda, Michael, 25
Kosinski, Jerzy, 191
Kosygin, Alexei, 191
Kravitz, Lennie, 72, 85
Kray, Ronnie, 79, 191
Kristel, Sylvia, 181, 182
Kristofferson, Kris, 21, 38, 91, 129
Kubrick, Stanley, 15, 26
Kwouk, Burt, 143
Kydd, Sam, 99

La Plante, Linda, 69
La Rue, Danny, 15, 56, 141, 174
LaBelle, Patti, 12
Lacroix, Christian, 31
Ladd, Cheryl, 47
Laine, Cleo, 34
Laine, Denny, 15
Ladd, Diane, 16
Laine, Frankie, 131
Lake, Ricki, 72
Lake, Veronica, 155, 181
Laker, Freddie, 34
Laker, Jim, 191
Lamarr, Hedy, 155
Lambert, Verity, 31, 184
Lambton, Lucinda, 165
Lamont, Norman, 46, 160
Lamour, Dorothy, 155, 179, 181
Lancaster, Burt, 101, 180, 187
Lanchester, Elsa, 7, 150
Land, Edwin, 191
Landen, Dinsdale, 36
Landon, Michael, 12

Longford, Lord, 44, 75, 173

Longley, Clifford, 187

Longthorne, Joe, 59, 112

Lonsborough, Anita, 95

Lord, Jack, 67

Lorean, John de, 160

Loren, Sophia, 25, 131, 186

Lorimer, Peter, 16

Louis, Joe, 177, 180

Louise, 63

Love, Courtney, 17, 111, 126, 170, 183

Love, Davis, 49

Love, Geoff, 192

Lovelace, Linda, 16

Lovett, Lyle, 61

Lowe, Arthur, 140

Lowe, Chris, 15, 35, 41

Lowe, Rob, 55, 148, 171

Lowell, Robert, 194

Lower, Jonathan, 76

Lowndes, Victor, 145

Luce, Clare Booth, 147

Lulu, 8, 52, 63, 98, 126, 166

Lumet, Sidney, 26

Lumley, Joanna, 34, 40, 107, 114, 144, 168

Lundgren, Dolph, 156

Lunghi, Cherie, 19, 114, 168

Lusardi, Linda, 44

Luthuli, Albert, 194

Lyle, Sandy, 13, 138, 155

Lynam, Desmond, 36, 57, 162

Lyndhurst, Nicholas, 43, 96, 119

Lynn, Jonathan, 32

Lynn, Loretta, 8

Lynn, Vera, 54, 66, 100, 122, 163, 168

Lynne, Gillian, 20, 141

Lynott, Phil, 120

Lyttelton, Humphrey, 105, 123

Mabbutt, Gary, 76

MacArthur, Douglas, 183

MacColl, Ewan, 24

MacColl, Kirsty, 24

MacCorkindale, Simon, 40

Macdonald, Aimi, 16

MacDonald, Ramsay, 188

MacDowell, Andie, 59

MacGowan, Shane, 46, 178

MacGraw, Ali, 77, 182

MacGregor, Sue, 92

Mackay, Fulton, 79

Mackintosh, Cameron, 31

Mackenzie, Compton, 180

Mackenzie, Kelvin, 90

MacLaine, Shirley, 43, 54, 60, 127, 148

MacLaurin, Lord, 33

Maclean, Don, 80

Macmillan, Harold, 54, 78

MacMurray, Fred, 192

Macnee, Patrick, 13, 36, 62, 100, 141

Macpherson, Elle, 52, 57, 94

Madeley, Richard, 58

Madison, Helen, 94

Madoc, Ruth, 42, 122

Madonna, 10, 45, 46, 47, 51, 63, 78, 84, 95, 106, 107, 111, 114, 124, 130, 138, 152, 159, 178

Madsen, Virginia, 176

Magnusson, Magnus, 35, 43, 115, 164

Magnusson, Sally, 174

Magritte, Rene, 157

Mahmood, Zia, 42

Mahoney, Jock, 23, 140

Mailer, Norman, 26, 83, 151, 163

Major, John, 13, 27, 35, 54, 75, 92, 98, 107, 166, 168

Major, Norma, 39, 86, 173

Major, Tom, 187

Major-Ball, Terry, 27, 54

Malcolm, Devon, 74

Malden, Karl, 149

Malick, Terrence, 38

Mallett, Timmy, 33, 46, 47, 97, 154, 167, 168

Mandela, Nelson, 75, 107, 117

Manilow, Barry, 53, 58, 106

Mankowitz, Wolf, 169

Mann, Manfred, 15, 26, 52

Manning, Bernard, 65, 76, 97, 179

Manning, Olivia, 116

Mansell, Nigel, 34, 74, 86, 89, 107, 122

Mansfield, Jayne, 120, 180, 181

Manson, Charles, 135

Mantegna, Joe, 139

Mantovani, 63

Maples, Maria, 181

Maradona, Diego, 79, 183

Marceau, Marcel, 26

Marcos, Imelda, 12, 51, 181

Marek, John, 9

Margaret, Princess, 57, 76, 174

Margolyes, Miriam, 19, 36

Marilyn, 63

Mark, Marky, 94

Markinson, Mary, 90

Markova, Alicia, 44

Marks, Alfred, 101, 191

Marley, Bob, 130, 179

Marriott, Steve, 134, 192

Marryat, Captain, 124

Marsden, Gary, 174

Marsh, Jean, 143

Marshall, Arthur, 193

Marshall, Malcolm, 155

Marshall, Penny, 139

Martika, 63

Martin, Dean, 23, 179

Martin, George, 83

Martin, Mary, 193

Martin, Millicent, 156

Martin, Steve, 149, 171

Martinez, Conchita, 127

Marx, Harpo, 12

Marx, Karl, 128

Marx, Zeppo, 193

Mary, Queen of Scots, 107

Mason, Jackie, 28, 139

Mason, James, 150

Mason, Marsha, 139

Mason, Nick, 49

Massey, Daniel, 28, 113

Massey, Raymond, 192

Massiel, 63

Mastrantonio, Mary Elizabeth, 63

Mates, James, 160

Mathias, Bob, 94

Mathis, Buster, 55

Mathis, Johnny, 146

Matlin, Marlee, 64

Matthau, Walter, 26, 101, 148, 150, 179

Matthew, Brian, 38

Matthews, Bernard, 12

Matthews, Meg, 135

Matthews, Stanley, 82

Matthews, Victor, 173

Maughan, William Somerset, 23, 190

Maurois, André, 193

Mawhinney, Brian, 125

Maxwell, Robert, 65, 104, 192

May, David, 29

May, Peter, 28

Mayall, John, 109

Mayall, Rik, 22, 43, 112, 136, 155, 156

Maynard, Bill, 72, 76, 82, 142

Mayo, Simon, 33, 75, 97, 121, 155, 174

McCall, Danny, 131

McCall, Oliver, 183

McCallum, David, 112

McCann, Barbara, 112

McCartney, Linda, 80, 129

McCartney, Paul, 24, 36, 54, 72, 86, 109, 111, 114, 117, 128, 129, 143, 145, 173, 186

McCartney, Stella, 24

McCaskill, Ian, 46, 58

McColgan, Liz, 14, 73, 95, 137

McCormack, Mark, 165

McCririck, John, 154

McCrum, Robert, 82

McCullough, Jimmy, 194

McCutcheon, Martine, 73, 134

McDermott, Kirsty, 72

McDonald, Trevor, 34, 162

McDormand, Frances, 29

McDowell, Malcolm, 21, 150

McEnroe, John, 43, 108, 120, 173, 177

McGann, Joe, 84, 96

McGann, Paul, 72, 121

McGillis, Kelly, 45

McGoohan, Patrick, 114, 151

McGough, Roger, 124, 160

McGovern, Jimmy, 70, 78

McGowan, Cathy, 76

McGrath, Rory, 32, 58, 97, 137

McGregor, Ewan, 147

McGuigan, Barry, 10, 56

McGuigan, Paul, 79

McGuinn, Roger, 16

McIntyre, Joey, 9

McKay, Peter, 96

McKellen, Ian, 36, 72

McKenna, Paul, 126

McKenna, Virginia, 20, 72, 161, 162

McKenzie, Duke, 79

McKenzie, Julia, 19, 79

McKenzie, Linsey Dawn, 112

McKern, Abigail, 24, 78

McKern, Leo, 24, 76, 78, 92, 137, 158

McKuen, Rod, 131

McLaren, Bill, 75

McLaren, Malcolm, 106

McLean, Don, 72

McMenemy, Lawrie, 162

McQueen, Alexander, 45, 62

McQueen, Steve, 175, 180

McShane, Ian, 88, 94

McShane, Mike, 20

Meacher, Michael, 36

Meade, Richard, 174

Meades, Jonathan, 27

Meatloaf, 15, 52

Meen, Sally, 41

Meir, Golda, 157

Melanie, 63

Mellencamp, John Cougar, 146

Mellish, Bob, 100

Mellor, David, 46, 96

Mellor, Will, 134

Melly, George, 35, 83, 123, 168

Mendes, Sam, 20, 76, 117

Menuhin, Lady, 123

Menuhin, Yehudi, 66, 168, 145

Menzies, Robert, 108

Meo, Tony, 15

Mercer, Joe, 173

Merchant, Piers, 72

Mercier, Sheila, 27, 54, 100

Mercury, Freddie, 130, 191

Meredith, Burgess, 132, 150

Merman, Ethel, 140

Merrington, Dave, 125

Merryfield, Buster, 136

Merson, Paul, 66, 183

Merton, Paul, 20, 58

Messenger, Melinda, 57

Messiaen, Olivier, 193

Miandad, Javed, 14

Michael, George, 8, 43, 58, 60, 74, 106, 120, 132, 156, 173, 175

Michell, Keith, 158, 161

Michelmore, Cliff, 181

Michener, James, 127

Mickelson, Phil, 43

Midler, Bette, 51, 57, 149

Milburn, Colin, 191

Milburn, Jackie, 25

Miles, Bernard, 192

Miles, Brenda, 64

Miles, Michael, 70

Miles, Sarah, 9, 148, 156

Miles, Stewart, 75

Mill, John Stuart, 28, 125

Milland, Ray, 179

Miller, Jonny Lee, 23, 63

Miller, Jonathan, 32, 109, 169

Miller, Max, 128

Milligan, Spike, 67, 70, 76, 103, 163, 168, 169

Millns, David, 42

Mills, Barbara, 35

Mills, Bob, 182

Mills, Caspian, 23

Mills, Hayley, 23, 72, 148

Mills, Heather, 25

Mills, John, 83, 190

Mills, Juliet, 15, 141

Milnes, A.A., 49, 126

Milton, John, 76

Minghella, Anthony, 164

Minnelli, Liza, 23, 77, 114, 119, 148

Minogue, Dannii, 110, 131

Minogue, Kylie, 57, 67, 93, 114, 152, 178

Minter, Alan, 56, 130

Mintoff, Dom, 38

Mirman, Sophie, 184

Mirren, Helen, 40, 45, 121, 163

Mishcon, Victor, 28

Mitchell, Austin, 174

Mitchell, Joni, 17, 62, 74, 134, 135

Mitchell, Warren, 98, 164

Mitchum, Robert, 133

Mitford, Jessica, 124

Mitterand, Francois, 107, 108

Mix, Tom, 177

Mizzi, Kate, 78

Mizzi, Suzanne, 47

Modine, Matthew, 22

Molby, Jan, 16

Monk, Thelonius, 56, 192

Monkhouse, Bob, 35, 57, 122, 141, 163, 179, 181

Monroe, Marilyn, 7, 17, 45, 84, 102, 106, 111, 128, 151, 153, 163, 180

Montgomerie, Colin, 85

Montgomery, Bernard, 65

Moody, Ron, 140, 181

Moon, Keith, 176, 180

Mooney, Bell, 36, 117

Moore, Bobby, 156, 179, 180

Moore, Brian, 33, 40, 97, 125, 159, 181

Moore, Charles, 27

Moore, Debbie, 37, 73

Moore, Demi, 7, 48, 51, 52, 58, 64, 139, 147, 159

Moore, Dudley, 22, 65, 56, 107, 110, 123, 141, 156, 171

Moore, Henry, 107

Moore, Jeremy, 157

Moore, Mary Tyler, 48, 63, 76, 77

Moore, Patrick, 46, 58, 64, 100, 107, 122, 167

Moore, Roger, 29, 48, 70, 155, 164, 184

Moores, John, 117

Moorhouse, Adrian, 14, 36, 174

Moran, Diana, 174

More, Kenneth, 116

Morecambe, Eric, 180

Morley, Eric, 89

Morley, Ken, 49

Morley, Robert, 133

Morrell, Penny, 71

Morris, Desmond, 36, 98, 168

Morris, Dewi, 73

Morris, Glenn, 94

Morris, Juliet, 43

Morrison, Danny, 82

Morrison, Jim, 175, 179

Morrison, Mark, 59, 186

Morrison, Van, 62

Morrissey, 22, 46, 63, 72, 106, 110

Morrissey, Neil, 21

Morrow, George, 188

Morrow, Vic, 151

Mortimer, Bob, 98, 117

Mortimer, John, 20, 34, 121, 126, 161, 166

Mortimer, Tony, 106

Morton, J.B., 120

Moses, Ed, 72

Mosimann, Anton, 19, 95, 163

Mosley, Bryan, 79

Mosley, Diana, 116

Moss, Kate, 56, 57, 60, 114

Moss, Stirling, 35, 93, 146, 154, 174

Most, Mickie, 141

Mother Teresa, 65

Motson, John, 15, 29, 36, 97, 153

Mountjoy, Doug, 65

Mowatt, Paul, 144

Mowlam, Mo, 39, 174

Moyet, Alison, 59, 71, 97, 156

Moynihan, Colin, 91

Mozart, Wolfgang, 80

Mr Motivator, 94

Muggeridge, Malcolm, 124, 180

Muir, Frank, 125, 154, 190

Mullen, Larry, 55

Mullery, Alan, 188

Mullville, Jimmy, 32, 183

Mulroney, Brian, 108

Munch, Edvard, 24, 188

Muni, Paul, 150

Murdoch, Iris, 20, 34, 36, 67, 116, 124

Murdoch, Rupert, 62

Murphy, Audie, 155, 179

Murphy, Davinia, 62

Murphy, Eamon, 75

Murphy, Eddie, 120, 132, 148

Murphy, Glen, 89

Murray, Jenni, 69

Murray, Pete, 38, 181

Muskie, Ed, 193

Mussolini, Alessandra, 25, 41

Mussolini, Benito, 129, 152, 172

Myers, Mike, 134

Myskow, Nina, 84

Mystic Meg, 184

Nadir, Asil, 134

Nail, Jimmy, 97, 186

Nannini, Alessandro, 112

Napoleon, 65

Nastase, Ilie, 12, 145

Naughtie, James, 62

Naughton, Bill, 194

Navratilova, Martina, 43, 72, 120, 154

Neal, Patricia, 118

Neame, Christopher, 9

Neeskens, Johan, 26

Neeson, Liam, 34, 61, 88

Neil, Andrew, 33, 92

Neill, Sam, 70, 139, 161

Nelson, Ricky, 191

Nena, 63

Nesmith, Michael, 151

Nettles, John, 20

Neuberger, Julia, 80, 83. 92, 117

Neville, Phil, 120

Newbon, Gary, 36

Newhart, Bob, 85, 178

Newley, Anthony, 43, 62, 115, 158

Newlove, Paul, 85

Newman, Andrea, 113

Newman, Nanette, 19, 23, 137, 168

Newman, Paul, 12, 16, 26, 42, 72, 87, 118, 120, 148, 170, 178

Newsome, Chloe, 42

Newton-John, Olivia, 18, 22, 26, 51, 80, 106

Newton, Isaac, 67

Newton, Tony, 35

Nicholas, Paul, 19, 43

Nicholls, Paul, 112

Nicholls, Sue, 131

Nicholson, Emma, 12, 36, 39, 40, 167

Nicholson, Jack, 18, 147, 159

Nicholson, Mavis, 160

Nicholson, Michael, 12, 117, 156, 181

Nicholson, Vanessa-Mae, 19

Nicklaus, Jack, 42

Nicks, Stevie, 72, 77

Nicole, 63

Nielsen, Brigitte, 45

Nielsen, Leslie, 64, 101

Nightingale, Anne, 36

Nilsson, 63

Nimmo, Derek, 164, 174, 190

Nimoy, Leonard, 109, 114, 132

Niven, David, 12, 173, 192

Nixon, Richard, 127

Nkrumah, Kwame, 194

Noah, Yannick, 66

Noakes, John, 112

Nobbs, David, 160

Nolan, Linda, 98

Nolte, Nick, 114, 186

Noor, Queen of Jordan, 41

Norden, Denis, 13, 35, 147, 163, 174

Noriega, Manuel, 7, 86

Norman, Barry, 15, 35, 113, 117, 162

Norman, Greg, 78, 119

Norris, Chuck, 89

Norris, Steven, 35, 69, 81

Nott, John, 86

Novak, Kim, 181

Nugent, Ted, 16

Numan, Gary, 52, 119, 155, 177

Nureyev, Rudolf, 80, 191

Nutkins, Terry, 44

O'Brien, Conor Cruise, 190

O'Brien, Edna, 96, 178

O'Brien, Vincent, 62

O'Connor, Andrew, 106, 115

O'Connor Jnr, Christy, 25, 55, 112

O'Connor Snr, Christy, 25

O'Connor, Christy, 55

O'Connor, Des, 57, 141, 175, 181

O'Connor, Sinead, 51, 57, 66, 118, 176

O'Connor, Tom, 174

O'Donnell, Rosie, 12

O'Grady, Paul (*see also* Lily Savage), 136

O'Mara, Kate, 78, 115, 143, 177

O'Neal, Ryan, 43, 62, 186

O'Neal, Tatum, 25, 148, 183

O'Neill, Jonjo, 80

O'Neill, Terry, 79

O'Reilly, Tony, 7, 116

O'Sullevan, Peter, 86, 169

O'Sullivan, Maureen, 23

O'Sullivan, Richard, 115

O'Sullivan, Ronnie, 25

O'Toole, Peter, 18, 47, 88, 183

Oakley, Robin, 36

Oaksey, John, 92, 96

Oberon, Merle, 25

Ocean, Billy, 53

Oddie, Bill, 15, 32

Ofarim, Abi, 129

Ofarim, Esther, 129

Offiah, Tommy, 154

Ogilvy, D.G.C.P., 61

Ogilvy, Ian, 15

Ogilvy, Marina, 144

Okri, Ben, 80

Olazabal, Jose Maria, 83

Oldfield, Bruce, 7, 21, 22, 122

Oldfield, Mike, 24, 85, 92

Oldman, Gary, 27, 59

Olivier, Laurence, 68, 116, 118, 150, 179, 180

Onassis, Aristotle, 78

Onassis, Jackie, 143

Ono, Yoko, 13, 23, 51, 106, 129, 146, 188

Oppenheim, Philip, 61

Oppenheimer, Robert, 188

Oppenheimer, Sally, 174

Orange, Jason, 72

Orbach, Susie, 124

Orbison, Roy, 145, 180

Ortega, Daniel, 188

Orwell, George, 12

Osbourne, Ozzy, 72, 77, 179, 186

Osmond, Donny, 27, 67

Osmond, Jason, 27

Osmond, Marie, 62, 155

Ovett, Steve, 43, 137

Ovid, 191

Owen, David, 36, 40, 108, 174, 190

Owen, Nick, 73, 95, 97

Owen, Sid, 53, 183

Owens, Jesse, 107

Oxenberg, Catherine, 72

Oyston, Vicki, 181

Ozbek, Rifat, 41

Pace, Norman, 61, 110
Pacino, Al, 58, 61, 114, 149
Pack, Roger Lloyd, 35, 63, 136, 161, 167
Packer, Kerry, 74, 93
Paddock, Charley, 94
Pagett, Nicola, 40, 67, 70, 161
Paige, Elaine, 22, 52, 92, 122, 141, 158
Paisley, Bob, 104
Paisley, Ian, 163
Palance, Jack, 53, 88, 132
Palin, Michael, 36, 57, 97, 126, 164, 177
Pallenberg, Anita, 82
Pallister, Gary, 90
Palma, Brian de, 24, 185
Palmer-Tomkinson, Charles, 87
Palmer-Tomkinson, Tara, 87
Palmer, Arnold, 160
Palmer, Geoffrey, 35, 137
Palmer, Patsy, 42, 81, 183, 189
Palmer, Robert, 13
Paltrow, Gwyneth, 110, 114, 144
Palumbo, Lord, 159
Palumbo, Peter, 33, 119
Pankhurst, Christabel, 193
Papandreou, Andreas, 193
Parfitt, Judy, 158, 168
Parfitt, Rick, 176, 183
Paris, Mica, 53
Park, Nick, 155
Parker Bowles, Brigadier, 124
Parker Bowles, Camilla, 28, 49, 51, 143
Parker, Bonnie, 129
Parker, Charlie, 111, 144
Parkin, Molly, 48, 72
Parkinson, C. Northcote, 193
Parkinson, Michael, 20, 21, 43, 80, 97, 174
Parnell, Charles Stewart, 191
Parnevik, Jesper, 74, 127

Parrott, John, 97
Parsons, Charlie, 161
Parsons, Nicholas, 48, 62, 90, 103, 125, 146, 161, 162, 187
Parsons, Tony, 168
Parton, Dolly, 58, 110, 120, 129
Pasquale, Joe, 112
Pastorius, Jaco, 191
Paterson, Jennifer, 40
Patten, Chris, 35, 113, 163, 165, 171
Patterson, Floyd, 12
Paul, Adrian, 112
Paul, Lynsey de, 122
Pavarotti, Luciano, 15, 58, 83, 107, 132, 164
Paxman, Jeremy, 27, 35, 40, 55, 169
Pearce, Billy, 75
Pearce, Stuart, 58, 137
Pearson, Neil, 121
Peasgood, Julie, 126
Peck, Gregory, 56, 62, 81, 140
Peel, John, 72
Pelé, 27, 63, 107, 111, 120, 146
Pellow, Marti, 97
Penhaligon, Susan, 143, 170
Penn, Arthur, 26
Penn, Sean, 129, 148, 186
Pennis, Dennis, 42, 74
Peppard, George, 84
Percival, Lance, 46
Perkins, Anthony, 151, 180, 190
Perkins, Carl, 16
Perlman, Itzhak, 74
Perlman, Rhea, 72
Perot, H. Ross, 153
Perrie, Lynne, 47, 48, 80, 178
Perry, Fred, 124, 191
Perry, Jimmy, 103
Pertwee, Jon, 67, 102, 140, 179
Pétain, Henri, 193
Peter the Great, 70
Peters, Andi, 58, 71, 73
Peters, Mary, 95, 126
Peterson, Oscar, 82

Pettifer, Julian, 161
Petty, Tom, 61
Pfeiffer, Michelle, 12, 110, 114, 139, 155
Philbin, Maggie, 171
Philip, Prince, 11, 33, 40, 54, 60, 105, 117, 152, 173
Phillips, Chynna, 146
Phillips, Trevor, 9, 62
Phillips, Leslie, 67, 136
Phillips, Lou Diamond, 27, 55
Phillips, Mark, 35
Phillips, Peter, 40
Phillips, Sian, 19, 161, 163, 168
Phillips, Trevor, 161
Phoenix, Pat, 44, 120
Phoenix, River, 151, 179, 180, 193
Piaf, Edith, 192
Picasso, Pablo, 44, 86, 120, 124, 145, 180
Picasso, Paloma, 23, 146
Pickett, Wilson, 186
Pickford, Mary, 118
Piggott, Lester, 19, 83, 186
Pigott-Smith, Tim, 143
Pinckney, Callan, 65
Pinsent, Matthew, 90, 122
Pinter, Harold, 19, 36, 117
Pinto, Antonio, 119
Piquet, Nelson, 153
Pissaro, Lucien, 188
Pitman, Mark, 93
Pitman, Richard, 152
Pitt, Brad, 62, 107, 114, 138, 170, 172
Pius XI, Pope, 189
Pizzey, Erin, 158
Planer, Nigel, 190
Plant, Robert, 97
Plater, Alan, 41, 91, 165
Plath, Sylvia, 120
Platt, David, 120, 137
Player, Gary, 34, 54
Pleasence, Donald, 102, 179
Pleasence, Fred, 191

Reid, Mike, 8

Reid, Pat, 192

Reiner, Rob, 140

Reinhardt, Django, 44

Remarque, Erich Maria, 146

Rendall, Paul, 13

Rendell, Ruth, 19, 72, 166

Renenberg, Richey, 75

Rennie, Michael, 140

Reubens, Paul, 185

Reynolds, Burt, 12, 29, 49, 58, 75, 85, 133, 182, 184

Reynolds, Dean, 97

Reynolds, Debbie, 23

Reynolds, Gillian, 35

Rhodes, Zandra, 22, 69, 141

Rhys-Jones, Sophie, 57

Rice, Anneka, 108, 155, 177, 184

Rice, Tim, 35, 70, 89, 117, 122, 128, 163

Rich, Buddy, 86

Rich, Charlie, 109

Richard, Cliff, 15, 52, 77, 110, 132, 157, 175

Richard, Eric, 15, 65

Richard, Wendy, 57, 80, 131, 161, 162, 168

Richards, Keith, 174, 183

Richards, Viv, 62, 78, 120, 141

Richardson, Joely, 23, 138

Richardson, Miranda, 155

Richardson, Ralph, 179

Richardson, Richie, 82

Richie, Lionel, 12

Richler, Mordecai, 91

Rickles, Don, 13

Ridgeon, Jon, 78

Ridgway, John, 12

Ridley, Joanne, 144

Ridley, Nicholas, 194

Rifkind, Malcolm, 15, 35

Rigg, Diana, 113, 148, 172

Rilke, Rainer Maria, 183

Rinder, Tommy, 191

Rippon, Angela, 59, 93, 141, 174

Ritchie, Shane, 42, 97, 112, 175

Rivers, Joan, 15, 24, 48, 53, 106, 146, 151

Rives, Jean Pierre, 9

Rix, Brian, 27, 33, 34, 35, 54, 89, 100, 174

Roach, Hal, 116

Roach, Pat, 88

Roache, Linus, 24, 90

Roache, William, 24, 43, 93, 122

Robards, Jason, 16

Robert the Bruce, 11

Roberts, Julia, 43, 45, 51, 142, 144, 149, 170

Robertson, Cliff, 148

Robertson, Denise, 34

Robinson, Edward G., 140

Robertson, Liz, 29

Robertson, Robbie, 16, 145

Robeson, Paul, 157

Robinson, Anne, 59

Robinson, Geoffrey, 36, 118

Robinson, Jancis, 80

Robinson, Mary, 107

Robinson, Tim, 16

Robinson, Tom, 14, 35

Robinson, Tony, 43, 60, 73, 76, 97, 121, 136

Robinson, Smokey, 129

Robinson, Sugar Ray, 193

Robson, Bobby, 13, 92, 95, 137, 174

Robson, Flora, 116

Robson, Linda, 58, 78, 174, 189

Roche, Stephen, 117

Rodber, Tim, 33

Roddenberry, Gene, 193

Roddick, Anita, 121, 123, 163, 174, 178

Rodgers, Ted, 181

Rodman, Dennis, 51

Rogers, Ginger, 150

Rogers, Kenny, 48, 177

Rogers, Mimi, 122

Rogers, Roy, 12

Rogers, Ted, 93, 175

Rogers, Will, 188

Rohe, Mies van der, 188

Romero, Caesar, 179

Romero, Eduardo, 81

Ronstadt, Linda, 12, 51

Rooney, Mickey, 56, 66, 141, 156

Roosevelt, Theodore, 152

Rose, Axl, 52, 53, 170, 185

Rose, Billy, 188, 192

Roseanne, 17 , 45, 48, 51, 66, 67, 176, 184

Rosenthal, Jack, 109

Rosenthal, Jim, 97

Roslin, Gaby, 57, 73

Ross, Diana, 106

Ross, Jonathan, 27, 137, 184

Ross, Katharine, 13

Ross, Nick, 96, 160, 176

Ross, Paul, 27

Rossellini, Isabella, 12, 170

Rossi, Francis, 168

Rossiter, Leonard, 137, 176

Roth, David Lee, 63, 86, 106

Roth, Tim, 50, 68, 114

Rotten, Johnny, 106

Roualt, Georges, 193

Rourke, Mickey, 88, 149, 178

Roux, Michel, 92, 119

Rowan, Dan, 191

Rowell, Jack, 34

Rowland, Tiny, 177

Rowse, A.L., 113

Roy of the Rovers, 112

Royal, Princess, 174

Royle, Joe, 83

Ruddock,. Joan, 161

Rudolph, Wilma, 74

Ruffelle, Frances, 35

Runcie, Robert, 84, 89, 100, 117, 165, 166

Runyon, Damon, 108

RuPaul, 63

Rusedski, Greg, 43

Rush, Ian, 43, 56

Rush, Jeffrey, 67
Rush, Jennifer, 132
Rushdie, Salman, 163
Rusk, Dean, 111
Ruskin, John, 192
Russell, Bertrand, 28, 124, 180
Russell, Jane, 12, 56, 62, 148, 150, 155
Russell, Ken, 35, 41, 67, 119
Russell, Kurt, 132
Russell, Theresa, 53
Russo, Rene, 179, 182
Rutherford, Margaret, 190, 192
Ryan, Meg, 16, 39, 53, 58, 114, 139
Ryder, Shaun, 85, 183
Ryder, Sue, 105
Ryder, Winona, 28, 52, 57, 84, 114, 138, 139

Sabrina, 63
Sachs, Andrew, 115, 136
Sacks, Jonathan, 160
Sachs, Leonard, 142
Sacks, Oliver, 70
Sackville-West, Vita, 44
Sade, 63
Sadler, Brent, 36, 92
Saeed, Jaffrey, 91
Sager, Carole Bayer, 12, 63
Salinger, Tom, 50
Salk, Jonas, 23
Sallis, Peter, 143
Salmond, Alex, 9
Salonga, Sian, 168
Salzmann, Josh, 28
Sampras, Pete, 156
Sanders, George, 54, 175
Sanders, Harland, 145
Sanderson, Tessa, 97, 110
Sandino, Augusto, 192
Sanger, Margaret, 192
Santana, Carlos, 185
Santer, Jacques, 29, 107
Sarandon, Susan, 126, 139

Sargent, Malcolm, 191
Sarne, Mike, 147
Sassoon, Vidal, 21, 26, 69
Saud, King Ibn, 192
Saunders, Jennifer, 43, 58, 142, 144, 155
Savage, Lily (see also Paul O'Grady), 136
Savalas, Telly, 28, 103, 180
Savident, John, 20
Savile, Sir Jimmy, 10, 22, 33, 34, 42, 47, 65, 104, 107, 141, 159
Sawalha, Julia, 24, 43, 112, 136, 152
Sawalha, Nadia, 173
Sawalha, Nadim, 24
Sayer, Leo, 38, 179
Sayle, Alexei, 21, 143, 178
Scacchi, Greta, 21, 58, 167
Scales, Prunella, 121, 161, 171
Scarfe, Gerald, 73, 160, 164
Scargill, Arthur, 108, 163, 165
Scheckter, Jody, 26
Scheider, Roy, 119
Scher, Anna, 189
Schiffer, Claudia, 94, 126
Schlesinger, John, 158
Schmeichel, Peter, 154
Schofield, Philip, 57, 95, 107
Schumacher, Michael, 84
Schumann, Robert, 71
Schwarzenegger, Arnold, 58, 61, 80, 87, 107, 114, 120, 138, 151, 159, 171
Schwarzkopf, Norman, 111, 118
Scofield, Paul, 34, 36, 62
Scott-Heron, Gil, 94
Scott, Brough, 36, 109
Scott, Nicholas, 12
Scott, Norman, 182
Scott, Peter, 28, 133
Scott, Randolph, 192
Scott, Roger, 182
Scott, Selina, 29, 57
Scott, Terry, 67, 105, 150
Scott, Walter, 74

Screaming Lord Sutch, 20, 56
Scudamore, Peter, 155
Seagal, Steven 73
Seagrove, Jenny, 69, 72, 73, 122, 161
Seal, 63, 72
Seaman, David, 57
Searle, Ronald, 27, 102
Seaward, Carolyn, 181
Secombe, Sir Harry, 76, 98, 137, 158, 163
Sedaka, Neil, 26
Sedgemore, Brian, 169
Segal, Erich, 28, 147
Segal, George, 114, 173
Seles, Monica, 43, 71
Self, Will, 183
Selleck, Tom, 139, 142, 149
Sellers, Peter, 100, 131, 179, 180
Senna, Ayrton, 107
Sennett, Mack, 192
Sergeyev, Konstantin, 193
Serle, Chris, 36
Sessions, John, 68, 117
Seurat, Georges, 188
Sewell, Brian, 126
Seyler, Athene, 116
Seymour, Jane, 24, 27, 36, 42, 51, 52, 107, 108, 111, 144, 160
Shadow, 183
Shaffer, Peter, 26
Shah of Iran, The, 115
Shakespeare, William, 54, 173
Shakin' Stevens, 52
Shand-Kydd, Frances, 28
Shane, Paul, 37, 43, 59, 87, 98, 142, 174
Shapiro, Helen, 15
Sharif, Omar, 16, 53, 141, 160, 166
Sharman, Helen, 107, 117, 174
Sharp, Cameron, 70
Sharp, Graeme, 15
Sharpe, Lee, 169
Sharpe, Tom, 35
Shastri, Lal, 191

Shatner, William, 13, 49, 57, 114, 171

Shaughnessy, Alfred, 173

Shaw, Artie, 23

Shaw, George Bernard, 128, 172, 180

Shaw, Martin, 72

Shaw, Robert, 144

Shaw, Sandie, 72, 126, 144, 156

Shaw, Tracy, 176

Sheen, Charlie, 54, 77, 138, 142

Sheen, Martin, 24, 53, 155

Sheene, Barry, 137, 141, 145

Sheldon, Sidney, 151

Shephard, Gillian, 39, 161,

Shepherd, Cybill, 93, 132, 148

Shepherd, Jack, 20

Sher, Anthony, 69, 121, 144

Sheringham, Teddy, 57

Sherman, Alfred, 124

Sherrin, Ned, 164, 165

Sherry, Gordon, 29

Shields, Brooke, 46, 61, 72, 138, 142, 182

Shilton, Peter, 108

Shinwell, Manny, 116

Shire, Talia, 54

Shore, Dinah, 103

Short, Clare, 17, 174

Short, Martin, 149

Short, Nigel, 36, 134

Shrimpton, Jean, 21, 43, 114, 159

Shultz, Georhe, 45

Siegel, Don, 192

Sieghart, Mary Ann, 167

Silkin, Lord, 191

Sillitoe, Alan, 75, 181

Silvera, Carmen, 143

Silvers, Phil, 179

Silverstone, Alicia, 26, 59, 114

Silverwood, Chris, 89

Simmons, Jack, 188

Simmons, Jean, 77, 146

Simon, Carly, 26, 68, 70, 128, 129

Simon, Neil, 62, 116, 119

Simpson, Alan, 75

Simpson, John, 36, 96, 123

Simpson, Judy, 80

Simpson, O.J., 41

Simpson, Valerie, 129

Simpson, Wallace, 194

Sims, Joan, 156

Sinatra, Frank, 49, 66, 79, 120, 140, 143, 151, 154, 166

Sinatra, Nancy, 135

Sinclair, Clive, 15, 122

Sinden, Sir Donald, 42, 89, 141

Singer, Isaac Bashevis, 28, 192

Singleton, Valerie, 38, 47, 58, 92, 158, 171

Sinitta, 63, 72

Sioux, Siouxsie, 14, 52, 72

Sissons, Peter, 35, 168

Skellern, Peter, 92

Skinner, Frank, 65, 98

Skinner, Mick, 155

Skinner, Richard, 47

Slater, Christian, 52, 56, 139, 186

Slater, Jim, 161

Slattery, Tony, 16, 32, 67, 86

Sleep, Wayne, 66, 110, 117, 141, 164

Smethurst, Jack, 16

Smillie, Carol, 58, 69, 176, 181

Smith, Andreas Whittam, 63

Smith, Anna Nicole, 48, 77

Smith, Arthur, 169

Smith, Chris, 30, 174

Smith, Cyril, 7

Smith, Delia, 124

Smith, Harvey, 16

Smith, Ian, 105

Smith, Jaclyn, 170

Smith, John, 107

Smith, Maggie, 36, 148, 156

Smith, Mandy, 73, 144, 176

Smith, Mel, 117

Smith, Michelle, 117

Smith, Mike, 112, 156, 170

Smith, Patti, 106

Smith, Robin, 44

Smith, Tommy, 83

Smith, Will, 22, 90

Smith, William Henry, 191

Smurfit, Victoria, 39

Snagge, John, 193

Snipes, Wesley, 61, 114

Snoop Doggy Dogg, 53

Snow, Peter, 36, 92

Snowdon, Lisa, 71

Snowdon, Lord, 41, 74, 91, 144

Soames, Emma, 124

Soames, Nicholas, 159

Sobers, Gary, 81

Sofia, Queen of Spain, 11

Somerville, Jimmy, 106, 178

Somerville, Julia, 70, 98, 162

Sonia, 122

Sopwith, Thomas, 116, 193

Soul, David, 112

Souness, Graeme, 47, 57

Southall, Neville, 155

Southgate, Gareth, 137

Spacek, Sissy, 133

Spackman, Nigel, 27

Spall, Timothy, 80, 147

Spark, Muriel, 26

Spassky, Boris, 13

Spear, Ruskin, 74

Spector, Phil, 12, 26, 89, 128

Spector, Ronnie, 12, 144

Speed, Gary, 91

Speight, Johnny, 130

Spelling, Aaron, 61, 85, 102, 168

Spencer, Countess, 66

Spencer, Earl, (9th Earl), 27, 145

Spencer, Earl, (8th Earl), 193

Spender, Stephen, 124, 165

Spiegel, Sam, 191

Spielberg, Steven, 12, 60

Spiers, Judi, 72

Spinetti, Victor, 113

Spitz, Mark, 43, 174

Spock, Benjamin, 87

Springer, Axel, 193

Springfield, Dusty, 55

Springsteen, Bruce, 106, 120, 124

St Clair, Lindi, 72

St Clement, Pam, 33, 121, 142

St Laurent, Yves, 67

Stack, Robert, 148

Stadler, Craig, 145

Staff, Kathy, 15, 112, 136, 142

Stalin, Josef, 192

Stallone, Sylvester, 58, 138, 149, 169, 171, 173, 185

Stamp, Terence, 72, 148

Stansfield, Lisa, 57

Stanshall, Vivian, 67, 182

Stanton, Harry Dean, 63

Stanwyck, Barbara, 150

Stanwyck, Stan, 12

Stapleton, John, 20, 22, 35, 98

Stardust, Alvin, 141

Stark, Freya, 116

Stark, Koo, 21, 126, 145, 158

Starkey, David, 20, 65, 126

Starr, Freddie, 13, 21, 53, 68, 71, 97, 109, 141, 178

Starr, Ringo, 43, 45, 66, 72, 80, 138, 151, 170, 173, 179

Staunton, Imelda, 72

Steel, David, 12, 29, 81, 167

Steele, Tommy, 56, 95, 154, 160, 164, 168

Steiger, Rod, 102

Stein, Rick, 25

Steinem, Gloria, 26

Stephanie, Princess of Monaco, 45, 133

Stephen, Jaci, 125

Stephenson, Pamela, 24, 126

Stevens, Cat (see also Yusuf Islam), 122

Stevens, Kirk, 15

Stevens, Ray, 15

Stevenson, Robert Louis, 11

Stewart, Alastair, 162

Stewart, Dave, 70, 81, 130

Stewart, Jackie, 14, 90, 141

Stewart, James, 103, 177

Stewart, Patrick, 121, 139

Stewart, Rod, 42, 58, 109, 123, 135, 179

Stewart, William G., 36, 59, 175

Stiles, Nobby, 141

Stilgoe, Richard, 188

Stills, Stephen, 16, 135

Stimson, Tess, 93

Sting, 8, 34, 53, 63, 98, 106, 138, 183

Stirling, David, 193

Stock, Francine, 39

Stockwell, Dean, 148

Stoker, Bram, 11

Stokes, Doris, 12

Stokowski, Leopold, 146, 180

Stone, Michael, 144

Stone, Norman, 173

Stone, Oliver, 15, 22, 126, 138, 186

Stone, Sharon, 89, 114, 122, 149, 159, 185

Stone, Steve, 35

Stoppard, Miriam, 92, 144, 162

Stoppard, Tom, 24, 151

Storey, David, 24, 87

Storey, Helen, 24

Stourton, Edward, 81

Strachan, Michaela, 58, 69, 83, 176

Stransky, Joel, 26

Strasberg, Lee, 192

Strauli, Christopher, 16

Straw, Jack, 120

Streep, Meryl, 15, 133, 139, 149

Street-Porter, Janet, 41, 43, 46, 59, 152, 166, 174

Streisand, Barbra, 31, 35, 51, 68, 79, 120, 131, 148, 166, 173

Strindberg, August, 189

Stringfellow, Peter, 22, 182

Strong, Roy, 30, 161

Strummer, Joe, 22, 129

Stubbs, Imogen, 30, 35, 190

Stubbs, Levi, 135

Stubbs, Una, 12, 84

Sturges, Preston, 188

Suchet, David, 88, 158, 190

Suchet, John, 158

Sugden, Mollie, 27, 35, 137, 161

Suggs, 22, 63

Sullivan, David, 84

Summer, Donna, 9, 53, 127

Summers, Andy, 9

Summers, Jill, 12

Sutcliffe, Stewart, 128, 192

Sutherland, Donald, 8, 24, 73, 139, 149

Sutherland, Joan, 166, 168

Sutherland, Kiefer, 24, 144

Sutherland, Rosalind, 176

Suzman, Janet, 164

Swann, Donald, 101

Swanson, Gloria, 12

Swanton, E.W., 100

Swayze, Patrick, 110, 133, 171

Sykes, Eric, 83, 163, 165, 181

Sylvia, 63

Syms, Sylvia, 12, 23, 74, 176

Taki, 63, 89, 186

Tarantino, Quentin, 61, 137, 176

Tarbuck, Jimmy, 96, 98, 122, 137, 154, 162, 175

Tarkington, Booth, 188

Tarrant, Chris, 15, 20, 48, 162, 172

Taylforth, Gillian, 57, 189

Taylor, A.J.P., 35, 124

Taylor, Birt, 35

Taylor, Dennis, 13, 46

Taylor, Elizabeth, 21, 47, 58, 65, 66, 71, 77, 78, 79, 80, 82, 83, 84, 85, 106, 112, 114, 118, 123, 135, 133, 140

Taylor, Graham, 137

Taylor, Helen, 95

Taylor, James, 13, 129, 134, 145

Taylor, John 144

Taylor, Laurie, 35, 110, 189

Tebbit, Norman, 36, 46, 108, 119, 181

Temple, Shirley, 128, 150

Temple, William, 192

Tendulkar, Sachin, 156

Tennyson, Alfred Lord, 49

Terry-Thomas, 35, 64

Terry, Ellen, 11

Testino, Mario, 144

Thackeray, William Makepeace, 116

Thatcher, Carol, 33

Thatcher, Denis, 67, 103, 159

Thatcher, Margaret, 33, 39, 77, 84, 115, 117, 120, 125, 174

Thatcher, Mark, 35

Thaw, John, 69, 109

Theroux, Paul, 147, 177

Thomas, Dylan, 128, 192

Thomas, Kristin Scott, 40

Thomas, Leslie, 13, 21, 89, 98, 158, 173, 174

Thompson, Daley, 15, 98, 155, 176

Thompson, Emma, 32, 36, 43, 57, 118, 174

Thomsett, Sally, 46

Thorndike, Sybil, 116

Thorne, Angela, 136

Thorne, Willie, 27, 98

Thornton, Frank, 115

Thorpe, Graham, 43

Thorpe, Jeremy, 109, 124

Thorpe, Jim, 94

Thurman, Uma, 55, 59, 61, 114, 126, 171

Tiegs, Cheryl, 22

Tiffany, 63

Tigana, Jean, 119

Tikaram, Tanita, 72

Tilberis, Liz, 12

Tilly, Jennifer, 159

Tilton, Charlene, 173

Timothy, Christopher, 15

Tinling, Teddy, 193

Titchmarsh, Alan, 93

Todd, Bob, 193

Todd, Mark, 92

Todd, Richard, 56, 100, 160

Toksvig, Sandi, 32, 92, 155

Tolden, Bill, 183

Tomalin, Claire, 168

Tomei, Marisa, 139

Tomelty, Frances, 135

Tomlin, Lily, 148

Tomlinson, David, 101

Tong, Pete, 56

Took, Barry, 89, 181, 190

Topol, 63, 141

Tork, Peter, 16

Torme, Mel, 26

Torn, Rip, 16

Torrance, Sam, 20, 76, 91

Torvill, Jayne, 95, 107, 117, 159

Tosh, Peter, 192

Tour, Andy de la, 84

Townsend, Sue, 73, 117

Townshend, Pete, 38, 49, 79, 106, 111, 183

Toyah, 63

Tracy, Spencer, 84

Travers, Ben, 191

Travers, Bill, 103

Travis, Dave Lee, 63, 115

Travolta, John, 13, 55, 119, 122, 149

Treacher, Bill, 14, 43, 92, 170, 181, 182

Trelford, Donald, 188

Tremain, Rose, 31, 164, 165

Trollope, Antony, 11

Trollope, Joanna, 11

Trotsky, Leon, 146

Trueman, Fred, 16, 115, 122, 157

Trump, Donald, 145, 188

Trump, Ivana, 47, 48, 59, 145

Tse-Tung, Mao, 189

Tucker, Sophie, 192

Tufnell, Phil, 85, 169

Tully, Susan, 98, 174, 189

Tunney, Gene, 157

Turlington, Christy, 45

Turner, Adair, 30

Turner, Anthea, 47, 48, 55, 57, 78, 110, 178, 189

Turner, Eva, 180

Turner, Ike, 29

Turner, Kathleen, 55, 139, 148

Turner, Ted, 49, 62, 71

Turner, Tina, 49, 51, 52, 54, 86, 120, 126, 129, 145, 178

Turpin, Randolph, 188

Tusa, John, 34, 95, 117

Tushingham, Rita, 72, 161

Tutin, Kathy, 136

Tweedie, Jill, 194

Twiggy, 37, 63, 66, 141, 154, 162, 163, 165

Twinkle, 63

Twitty, Conway, 146

Twose, Roger, 93

Tyler, Bonnie, 98

Tynan, Kenneth, 64

Tyrrell, Ken, 37

Tyson, Mike, 7, 114, 122, 188

ul-Haq, Zia, 191

Ullman, Tracey, 65, 93, 139

Umberto I, King, 194

Underwood, Rory, 14, 35

Ustinov, Peter, 20, 34, 92, 99, 118, 119, 137, 173

Valentine, Anthony, 140

Valli, Frankie, 124

Van Buren, Martin, 11

Van Damme, Jean-Claude, 52, 142, 183

Van Der Post, Laurens, 103

Van Dyke, Dick, 66

Van Gogh, Vincent, 70, 71, 79, 180

Van Renderwick, Issy, 11

Van Rensburg, Christo, 118

Vance, Cyrus, 111

Vandross, Luther, 13, 61, 76, 128

Vangelis, 63

Vanilla Ice, 45, 66

Varadi, Imre, 16

Varney, Paul, 79

Vaughan, Frankie, 56

Vaughan, Johnny, 186
Vaughan, Peter, 23, 82, 123
Vaz, Keith, 30, 61, 188
Venables, Terry, 19, 43, 107, 109, 122, 137
Vereen, Ben, 119
Verhoeven, Paul, 12
Verne, Jules, 180
Vernon, Richard, 141
Versalle, Richard, 176
Verwoerd, Hendrik, 192
Vicious, Sid,
Victoria, Queen, 11, 115, 192, 194
Vidal, Gore, 116, 145
Villeneuve, Giles, 24
Villeneuve, Jacques, 24
Villeneuve, Justin de, 109
Vincent, Lorna, 13
Vincent, Tim, 144
Vincenzi, Penny, 19
Virgo, John, 98, 162
Voight, Jon, 16, 23, 149
Vorderman, Carol, 9, 47, 69, 187
Vranch, Richard, 32
Vreeland, Diana, 191

Waddle, Chris, 137
Wade, Kirsty, 72
Wade, Virginia, 15, 29, 34, 95
Wagner, Lindsay, 15, 17
Wagner, Robert, 22
Wahlberg, Donnie, 188
Wainwright, Loudon, 49
Waite, Terry, 29, 34, 43, 56, 153, 156
Waldegrave, Carole, 95
Waldegrave, William, 159
Walden, Brian, 62, 167
Waldheim, Kurt, 111
Walesa, Lech, 145
Walken, Christopher, 53, 139
Walker, Anna, 96
Walker, Jack, 157
Walker, Johnnie, 36, 161
Walker, Murray, 82, 137

Walker, Roy, 15, 97
Walker, Scott, 13, 20
Wall, Max, 142, 192
Wallace, Jim, 15
Wallace, Julie T., 152
Wallach, Eli, 100
Walsh, Bradley, 58
Walters, Julie, 21, 33, 66
Wangford, Hank, 144
Ward, Simon, 24, 36
Ward, Sophie, 24
Ward, Tracy, 72
Warhol, Andy, 106
Warner, Marina, 124
Warren, Leonard, 176
Warrior, 154
Warwick, Dionne, 62, 146
Washington, Denzel, 29, 54
Washington, Desiree, 181
Washington, George, 152
Waterman, Dennis, 21, 90, 115, 137
Waterman, Peter, 167, 168, 169
Waters, Muddy, 191
Watt, Jim, 141
Watt, Tom, 121, 131
Watts, Charlie, 14, 50, 72, 144, 178
Waugh, Auberon, 44, 65, 75, 167
Waugh, Evelyn, 116
Wax, Ruby, 20
Way, Paul, 80
Wayne, John 133, 180
Weatherill, Bernard, 102
Weaver, Jason, 94
Weaver, Dennis, 72, 132
Weaver, Sigourney, 52, 58, 139, 147
Webster, Gary, 87, 90
Webster, William, 123
Weeks, Alan, 101, 182
Weidenfeld, Lord George, 105
Weinberger, Caspar, 111
Weir, Dodie, 79
Weissmuller, Johnny, 94
Welch, Bruce, 15
Welch, Denise, 85

Welch, Raquel, 15, 94, 106, 109, 133, 155
Weld, Tuesday, 66
Weldon, Fay, 36, 48
Welland, Colin, 12, 121, 150
Weller, Paul, 121, 130, 155
Welles, Orson, 148, 192
Wells, H.G., 128, 150
Wells, John, 29, 109, 147
Wenders, Wim, 41
Wesker, Arnold, 123, 181
Wesley, Mary, 82, 116
West, Mae, 128, 144, 172
West, Timothy, 117, 121
Westbrook, Daniella, 66, 84, 183
Westheimer, Ruth, 105, 146, 153
Westminster, Duke of, 96
Westwood, Vivienne, 164
Whale, James, 87
Whalley, Joanne, 142
Whateley, Kevin, 35, 90, 121
Wheeler, Charles, 188
Wheeler, Sara, 124
Whicker, Alan, 162
Whigfield, 63, 85
Whitbread, Fatima, 95, 108, 122
White, Jimmy, 43, 154
Whitelaw, Viscount, 104
Whitfield, June, 97, 142
Whittaker, Roger, 97, 161
Widdecombe, Ann, 40, 81, 174
Wiesenthal, Simon, 9
Wilcox, Desmond, 27, 83, 93, 117, 118
Wild, Jack, 112
Wilde, Kim, 24, 179
Wilde, Marty, 24, 56
Wilde, Oscar, 107, 128, 183
Wilder, Gene, 14, 133
Wilhelm II, Kaiser, 108, 129
Wilkins, Ray, 15
Willcox, Toyah, 73, 84, 155
Willey, Peter, 188
William of Orange, 11

William, Prince, 43
Williams, Andy, 146
Williams, Emlyn, 193
Williams, Finty, 23
Williams, Frank, 125
Williams, Hank, 129
Williams, J.P.R., 13
Williams, Kenneth, 180
Williams, Leila, 181
Williams, Rachel, 45
Williams, Rex, 67
Williams, Robbie, 98, 161
Williams, Robin, 39, 58, 86, 114, 140, 148, 154, 183
Williams, Shirley, 23, 109
Williams, Vanessa, 72
Williamson, Malcolm, 61
Willis, Bob, 35, 122
Willis, Bruce, 62, 65, 70, 95, 132, 138, 147, 148, 159, 166
Wilson, A.N., 116, 118, 168
Wilson, Bob, 55
Wilson, Brian, 67
Wilson, Carl, 23, 76
Wilson, Jackie, 129, 130
Wilson, Julian, 79, 97
Wilson, Harold, 62, 133, 157
Wilson, Richard, 34, 57, 94, 95, 117, 121
Wilson, Woodrow, 145
Windsor, Barbara, 19, 22, 40, 57, 74, 82
Windsor, Duchess of, 7
Windsor, Frank, 140
Winfrey, Oprah, 7, 17, 43, 59, 61, 77, 107
Wing, Anna, 127
Winger, Debra, 14, 26, 105, 188
Winner, Michael, 36, 122
Winslet, Kate, 10, 39, 60, 169, 179, 184
Winstone, Ray, 136
Winter, Fred, 27
Winters, Bernie, 182, 191
Winters, Jack, 182

Winters, Sheila, 140
Winton, Dale, 19, 47, 60
Winwood, Steve, 13
Wisdom, Norman, 117, 148, 174
Wise, Dennis, 90
Witchell, Nicholas, 42
Withers, Bill, 178
Woddis, Roger, 124
Wodehouse, P.G., 180, 191
Wogan, Terry, 49, 76, 90, 108, 112, 156, 164, 165
Wolf, 97, 157
Wolf, Naomi, 38
Wolfe, Tom, 16, 183
Wollard, William, 72
Wolstenholme, Kenneth, 101
Womack, 129
Wonder, Stevie, 14, 52, 114, 120
Wood, Natalie, 84, 151, 180
Wood, Ronnie, 14
Wood, Victoria, 34, 58, 142
Woods, James, 153
Woods, Tiger, 59
Woodward, Joanne, 12, 118, 148
Woodward, Edward, 174, 178
Woodyatt, Adam, 73, 157
Woolf, Virginia, 108, 188
Woosnam, Ian, 91, 93, 155, 167
Worrall-Thompson, Antony, 158
Worsthorne, Sir Peregrine, 124, 159
Wray, Link, 65, 109
Wren, P.C., 188
Wright, Billy, 100
Wright, Fanny, 191
Wright, Fiona, 85
Wright, Ian, 12, 59, 73, 96, 114
Wright, Linda, 176
Wright, Orville, 108, 192
Wright, Steve, 22, 57, 60, 70, 73, 86, 178
Wyatt, Robert, 21
Wyatt, Woodrow, 102, 154
Wyle, Noah, 142
Wyman, Bill, 21, 53, 98, 122, 144, 181

Wyman, Jane, 118
Wynette, Tammy, 20, 28, 53, 77
Wyngarde, Peter, 140, 143
Wynne, Greville, 191

X, Malcolm, 122

Yacoub, Magdi, 84
Yardley, Norman, 193
Yarwood, Mike, 14, 66, 67, 87, 90, 178
Yates, Jess, 71
Yates, Paula, 13, 20, 45, 95, 183
Yazz, 63
Yeltsin, Boris, 82, 107
York, Duchess of, 33, 39, 42, 51, 71, 73, 77, 84, 85, 92, 108, 117, 142, 144, 154, 169
York, Michael, 65, 148
York, Susannah, 13, 148, 161,
Young, Faron, 109, 146
Young, Jimmy, 19, 22, 49, 56, 82, 99
Young, Lord, 44
Young, Neil, 22, 74
Young, Paul, 70, 128, 135, 178
Young, Sean, 62

Zeffirelli, Franco, 7
Zephaniah, Benjamin, 163
Zimbalist, Efrem, 55
Zinnemann, Fred, 24
Zola, Emile, 150